# Julia

*by Julia Mitchell*

Copyright © 2008 by Julia Mitchell

All rights reserved. No part of this publication may be reproduced or transmitted in any form or by any means, electronic or mechanical including photocopying, recording or any information storage or retrieval system, without prior permission in writing from the publishers.

First published in the United Kingdom in 2008 by
Julia Mitchell

ISBN 978-09559967-0-2

**The moral right of the author has been asserted.**

Book production by
Action Publishing Technology Limited
Gloucester GL1 5SR
Printed in Great Britain

# Contents

|  |  |  |
|---|---|---|
| | Acknowledgments | v |
| | Introduction | 1 |
| Chapter One | Preparing | 2 |
| Chapter Two | Coming Home | 5 |
| Chapter Three | Different | 7 |
| Chapter Four | Squint | 9 |
| Chapter Five | The Wanderer | 12 |
| Chapter Six | In To School | 15 |
| Chapter Seven | Highs and Lows of Growing Up | 18 |
| Chapter Eight | Frustration | 24 |
| Chapter Nine | Guiding | 28 |
| Chapter Ten | Mischief | 31 |
| Chapter Eleven | Learning to Swim | 33 |
| Chapter Twelve | Practise makes Perfect | 35 |
| Chapter Thirteen | The Dentist | 37 |
| Chapter Fourteen | Pets | 44 |
| Chapter Fifteen | Back to Work and Changes for Mum | 47 |
| Chapter Sixteen | Learning to Cope | 52 |
| Chapter Seventeen | Mum and Dad | 60 |
| Chapter Eighteen | Charlton Park | 68 |
| Chapter Nineteen | Valium | 79 |
| Chapter Twenty | Reflecting Back | 83 |
| Chapter Twenty One | Clubs | 84 |
| Chapter Twenty Two | Trinity (Part One) | 94 |
| Chapter Twenty Three | Bromley Workshop | 99 |
| Chapter Twenty Four | Trinity (Part Two) | 103 |
| Chapter Twenty Five | Portland Training College | 110 |
| Chapter Twenty Six | Trinity (Part Three) | 118 |
| Chapter Twenty Seven | New Ladywell Centre | 122 |
| Chapter Twenty Eight | Pauline's Marriage | 132 |
| Chapter Twenty Nine | Becoming Independent | 136 |
| Chapter Thirty | Teddy Bears | 147 |
| Chapter Thirty One | Counselling and Teaching | 149 |
| Chapter Thirty Two | Work | 154 |

| | | |
|---|---|---|
| Chapter Thirty Three | Dad Passing Away | 158 |
| Chapter Thirty Four | Holiday | 165 |
| Chapter Thirty Five | Verdant Lane | 178 |
| Chapter Thirty Six | Forest Hill | 185 |
| Chapter Thirty Seven | Friends | 187 |
| Chapter Thirty Eight | Romania | 192 |
| Chapter Thirty Nine | Open University | 199 |
| Chapter Forty | Religion | 212 |
| Chapter Forty One | Mum | 221 |
| Chapter Forty Two | Ladywell Part 2 | 226 |
| Chapter Forty Three | Mum's Will | 235 |
| Chapter Forty Four | On the Buses and in Public | 239 |
| Chapter Forty Five | Moving to Woolwich | 244 |
| Chapter Forty Six | Blindness | 264 |
| Chapter Forty Seven | Rosie | 276 |
| Chapter Forty Eight | A Very Nerve Racking Day | 279 |
| Chapter Forty Nine | Hopes for the Future | 286 |
| | Conclusion | 290 |
| Appendix | General Hints on Disability Awareness | 292 |

# Acknowledgements

I would like to thank Mollie Robertson for helping me to write this book at the very beginning in the 1970s. During the 1980s and 90s, I would like to thank Virginia at Lewisham College for correcting the first sixteen chapters of this book and for allowing me to scan all the text onto my new computer disk.

I am also very grateful to John Ryan who helped me here and there with some difficult parts.

Lastly, I would like to thank Helen Redding who really helped me to make it possible to finish this book and to try to get it published.

*This book is dedicated to the memory of my parents, Ernie and Doris Mitchell. For the love and support they always gave me.*

## What is Life?

What is life?
You are born with nothing
You die with nothing
Your upbringing and education
Decide who you are going to be
Three things we all do
Eat, work and sleep
We eat to live
We work to pay our way
For those who can, live comfortable
For those who can't, struggle
We sleep a quarter of our life
So what is life?
Is life what you make it?
God has given you a choice
To follow Him or go your own way
To go your own way
No hope, no future
To follow Christ
Hope and a future

By Julia Mitchell
July 23 2001

# Introduction

I am 55 years old and was born with Cerebral Palsy. I have achieved a lot in my life and I wanted to write a book which would keep the reader entertained and also give encouragement to readers with Cerebral Palsy and other disabilities.

Over the years, I have learned that people who are born with mild or moderate Cerebral Palsy can be greatly helped if they are taught to cope with their disability early on in life – ideally before school age.

When I reached the age of fourteen years old, the doctor told my mother to stop doing so much for me, and to let me decide which way I wanted to go, so that I could become more independent and to begin to make my own way in life.

This book will give an idea of how I coped with the disabilities I have and the various barriers I faced.

The initial chapters of this book are written from what I remember over the years when my parents had been talking to people about me. The rest of the book is written from the way I remember the events happening and from my own experiences and perspective.

I realise that this book is very personal and is written solely from my point of view. If I have hurt anyone's feelings in this book, it was not intentional.

My reason for writing the book was to put down in words my appreciation of what my parents did for me and to show people what can be achieved with love, care and the right training and support.

Despite my disability, I feel nothing is impossible and that disabled people can lead 'normal' lives.

## Chapter One

# Preparing

In 1939 my grandparents rented a house in Fordel Road, Catford in South East London. My mother and her sister lived with them. When my mother's sister married, she and her husband moved into a pre-fab – these were temporary houses built to replace bombed, ruined ones.

In June 1941, my dad came home on leave for ten days to get married to my mum and they made their home with Granddad and Nan. In 1945, my dad came home for good. Unfortunately, in December of that year my grandfather died. After a couple of years, mum and dad made a flat upstairs for Nan and they lived downstairs. My mum and dad decided to start their family, and in May 1951 my mum had my sister, Pauline. As the family expanded, mum and dad went on to buy the house from Nan, and Nan moved to a flat in Brockley.

I was born in December 1952. One of my earliest memories was that my nan seemed to love my sister Pauline more than she loved me. She seemed to have a different attitude towards me. I think it was because I was disabled. A year after I was born, Nan had an accident and broke her elbow so she came to live with us. She had to have a pin in her elbow and stayed with us until she was better. She then moved to Waters Road, Catford. However, she never fully regained the use of her arm.

It was a bitterly cold day in December 1952 when my mum had an appointment to go to hospital for a check up to see how I, her unborn baby, was getting on. On that day, my mum wasn't feeling very well but instead of staying in the warm, she decided that she would go and keep her appointment. When she came back from the hospital, she wasn't feeling any better. When my dad came home from work, he took one look at her and told her to go to bed, which she did. My dad had to feed Pauline and then put her to bed.

Pauline used to be naughty and she always played up when it was bedtime. At the time when Pauline was young, parents were advised to go to their child every time they cried. Usually, my mum had to stay upstairs with Pauline, holding her hand until she dropped off to sleep. Sometimes when Pauline dropped off and mum let go of her hand, Pauline would start to cry and mum had to go back and hold her hand and start all over again. It was often gone ten o'clock before Pauline got to sleep. But on that night, I don't think dad stayed up there very long; she soon went to sleep!

At about nine o'clock, dad went up to see how mum was and saw that she was getting worse. He called the doctor. The doctor told dad that mum had to go into hospital because she had pneumonia.

Dad called an ambulance and mum was soon on her way to hospital. However, because of the difficulty that she had in breathing, she could not lie down in the ambulance. Instead, she had to sit up all the way, which was very painful for her, as my head was being pushed against her pelvis.

When mum got into the hospital, the consultant said, "Didn't this patient come in this morning for a check up?" The sister replied that she did. He then turned to mum and asked her if she knew which doctor she had seen that morning, but my mum was too ill to remember. The consultant told the sister to get together all the doctors who had been on duty that morning.

When the doctors came in, Dr. Cowan said, "Which one of you saw this patient this morning?"

Dr. Henn answered "I did – Why?"

Dr. Cowan told Dr. Henn to go to his office and wait until he came. After that, Dr. Cowan told my mum that he was going to give her an injection every four hours to try and help her worsening condition.

Mum was seven months pregnant with me and still in hospital when, on 17th December 1952 at about 10.30pm, she told the sister that she had a pain. The sister called Dr. Cowan and at 11.30pm I was born. They took me away from mum and put me in an incubator and mum was put back in the ward. As far as my mum and the doctors were concerned, I was doing fine for such a premature baby.

Dr. Cowan told mum that she was lucky to be alive. If she had been in the same position two years earlier, it could have proven fatal. He also told her that he was taking her off the injections and that in a couple of days she would be able to get up for an hour or two each day. A week later, mum was able to stay out of bed practically all day. She used to go round the ward talking to some of the other patients. Soon, she wanted to go home.

Sister said, "If I let you go home, I know exactly what will happen. You will go back to housework and everything else. No, you can stay here for a while longer."

Mum had been in hospital for three weeks when Christmas came and she was not very pleased that she was still in there! However, on Christmas morning all the nurses came in, singing Christmas carols and walking round with candle lamps in their hands. Then the doctors came in with bottles of drink for the nurses and the patients. Later on, the patients' husbands came in with Christmas presents for their wives. After the husbands had come and gone, the nurses got all the patients organised and the babies back in their cots for their morning sleep. After that, the patients were got ready for their Christmas dinner.

Mum said, "It was not all that bad, but not like being at home."

Four days after Christmas, she asked Dr. Cowan if she could go home. Dr. Cowan knew my mum was a sensible person and said, "Well, I don't see why not, providing you take it easy for a while. Your daughter is coming on nicely. She has caught up on her weight, so you can go home together."

When dad came to see mum that night, she told him the good news. Dad was delighted and went to see the sister, asking when he could take us home. He was told that he could take mum and me home in two days' time.

The two days went by pretty quickly and when dad got to the hospital, mum was saying her goodbyes to the other patients. Then a nurse came in with me in her arms and she handed me over to mum. Mum and dad thanked the Sister for everything and we got into our taxi and went home.

## Chapter Two
# Coming Home

When mum and dad got home, they found that Nan and Pauline had been getting on very well together. Mum got back to normal within a few hours.

It was nearly time to feed Pauline, so mum got her meal ready. Pauline was just 19 months old. Just as she was going to feed her, Pauline started to cry. Mum began to get a bit worried and she wondered what was wrong. She went to get Nan to see if she could help. As soon as Pauline saw Nan coming towards her, she stopped crying. After a few minutes they found out what was wrong. It was only that Pauline wanted Nan to feed her. This went on for a week, then Nan went back to her own home and Pauline had to get used to mum feeding her again. Mum had stopped breastfeeding Pauline when she was four months old, and Pauline had never liked the feeding bottle. It didn't matter how hard mum tried, there was always a battle. In the end, mum gave her her milk by spoon-feeding her from a cup, which took ages.

Pauline also had a habit of holding her breath. Mum didn't know that this was not unusual for babies. One day, mum went to give Pauline her meal and after a couple of mouthfuls, Pauline went quite blue in the face. Mum thought she was choking. However, she soon started breathing again and mum was relieved to see her back to normal.

On one occasion, Pauline held her breath when we were at the hospital. Mum had taken her for a smallpox vaccination and just as the doctor was ready to give her the injection, Pauline's face went blue.

"Oh dear!" said the doctor, "You've got one of those babies who holds their breath! What do you do when she does it?"

"Well," said mum "At first I did nothing, but now I usually slap her on the leg."

The doctor replied that it might be a good idea to do this now!

mum asked the doctor why Pauline did this and was told that all babies did it to some extent and sometimes use it to get their own way. Mum was frightened by the number of times that Pauline held her breath.

In our back room, we used to have a big water tank in the corner, fed by a pipe which went down the side of the wall. At one end of the tank, only a couple of inches from the floor, was a tap. Pauline had a rag doll and one morning, fascinated by the tap, she put her rag doll in the corner and decided to turn on the tap, sending water everywhere. Terrified, Pauline burst into tears and when mum came in from the kitchen, the floor was covered with water. Mum went mad! However, when mum saw Pauline crying her eyes out, holding on to her soaking rag doll, she tried to cheer her up and comfort her. After that, poor mum had to clear up that mess before dad came home. And what a job it was!

## Chapter Three
# Different

By the time I was thirteen months, mum began to realise that there was something wrong with me. She used to take me to Lewisham Hospital once a month, and as time went by she began comparing me with Pauline. At the same age, Pauline could sit up unaided and I could not. I couldn't keep my head still. Mum asked dad if he thought that there was something wrong with me but he didn't think so. mum tried not to worry, but a couple of weeks later she decided to take me to Lewisham Hospital to see Dr. Gann, a children's specialist. Dr. Gann, however, just told mum that I was "making the grade".

A couple of months went by and mum asked dad again if he thought there was something wrong with me.

Dad said, "No. Why do you ask?"

Mum said, "It's not only her head, it's her arms and legs."

Then dad said that when she next took me to hospital in three weeks' time she should ask the doctor about it then.

Soon it was time for mum to take me back to Lewisham Hospital to see Dr Gann. This time he told her nearly everything she wanted to know.

He said, "Julia has slight brain damage and it is called Cerebral Palsy. We don't know how serious it is, but as she grows up we will see how it develops. Cerebral Palsy can affect people in different ways. Julia will not be able to walk until she is about three and a half years old." Then he told mum, "It will be up to you to help her."

This confirmed to my mum what she had been fearing and thinking – that there was something wrong.

The most common cause of cerebral palsy is when a baby gets the umbilical cord wrapped around its neck, and is starved of oxygen for a few vital minutes. Mum was sure that this had not happened to me at birth, and was almost certain that the damage had been caused when she was taken to hospital by ambulance when she was ill and I was squashed up inside her.

Because mum had noticed that I had developed a bit of a squint, she asked him about my eyes and Dr Gann told her to take me to Moorfields. He also asked mum if she would take me to see Dr

McKeith, a paediatrician and a specialist in cerebral palsy, at Guy's Hospital. All mum could say was that she didn't mind – but I think she did really because it was a long journey for her. Dr Gann made an appointment and said that he would see mum and me again in three months' time.

Two weeks after this, mum and dad had a letter from Guy's Hospital, asking her to take me up to the hospital the following Tuesday at ten o'clock.

On Tuesday morning, mum got up at six o'clock to get breakfast ready for us all. Then dad got up, had his breakfast, and went off to work. At quarter past seven, mum went to get Pauline up. She washed and dressed us both and gave us breakfast. By the time it was eight o'clock, mum had washed up and tidied the room. By half past eight, mum was sitting in the armchair, waiting for Nan to come and look after Pauline, who was by now sitting on the floor playing with her rag doll. I was in the chair with mum. Nan arrived about fifteen minutes later and we set off for hospital at about nine o'clock .

We caught the 124 bus to Catford station and then took a train to London Bridge and a short walk to the hospital. It was just ten o'clock when we got into the out-patient's department. I was taken to be weighed, which was done every time I went to the hospital. We then went into Dr McKeith's room. The doctor asked mum lots of questions about me and then examined me very thoroughly. He told mum that he thought I wouldn't be able to walk and I would be in a wheelchair. Mum was naturally very upset at this. The doctor said that he would like to see us both in a year's time.

On the way back home, mum thought about all the things Dr Gann and Dr McKeith had said – the first doctor saying that I would walk when I was three and a half years old, and then Dr McKeith saying that I would never be able to walk.

Mum thought, "We'll wait and see."

When we went up to Guy's Hospital a year later, to see Dr McKeith, he was very pleased to see the overall progress I had made. Mum's efforts were starting to pay off.

## Chapter Four
# Squint

When I was fourteen months old, mum had a sore eye so she went to the doctor to see what he could do for her. When she got into Dr. Gann's room he asked her questions and took a look at her eye. He told her that he could see about twenty little ulcers around the iris of her eye. Dr Gann asked mum if he could bring in three other doctors to have a look. Mum said that she didn't mind.

In a few minutes the doctors came in one by one and they took it in turns to look at mum's eye. They all agreed that it was very unusual to have ulcers around the iris and they hadn't seen anything like it before. When the doctors went back to their own patients, Dr Gann told mum she would have to go to Moorfields Eye hospital in London to have special treatment. A few days later, mum had an appointment to see Dr. Bross. When he saw mum's eye, he also said how unusual it was to find ulcers around the iris, and gave her about three different kinds of drops for her eye, and a cream for around the eye. He told her to come back and see him in two weeks' time.

When mum went back to Moorfields on the following Wednesday, Dr Bross was very pleased, and gave her some more eye drops. Whilst he was writing the notes, mum asked him if he would mind having a look at my eyes if she brought me up next time.

Mr Bross agreed and said that he wouldn't be seeing mum again for another four weeks, but would see me then.

When I was 17 months old, mum had to go back to Moorfields to see Mr. Bross. When he examined mum's eye, he was very pleased and said, "Good, you don't need any more treatment." Mum was thankful.

When mum reminded him about my eyes, Mr. Bross remembered and agreed to examine me. After the examination, he told mum that I had a squint in both my eyes and that the right one was pretty bad. He said, "I think we ought to operate on the right eye and leave the left eye, as it is not so bad."

He put me on the waiting list and made an appointment to see me again in two months' time.

Two weeks later, we had a letter from Moorfields to say they were ready to do the operation on my eye on Tuesday 10th June – in two weeks' time.

The time soon went by, and mum agreed that Nan and Pauline would come with us to the hospital. Early on the Tuesday morning, Nan came in to help get Pauline and me ready. We were all ready by 8.45am in order to leave the house at 9.00am and be at the hospital for 10.00am. We arrived in good time and a porter told us where to go – through the Out Patients' department, turn left and go up to the second floor.

When we came to the stairs, there were four flights of steps with twenty steps in each flight! When we reached the second floor, mum and Nan were glad that they didn't have to climb to the third floor! A nurse came out of one of the side rooms and looked at us all and said, "You look worn out!"

Mum said, "Yes we are. We've just walked up four flights of stairs."

The nurse said, "Why? What way did you come in? Didn't he tell you that there is a lift on the other side?" Mum was not amused!

The nurse asked mum which department she was looking for. Mum showed her the letter that she had from the hospital and the nurse said we were on the right floor. She directed us to walk through the corridor on the right and we would see a room where a Sister was.

"Sister will tell you where to go and what to do," she said.

The Sister told my mum everything that she wanted to know about the operation. Mum told her that she would not be able to come to see me until the weekend.

Sister said, "Oh, that's all right, we have a lot of parents who do that. In fact it makes it a lot easier for us. Now, I will get one of the nurses to show you where Julia will be sleeping. Perhaps you would like to stay for a while and have a cup of tea?"

Mum and Nan said, "Yes please! We would love a cup of tea!"

After they had drunk their tea, mum decided to take a look to see if I was all right, but I was asleep. By this time, Pauline was getting tired and fed up, so mum and Nan said their goodbyes to the nurses and the Sister. They remembered to go down in the lift and not down four flights of stairs. Mum was feeling a bit upset, so they didn't go straight home. They went to see Auntie Eva in Catford, where they had a chat and a cup of coffee and Pauline had a glass of milk. Auntie Eva asked how they had got on that morning. Mum told her the story of us all climbing the stairs and not using the lift. They all burst out laughing which made Pauline jump and start crying. Mum picked her up and gave her a little cuddle, which calmed her down.

After a while, mum said that they must be going. They went shopping and were very tired by the time they got home.

I had the eye operation on the Thursday and on Saturday mum and dad came to Moorfields to see me. When they arrived they found me in one of the nurse's arms. When she saw them she put me back in the cot! Nurse told mum that I was a lovely little baby, and that she'd heard that

I was going home on the next Tuesday and she would miss me. Mum didn't know that it only took a week to recover from the eye operation. My parents stayed with me for half an hour and then went to see Sister to ask about me coming home. Sister told them what time to come the next Tuesday and for them to see the doctor before we went home.

On Monday, Nan came over as she did every day, and mum told her about picking me up from the hospital the next day. Dad took the day off and they all went together – mum, dad, Nan and Pauline. Nan had come at half past eight on that morning and they left the house at nine o'clock and arrived at the hospital by ten. The nurses had me ready and my parents thanked them, said goodbye, and went to Sister's office. Dr. Bross came in and talked to mum and dad about the operation. He said he'd like to see me in six weeks' time and after that perhaps once a year. We went down, by lift, to the Out Patients' Department to make the appointment for six weeks' time. By this time it was half past eleven. We went straight home and were home by 1pm for dinner.

## Chapter Five
# The Wanderer

One afternoon, mum put me in the pushchair to take me down to Catford to do some shopping. We had finished most of the shopping when mum suddenly decided to go into Woolworths. She thought it would be quicker to leave me outside and go in on her own – which you could do in those days! While she was in Woolworths, I managed to undo the strap of the chair and crawled on my hands and knees into the shop.

When mum came out of the shop and saw the empty pushchair she could not believe her eyes! Where had I gone! She did not think it was possible that I could undo the strap. Mum panicked and turned around to search for me. Just then, a lady outside the shop, who knew us, saw mum looking and told her where I was. Mum went back into Woolworths, where a shop assistant had picked me up. Mum was always puzzled about me getting out of that pushchair and never worked out how I did it. She always said that I could not have managed it because of the way my disability restricted my hands. As I was so young at the time, I could never remember!

Another time, when we were in Catford, mum left me outside a shop and a lady gave me a piece of chocolate. The lady knew I could not use my hands so she put it in my mouth and walked away. When mum came out of the shop and looked at me she went mad!

"Who gave you that chocolate and then left you? Just look at you! Chocolate round you mouth, hands and all over your dress!"

We had to leave the shopping and go home. When we got home, the pushchair, my dress and I got a good wash! Well! It was not my fault that a lady gave me a piece of chocolate!

As I have not told you about wearing glasses I will do it now while I remember. About three years after my operation, I had to wear glasses to straighten my left eye, which was not bad enough to be operated on. Every morning, mum had to put my glasses on for me.

My education began when I was two and a half years old. Mum knew it was up to her to make me do and say the things a 'normal' child of two and a half would do. Every day, mum used to take me round the kitchen and bathroom and show me where everything was. Then mum used to say "table", "cup" and the names of everything around. I had to point at them and try to say the name. As hard as I tried, I could not say it properly and it was very hard for mum to tell what I saying, but she would not give up. She knew it would be worthwhile in the end.

When I was four years old, I could just about say all the names of the objects around us and mum was very pleased. It had taken over a year to accomplish this. Now she became concerned about teaching me to read. So she brought the Janet and John reading books. They came in books 1, 2, 3, 4 and 5. Every day, mum used to sit down with me and read one page at a time. Then she used to make me say it after her. Sometimes she was not sure of what I was saying so she used to make me read the line or page again. By the time I was four and a half years old, I could read any of the Janet and John books.

When I was nearly five, mum bought me a reading book and was surprised, I think, to find that I could read it straight away. So that was another job over!

You will remember that Dr. Gann said that I would not be able to walk until I was about three and a half years old. Dr. McKeith at Guy's Hospital said that I would never be able to walk. However, when I was nearly three, mum wanted to start trying to get me to walk, so she asked dad if he would help her with this. At first, mum and dad used to take me into the hall or garden, depending on the weather. They got on their knees about five or six steps away from each other, with me in the middle between them. Mum had me first and I had to get to Dad. Then he would turn me round and I had to get to mum. It was all a very slow business and it went on week after week. In the meantime, mum got me to do a lot of leg exercises.

As the months went by, mum and dad were able to move gradually a little further away from each other. After eight months of hard work on everyone's part, I managed to walk four steps on my own. Mum and dad were delighted and felt it had all been worthwhile. A bit later, dad bought me a doll's pram to help me walk better and better.

When I was exactly three and a half years old, mum had her appointment at Lewisham Hospital to see Dr. Gann. Mum wanted to tell him the good news so she put me down on my feet and kept her fingers crossed that I would walk. But no, I would not move! I just stood there.

Dr. Gann said "Do not worry, I know she can do it".

Mum asked him if I would ever be able to use my hands and he said, "It will be a long time yet before Julia will be able to do that."

Then he said that he wanted to see me in six months' time. When we got home that day, mum was very cross with me because I would not walk in front of Dr. Gann!

"Wait until your father gets home. He will not be pleased either," she said.

Dad did not say much but I knew he was cross with me.

Mum said, "I hope she doesn't behave like that when I take her to Guy's Hospital."

Dad replied, "Well, you will have to wait and see."

Three months later, mum kept the appointment to take me to see Dr. McKeith at Guy's Hospital. She kept her fingers crossed in the hope that I would walk about if Dr. McKeith asked me to do so.

Dr. McKeith asked mum some questions about my progress, and he asked about me walking. When mum told him, he said, "Good! Let me see her doing it!" Poor mum crossed her fingers as she put me down on my two feet! She didn't know whether to watch or look the other way! However, she decided to watch me. Just as she turned her head towards me, she saw that I was walking across the room! Both mum and Dr. McKeith were very pleased with me.

Dr. McKeith told mum that she had done a wonderful job teaching me to walk and that he was delighted with both of us. He said that he had never thought of me being able to walk at all. He added that he wanted to see me in a year's time.

When dad came home that evening, mum told him all that had happened at the hospital. They were both really pleased with me and with themselves.

All this happened before I went to school.

In order to teach me my colours, mum used to buy me sweets. She would tell me the colour of the sweet and then mix them up and say the name of a colour and ask me to pick out the sweets of that colour. I soon learned colours because if I was right I had some sweets at the end of the lesson.

In Hungary, they have something called Constructive Education, which is eight hours of exercise for children with physical disabilities (mainly Cerebral Palsy). Looking back, I believe that the continuous effort mum made with my exercise at such a young age, was key to my being able to walk, talk and develop as well as I did.

*Chapter Six*
# In To School

When I was nearly five years old, my parents started to worry about which school to send me to. At first they did think of sending me to a boarding school for the disabled. However my doctor thought it may not be a good idea and that I might end up copying other children's ways and picking up some of their mannerisms, rather than developing naturally on my own. Dr. Gann suggested that I should go to Plassey Road School, which had a special unit for disabled children, added on to the mainstream school. Mum and dad agreed that they should try to get me accepted there, and so I was!

First of all, in the mornings, mum would get Pauline up and then me. Dad, by that time, was already on his way to work. Mum gave us our breakfast, fed me and then got us ready for school. At about half past eight, mum took Pauline to Sandhurst Road School and then she had to run back home to get me out for the school bus about 8.45am. As the days went by, mum got to know the bus driver and bus attendant very well. They understood how mum sometimes found it hard to have me ready and waiting for the bus, so the driver would always wait a few minutes.

First, I'll talk about the school itself and then I'll talk about some of the things that happened there. Plassey Road School was made up of three separate buildings. There was the Girl's Primary school, a Girl's Secondary School, and our school – a building for the physically disabled, which was on the other side of the main wall. It was made up of two small buildings with four rooms in each building on the ground floor. When the boys were eleven years old, they changed schools and went to Lee Manor, but the girls stayed on at Plassey Road.

My first class was with Miss Senior. She was very pleasant and extremely understanding. Miss Senior was very surprised to find that I was already able to read and count. I had been at school for six weeks when I was due for a medical. The Sister was very kind and whilst mum and I were waiting, she gave me a doll to play with. Afterwards the medical sister put the doll back in the box, but told me I could have it again next time, and mum took me back to my class. Then she had a long chat with Miss Senior.

When my teacher learned that mum and dad had taught me to read, count, speak and walk, she was quite amazed and said they'd worked a miracle!

After a couple of months at school, Miss Senior began to think I might be a little deaf, so a letter was written to mum and dad telling them this.

Mum said, "Oh no! Not another problem!"

Dr Gann confirmed that, yes, I was slightly deaf.

Dr Gann suggested that mum should take me to see Dr. Fish at the Ear, Nose and Throat Hospital in Grays Inn Road. He said that he would make the appointment and a few weeks later we had an appointment letter from the hospital.

When we saw Dr. Fish, he gave me the usual hearing test and some different ones, which proved that I was deaf. He told mum that I was high tone deaf in my left ear.

Mum said, "How can she be deaf if she can hear everything I say?"

Dr. Fish said that the reason for this was that I could recognise mum's voice.

Mum said, "What can we do now?"

Dr. Fish replied that they would give me a hearing aid.

My first hearing aid was an ugly old thing with two big batteries at the back and two in the front with a cord which went round the back of my neck and into my left ear.

After a few weeks, mum and I decided that we didn't like this hearing aid, so mum let me wear it only when I was at school, as I was supposed to wear it permanently. A few months later, a new type of hearing aid came out. It was square shaped and only took two smaller batteries with a similar cord and ear mould. We liked it better because it wasn't big and clumsy with four batteries. It was lighter and easier to wear, but there was one big problem – whatever I wore, mum had to make a pocket for the hearing aid. She used to get quite mad about this because it used to spoil all my clothes.

When I was in my secondary school at Plassey Place, I liked one of the teachers very much. Her name was Miss Lloyd. I was sorry when she left our school to work in a convent. After she'd been gone for some time, we were invited to spend a day with her and the nuns. When we arrived there, we were given a 'mother' to take us on a tour of the building, and a nun also showed me over the school. We had plenty of time left on our hands, so she asked me if I would like to go for a walk in the woods.

I said, "Oh, yes, I'd love to do that!"

So she took hold of my hand and off we went. About half an hour later we came back, but as we still had some time left, we went for another walk in a different direction. This took another half an hour and I admit we were walking quicker on the way back, as time was running out. Sister kept looking at her watch!

When we did get back, it was too late; the school bus had gone and left me behind, and I don't think Miss Lloyd was very pleased with us! However, she phoned the school and told them that I had been left behind. My teacher said that they were waiting for the school bus to return, and she would tell the driver that I was still at the convent and someone would come and pick me up.

Whilst I was waiting, the driver of the bus was supposed to call round to my home to tell mum what had happened. I don't know what mum thought!

About an hour and a half later, Miss Senior walked in. I think she gave me a funny look, but I don't think she was very cross with me. After all, it wasn't my fault I had been left behind!

Sister and Miss Lloyd had been very kind and had given me something to eat, but I said "goodbye" to them, and Miss Senior took me home. Mum thanked her for going to the convent to collect me. Mum told me that she was very worried because no one from the school had been to tell her until half an hour before I got home. I can't remember all that mum said, and I don't really care, as I had enjoyed every minute of my adventure. It had been good fun – but poor Miss Senior!

## *Chapter Seven*

# Highs and Lows of Growing Up

One day when I was at school getting my coat on (I was about 6 years old), a girl named Roseanna, who knew that I wasn't steady on my legs, came up to me, took off my glasses and threw them on the floor. I started to cry and she ran off and left me. She then came back and picked them up; but as she bent down, she pushed me over and I fell, which started me crying again. From that day onwards, ironically, we gradually became good friends. As I go along with my story, I will tell you about the things we did together. Another time I remember was when a boy threw sand in my eye and the school nurse had to spend time washing it out. My teacher had to write a letter to mum explaining how it happened.

One of the teachers at school used to run a Bible Club on Tuesdays. We called it "The Quarter To One Club" because it was held in our dinner hour. Generally it was interesting but at times it got rather boring and dull. I think the reason I went was that I wanted to avoid going out into the playground in the very hot or cold weather, because at that time I couldn't bear the hot sun. I seemed to be prone to heat stroke and just turn bright red. My sister could sunbathe and turn red and go then brown – but not me! I burnt or stayed white! However, I can say now that for the last ten years or more, I have been able to sunbathe and in fact I tan more quickly than my sister!

By the time I was seven, Pauline was eight and used to bring her two friends down from along the road to play with her. When I wanted to play with them, they used to tease and torment me, and I would begin to cry, and then mum would tell them off!

At that time, Pauline and I used to share a bedroom and sometimes I would wake up at about 3.30am. I would get out of bed and go to Pauline and make noises and then get into bed before she saw me. She would wake up thinking something was in the room. She would come to my bed and wake me up to tell me about it. I would say, "Go and tell mum, because I didn't hear anything." Whilst she was gone, I made myself comfortable and pretended to be asleep. When mum came back she looked at me and then put Pauline back to bed and no more was said about it for several weeks.

Pauline had two friends, whose names were Carol and Jenny. They were twins, a year older than Pauline and two and a half years older than me.

Sometimes, I used to get on well with them, but many times I did not!

When Pauline and I were given sweets, I would make mine last a long time, but Pauline used to eat hers up quickly, whatever they were. I had a habit of leaving my sweets on the sideboard, the window sill or on the table. When I wasn't around Pauline would take one, and I didn't find out for weeks. So many seemed to disappear that I told mum and dad about it and they said that they didn't know how I managed to keep my sweets for so long. They gave me an idea – to hide my sweets! I did that, and from that time, Pauline couldn't get any! Then she used to have to come and ask me for one whenever she felt like having one! Later, I found that Carol and Jenny used to take my sweets as well. In fact, mum told me that the twins took more than Pauline did!

When I was ten, my friend Roseanna, who went to the Deptford Mission Club on Monday nights, asked me if I would like to join.

I said, "Yes I would but I must ask mum and dad first."

They said that I could go.

Deptford Mission was held at a Methodist Church. It was not a very old building. The church was on the left of a big hall which had a stage at one end with a dark blue curtain. To the left of the stage was a kitchen. There was a lift in the church which took you up to the next floor. There were a number of rooms up there. When I first started the club, we used to go into one of those rooms, which really was quite dirty, with very old chairs. During the daytime, it was used by a Centre or a school. Roseanna and I always used to be together. Now the person who was running the club at that time was Jenny. I can't remember whether or not she was married, but I am sure that she used to go around with a man named Tony. Roseanna and I used to play games together, sometimes also with Jenny, and we had a good time.

The furniture in the club was old and rather scruffy and dirty and I used to sit in one of the decrepit armchairs because it was still comfortable. One thing that mum didn't like about the club was that every week when the coach brought me home, I was so dirty that I always needed a bath! Mum used to go up the wall about me!

The day after I came home from the club one week, I began to scratch my head to wildly that my mum began to wonder what was wrong, so she asked me to sit on the floor. She began to part my hair with a comb and she found some nits. She was very upset and quite cross because she said, "I know that you caught them at that club of yours! It's disgraceful that it is not kept clean!"

She had to wait until the next day before she could get a special soap to shampoo my hair regularly for some days, and every day she had to comb out any nits with a specially fine comb while my hair was wet. Every few days after my head and hair were clear, mum looked through my hair and frequently used the soap to be sure. I did not pick up any more lice. I must admit I enjoyed the feel of the comb and mum's fingers going through my hair. I have always liked to have my hair brushed and combed.

One Monday night, Roseanna and I decided to write a song for Jenny because we liked her very much. But we didn't expect it to come out like this:

"We love JENNY
We love Jenny
We know we do
And we're sure we do
We love JENNY!

On most Monday nights, we used to sing this song to Jenny. I think the reason we liked her so much was because she was different from the other leaders. We used to have a lot of fun with her. However, after a while, she left and two new leaders took over.

One Saturday night, we were in the club in the hall downstairs. I wanted to go to the loo, so I asked Roseanna if she would come too. In the toilet there was a right-angled wall on which was fixed a wash basin and all around there were tiles but on the corner there was a broken tile with a very sharp edge. I was washing my hands while Roseanna was in the toilet, but as I was waiting for her I fell down and as I fell I cut my thumb badly on the broken tile. Roseanna came running, wondering what I had done, but she couldn't do anything. I was crying and I was bleeding. There was blood running down the wall and the floor. There was only one thing for Roseanna to do, and that was to go for help. Two people came back with her. They picked me up from the floor, sat me on a chair and tried to stop my hand from bleeding, but they couldn't. Eva and Peter, the leaders of the club, were going to take me to the hospital, but I started to cry and said,

"No, you're not going to take me to the hospital – I won't let you!"

They decided to bandage my hand up, and again they wanted to take me to hospital, but I still said "No!" They finally said,

"All right, Julia, we will take you home."

When I got home, mum and dad were not very pleased when they heard about my accident, but there was nothing they could do except to thank Eva and Peter for bringing me home. Later on in the evening, Eva and Peter came down to see how I was and they brought me a present. I thought it was very nice of them to come and see me. I shall never forget them. However, I do remember that I was rude sometimes, not only to them but to the whole Deptford Mission Club.

My parents had to feed me at all times until I was nine years old, when mum bought me a special bowl which prevented the food from spilling over the edge. It was jolly hard work trying to get the food on to the spoon and into my mouth. By the time I got the spoon to my mouth, there was nothing on it – the food was everywhere but the spoon! In the end, mum had to feed me. However, by the time I was eleven, I was able to feed myself, but I could not cut up my food. Mum or dad always had to feed me with gravy or custard, with the last pieces of food on the plate. When I was at school, I didn't have gravy or custard because my hand shook and it went all down me. For years after, I only had gravy or custard if there was someone there who could feed me. These days, I don't really need any help with feeding, but sometimes I ask for help for quickness.

Mum always had to wash and dress me when I was young. Mum would get up at six o'clock, and wash and dress herself before calling dad. She would then get Pauline up and while Pauline was washing she would get breakfast ready. Dad would have his breakfast and immediately leave for work. Then, while Pauline was having her breakfast, mum would get me ready. If I was going to school she would do everything for me, just for quickness.

When I was on school holidays, mum used to spend time teaching me to first wash my hands, and then my face, etc. By the time I was fourteen, I was able to wash and dress myself, but I could not do up buttons or tie shoe laces. At this time, I still had the terrible habit of getting mum to do things that I couldn't do on my own. Sometimes, my sister Pauline would get really cross with me and say, "If you can do it, do it, instead of getting mum to do it for you!"

I would reply, "mum can do it a lot quicker than I can!"

Pauline would then say, "That is not the point at all!"

When I was young, I could not hold a cup, although dad showed me the different ways of holding one. So dad then bought me cups and mugs of different shapes and sizes until at last we found the right mug for me. I could hold and lift it by holding it with my thumb through the handle and my other hand round the body of the mug. Unfortunately, when I lifted it with the drink in it, I could not stop shaking and often would spill half of it down me or on the table or floor.

Sometimes, mum got mad, especially if she had just washed the floor. As it did not work, dad put me back on drinking straws again. A couple of years later, we tried again and this time I could drink from a mug if it was half full. Then I got into the habit of drinking a full mug without picking it up. One day, dad made me a full mug of cocoa – I couldn't pick it up so I brought my head down and drank as if I were an animal holding the edge of the mug with my mouth! I don't know what really happened but I think it was because my head jerked. The mug tipped over and the cocoa went everywhere. Down me, all over the table, and on the floor! My parents were really mad with me. All I could say was, "Oh! It was an accident."

After a long period of practise, I found I could manage a full mug without spilling any liquid.

Mum always cleaned my teeth for me until I was fourteen. It must be hard cleaning another person's teeth and I don't know how mum managed it, but she did it quite well. When I went on holiday or camping I could not clean my teeth with a brush but I put toothpaste on my tongue and rubbed my tongue around my teeth. Then I drank a glass of water and it all went down into my stomach. Ugh!!

For a while, I did use my finger as a toothbrush when I tried to brush my teeth independently. After years of practise with mum showing me how to do it, I could manage on my own with a tootbrush, as long as I brushed from side to side. Mum had (what was to me) a terrible habit of making sure I cleaned my teeth properly and I used to get cross with her, asking, "What difference does it make how you clean your teeth?"

Mum would just answer, "It does matter how you do it".

When I was fourteen, I was able to brush my teeth without mum being there to watch me and telling me to brush them up and down a bit more. It was a lovely feeling to be able to do it on my own. I can now do it the right way.

Mum used to have a real problem when it came to washing my hair because I didn't like the shampoo or water getting in my eyes and up my nose. Every time mum shampooed my hair, we went through a crying session! mum tried every different way she knew how, but whatever she did I always used to play up. In the end, mum found the way to do it was in the bath. Sometimes I would scream my head off and then mum would get really cross with me. Then, quite suddenly, I grew out of it, and wasn't mum pleased!

When I was quite small, mum could not take me to the hairdresser because I could not keep my head still. So that meant that she had to cut my hair for me. This is how she did it: She would sit me on the table and get dad to hold my head still whilst she cut my hair. However, just holding my head did not stop it from jerking and when dad was holding my head, it jerked. It was quite painful! mum managed to cut my hair quite well under these circumstances! When I got older, my sister Pauline used to cut my hair. Sometimes she did it better than others, but mum or dad always had to hold my head.

One day, mum had washed my hair, but instead of sitting on a table I sat on a chair with a towel around my neck. Pauline took the scissors and began cutting, but my head suddenly jerked and instead of cutting my hair she cut my neck! I began to cry but I can't remember what happened after that except that Pauline had to carry on cutting my hair. I think she made a good job of it that time!

Another time, Pauline just wanted to cut someone's hair and it looked that way when she had finished! I was sitting on a chair with a towel around my neck. No one was holding my head, and Pauline was cutting my hair. Mum was sitting on the armchair behind Pauline, watching us.

Mum began to realise that what Pauline was doing was not improving my hairstyle! First Pauline cut one side then the other, but she noticed after a minute or two that first one side seemed longer and then the other side seemed longer, and whichever side she cut, my hair did not seem to look even and level! Each time Pauline tried to get my hair even, she was cutting it shorter and shorter! I was glad when she decided to stop cutting it! When mum saw it, she was not pleased with her, and or was I! I felt terrible because it looked as if rats had been gnawing my hair as it was cropped so badly and so short! But I couldn't really be mad with Pauline!

Mum began to think of another way to get my hair cut. She wondered if she could take me to her hairdresser and get it done professionally, but she felt a bit worried about it. However, she decided to ask the hairdresser next time she went, and see what she had to say about it.

Mum used to visit her hairdresser every other Saturday and do her shopping afterwards. She explained to her hairdresser about my disability and the hairdresser made an appointment for Wednesday afternoon at 4 o'clock, after I came back from school.

The following Wednesday when I came home, mum said, "Come on Julia, we're going to get your hair cut!"

I said "Oh mum, do we have to?"

Mum replied, "Oh Julia! It's only round the corner in Brownhill Road, just past the Catford County Boys' School." This school is no longer there.

I believe the shop was called "Tina". My hair was in such a state that Tina really didn't know what to do. In the end we decided that there was only one way to deal with it, and that was to layer cut it as it was already short. Mum and Tina took so long discussing my hair that I said to myself, "Oh come on, just get on with it!"

Anyway, when Tina had finished my hair she had made a very good job of it. After that, I had it cut about every six weeks, but when I was fifteen I decided to grow it long.

Having my toenails cut was the same as having my hair washed! But instead of mum it was dad who used to do this for me. I used to play up and he would get really cross with me. I remember one thing he said, which was, "There is only one way of cutting toe nails. It is not like washing your hair".

Just the same as with my hair, I grew out of making a fuss!

One Sunday afternoon at about three o'clock when "Tonibell" ice cream van came down the road, and Pauline had her friends down at our house, we all wanted an ice-cream. Dad gave Pauline the money to get four cornets. As she was on her way back near the gate she accidentally dropped one of the cornets. That meant Carol, Jenny and Pauline got their ice-cream but I didn't get one that afternoon and Pauline was laughing her head off. But don't worry, I got her back next time and got a bigger one.

## *Chapter Eight*
# Frustration

As I began to get older, about eight or nine, something was beginning to happen to me. I sometimes lost my temper with my parents because there were some words that I could not say properly and I used to tell them off because they couldn't understand what I was trying to say. This went on for many months. After a while, my parents decided that this was getting us nowhere.

The next time I lost my temper with them I was crying my eyes out. They waited until I had calmed down and then they told me that if I were to slow down and take my time over what I was trying to say, perhaps we might get somewhere and I might not have to lose my temper so much. So I did just as they said and it made all the difference, but there were always one or two words that they couldn't understand. I soon got over that by using another word that meant the same as the one I couldn't say clearly. I found that it worked most of the time!

At first, when I was seven years old and mum and Nan took me shopping without my pushchair, mum really pulled me along the road and I couldn't keep up with them. People who knew me and my family used to say, "How could you pull Julia along the road like that? Poor little thing."

After about a year of this, some things were beginning to change. My legs were getting stronger and I could walk a lot better without falling over so often, so that meant that mum didn't have to pull me along. But she still held my hand and sometimes she hurt me. It was lovely to walk without being pulled here and there.

As I gradually grew stronger, mum decided to let me walk by myself, but she knew that if I fell over she would not be able to save me as she did when she was holding my hand, but it was the only way! mum had to let me stand on my own two feet (literally!) and when I fell over, I could gradually learn to cope with it! mum thought that this would be the best way to teach me to be independent.

At first when I fell over, I always used to hurt my knees and head, never my hands. My parents were amazed at this, but I knew why this used to happen. I had the habit of walking with my hands in my pockets in order to keep control of them. This meant that if I fell, I couldn't get my hands out of my pockets in time to save my head. Dad was always telling me off about putting my hands in my pockets, but he knew I would have to learn the hard way, as I always had done.

One of the falls I can remember very clearly. A woman was walking by with a baby in a pushchair. Mum and Nan were a little way behind me. Maybe I wasn't looking where I was going (which was just like me), but I fell over the pushchair, my head went down first so that my teeth went through my lower lip! Mum picked me up from the ground and the woman apologised to mum, although it wasn't really her fault. My lip was bleeding like mad all down my coat. Mum had some tissues in her pocket so she used them to wipe my mouth. Everybody was looking at us. They said that mum should take me to hospital, but she didn't because she knew how hospitals upset me and she thought that I was upset enough.

My lip was swelling and all mum wanted to do was to get home. Even so, she managed to do most of her shopping and poor Nan had to carry it, because mum was carrying me. My mouth was so bad that I couldn't bite anything. Mum had to break up everything I ate into tiny pieces. This went on for about two months and after that it got better. Honestly – the things mum went through on my account!

I gradually got out of the habit of walking with my hands in my pockets, but unfortunately, I began to get into another habit which I now think was worse. I began to walk with my arms sticking out behind my back. This made me look a lot worse than walking with my hands in my pockets. More people were looking at me and this made me worse. In fact, sometimes it would make me more self-conscious and appear a lot worse than I normally would be. However, if I didn't think anyone was looking at me, I would be all right. It still didn't help my falling over though, so I went back to putting my hands in my pockets! Really, I was glad to do this because it made me look much better. Gradually, however, I managed to get out of this bad habit and walk with my hands at my side. This was hard work and it took a lot of physiotherapy and patience.

Coming down the stairs was always a problem for me. I could manage to walk upstairs, but could not manage to walk downstairs. I had to think of a way to get downstairs without asking mum or dad to carry me.

One day, I was sitting on the top step waiting for someone to come and carry me down, when all of a sudden I came up with a great idea of how to get down by myself, and it worked perfectly. This is what I did. I would sit on the top step with my feet on the third step and wriggle my bottom until I could slide down on to the next step. I continued wriggling and sliding until I reached the last step and then I would stand up. The first time I managed this, I was very pleased with myself!

After five years I learnt to walk down our stairs, but still did it sometimes – especially when there was a bend or when I had to carry something downstairs. Dad used to say that I sounded like an elephant the way I clumped down those stairs of ours. Of course, I never came downstairs like that in public or in other people's homes! But I have done here and there and honestly the looks people have given me!

My sister had a three-wheeler bike that she had grown out of, so when I was about twelve it was passed on to me. I had always wanted to ride it when I was younger but couldn't because I was not steady enough.

One day, the bicycle was in the garden and I believe that Pauline was out with her friends and mum was working upstairs. I managed to get out into the garden and onto the bike without mum seeing me. After a while, mum saw me riding the bike around the garden. She was very surprised and pleased with what I was doing but of course as soon as I saw mum watching me I promptly fell off and cut my knees! Mum came running out and picked me up and took me indoors to clean me up. I felt shaken up but I was glad that I had proved that I could ride the bike. When dad heard of my adventure, he was very pleased with me and told me to practise every day!

As the year went by, I was getting stronger. That meant that I had permission to ride out on the pavement. One day, I rode to the top of Fordel Road, and I had to get off the bike in order to turn it round. I managed that quite well, but half way down the road, I think the bike must have run over something and it and me tipped over and I fell and hurt myself quite badly. I cut my head open and grazed and cut my hands and knees. I don't really know what happened, but somebody picked me up and took me home and I remember I was told off. Dad said that I wasn't allowed to ride the bike any more. "Back in the garden," he said.

I was really upset.

I said, "Oh, mum! Just because I've had an accident it shouldn't mean that I can't ride the bike any more."

Mum said, "Don't worry. I will see if I can get round him. But do as he says for the moment."

It took six months before dad said I could ride the bike on the pavement once more. This time I was able to turn the bike without getting off.

One sunny Wednesday afternoon, during a school holiday, my sister Pauline was at a friend's house and mum was going to wash her hair. It was about two o'clock and as I was riding the bike down the road. Pauline and her two friends came out of the friend's house and were walking beside me. Suddenly, the bike and I went over! Pauline came running up and she tried to pick me up but couldn't do it, so she left me on the ground with Carol and Jenny while she went to get mum. Carol and Jenny just stood there looking down at me. My head, nose, hands and knees were bleeding. After about five minutes, mum came running down the road with her hair wrapped in a towel because she had just finished washing her hair and it was dripping wet. Anyway, mum picked me up and carried me home while Pauline, Carol and Jenny came walking behind with the bike. Then they left the bike in the garden and carried on with whatever they were going to do.

Mum sat me on a chair in the kitchen and did her hair up properly with the towel before she cleaned me up. Mum washed off the blood and dirt from my cuts and she saw I had a big bump and a nasty cut on my head. She put plasters on my knees and a large one on my head.

The plaster on my head stayed on for four days, but when dad decided to change it he found my head wasn't any better and he didn't know what to do. He went to get Uncle Fred to come and have a look at it. In the end, they decided to take me to the hospital, so Uncle Fred took us in his car.

When we got there the nurse wanted to pull the plaster off and I started to cry, so she said, "I think we had better get her father to take it off."

Dad took the plaster off and the nurse said, "Oh! You'll have to see the Doctor."

We went into the waiting room but it was about one-and-a-half hours later when the nurse called me in. Because mum wasn't allowed to come in with me, I was really upset and could not stop crying. They put me in a cubicle and that made me even worse! Everyone on the ward could hear me, especially when they gave me an injection for tetanus in my arm and sent me back to mum and dad.

About ten minutes later, they called me in again and put me on the bed and gave me another injection in my backside! When I came out and told my parents what the nurses had done to me, they just sat there laughing at the way I told them, so that set me off crying again!

About fifteen minutes later, the nurse called me in for the last time. All they did this time was put some red "stuff" on my head. Because of the big lump on my head, it could not be stitched. It looked as if my head was bleeding and the blood was running down my face. When mum saw me she was shocked and I think she felt a bit faint! At last, we were allowed to go home and we thanked Uncle Fred for taking us and bringing us home. We did not have a car at the time.

Mum said, "Oh, You can't go so school looking like that!" so I had two days off school!

I carried on riding the bike until I got too big for it and then dad got rid of it.

# Chapter Nine
# Guiding

A couple of months before I went to secondary school, I wanted to be a Brownie. Before I tell you about this, I'll quickly tell you how they operated. The Brownie meeting was held during Tuesday lunch times and some of the girls went to it instead of going out to play. I wanted to be a Brownie but I was told that it wasn't worthwhile as in a few months' time I would be moving to the secondary school, so that meant I could go straight into Guides. I was let in by the leader for that Tuesday. I enjoyed it and it was better than being in the cold playground with the other children.

The following Tuesday, I wanted to go again but the leaders said I couldn't unless I had a medical certificate to say that I was fit enough to be a Brownie. I was very upset and started to cry. Then I went out to play with the other children.

A couple of weeks later, I had a medical and the doctor said that I was fit enough to join the Brownies. However, I didn't become a Brownie because I wasn't going to be in the pack long enough, but I certainly learned a lot about Brownies.

When I joined the Guides, the Guider came to the school on Wednesday at about 12.30pm. I liked Guides very much – there were so many things to do and so many things to learn about myself, other people, nature, in fact the whole world. We were taught that we should help other people, whether or not we knew them personally, or whether or not we liked them.

While I was in the Guides, I belonged to the Swallow Patrol. I have always been able to remember the promise, but I just couldn't learn all the Guide Laws, but I did remember some. I passed a number of tests and earned my Second Class badge. I got nearly three-quarters of the way through the tests for the First Class badge when the new way was started. Now Guides and Brownies can pick a subject, e.g. swimming, cookery, animal care, etc., and if they pass, they get the badge.

I did the Collector's badge, and I chose stamp collecting. I had to learn about the stamps as well as collecting them. Then I did the "Friend to the Deaf" badge, and I had to learn finger spelling and about the deaf. After that I was working for my "Child Nursing" badge, but halfway through I had to move up to Rangers.

As Plassey Road school closed down, the Guide's company moved to

Sydenham Girls' School and we held the meetings on the second Saturday of each month, in the afternoon from 3.00pm until 6.00pm. It used to be called post-guides. There used to be seven groups; one group was for learning difficulties and the other for the physically disabled – two for Brownies, two for Guides, two for Rangers and one group for the Trefoil Guides. They came from these areas – Lewisham, Greenwich, Lambeth, Southwark and possibly Bromley. Most children were picked up by ILEA (Inner London Education Authority) buses before it was abolished (in March 1990) and the local council took over. The transport lady for Lewisham told me once that she had more problems with the Borough of Lewisham transport than with any other borough.

Every year while I was in the Guides, we went camping. My first camp was a weekend at Cudham. On the way down on Friday evening I cried. I cried again when I went to bed. I was all right during the day time but on Saturday night I cried again. However, on Sunday I was great and I didn't want to come home. Every year after that I enjoyed every bit of camping and I got a great deal of fun out of it.

I was in the Guides from eleven years old to sixteen, and then moved up to the Rangers until I was in my twenties. Then I gave it up. A couple of years later, Fluty (one of the Guide Leaders) came to see me and asked if I would come back to Guiders and be a helper. I said that I would love to.

My friend and I were escorts for Brownies and Guides on the social services buses, which meant we were picked up at about one o'clock on Saturday. At mid-day I would receive a phone call from the lady dealing with transport, telling me who was not coming. Eight out of ten of the drivers would pick up one or two children on their way to collect me. Sometimes they would get cross if one didn't come. I would say, "Yes, I knew she wasn't coming and if you had picked me up first, I could have told you!"

Because we were escorts on the bus, we should have been dropped off last, but some of the drivers would take me and my friend home before finishing the round and I used to feel cross about this. I'm pretty sure they did it for quickness. Sometimes I would report them to Sheila the transport lady. I kept up the escorting for a good few years before I gave it up.

As I used to help Denise (another Guide Leader) with her Guides or Brownies, I gradually got to know to Diane, who took the Brownie pack. I grew to like her very much but that wasn't until 1987 when Diane asked me if I would like to join the Gang Show. I hesitated for a while, as I wasn't sure if I could cope. Diane assured me that she would take care of me and help me with the things I couldn't do. I thought Diane didn't sound like a person who would let you down after she has promised you something, so in the end I said I would join.

We met in a school near Charlton House every Sunday in the afternoon for about three months. The first couple of weeks was just to find out what you were good at. For example – singing, dancing or having a good voice for acting etc. I wanted to be part of it without having any major parts because I wasn't sure how my cerebral palsy would affect me. Then the Gang Show team would plan the show giving everybody their parts and words to learn.

The Gang Show was made up from extracts of James Bond films. I remember some of the titles we sang – 'For Your Eyes Only', 'Diamonds are Forever' and 'From Russia with Love'. Then 'Day by Day', 'I Don't Know How To Love Him' and many more. Diane sang the first bit of 'I Don't Know How To Love Him' on her own then the rest joined in. I thought she had a good voice.

While doing the gang show I just couldn't understand what was going on with my cerebral palsy. I would learn the words and could say them very well. But when at the school or on the stage, I had problems, yet I knew I could do it. My cerebral palsy would play up and I just couldn't control it. I knew that part of it was nerves but not all of it. The physiotherapist at the Ladywell Centre told me that when you do something new or different with cerebral palsy, your body takes time to learn to control the new movements. Diane was fantastic; she helped me whenever I needed it, including helping me to change my clothes during the show. She really was like a sister, and everyone thought we were related as we spent a lot of time together. We kept in touch for a while and then we lost contact, but I did enjoy doing the Gang Show. I would love to do it again and maybe meet up with Diane again some time. I often wonder what Diane is doing now.

I gave up Guiding when they had to leave Sydenham Girls' School because finance was becoming a problem with the cut backs. The Brownies, Guides and Rangers split up and they weren't all together under one roof. I wasn't very keen on their new meeting place, so I left.

I had suggested in previous years that the Guide meetings be held at Ladywell. It was just the place for the disabled children and youngsters. It had all the facilities they needed and a park, which would be great in summer. In 1992, I heard that there were problems with booking one hall and Sydenham School were charging about £100-200 a time. I rang June (the secretary in the Guides), and an appointment was made for her to have a look around and meet the manager at the Ladywell Centre. The Centre was fully booked on the second Saturday of each month, so they moved it to the first Saturday of each month and in September the Guides moved to Ladywell Centre. Everybody loved it there. I liked it because we were all in one building again as we were when we first started. I am not sure whether I would go back and be a committed guider now though – who knows what the future holds.

## Chapter Ten
# Mischief

One day when I was about 10 years old, the wardrobe fell on me, which was quite funny even at the time! On this day, mum and dad were out and Pauline and her friends, Carol and Jenny, had come around. I went upstairs to get something out of my wardrobe. I don't know how it happened but the wardrobe fell on top of me. Pauline and Carol came running upstairs to find out what the 'bang' was. When Pauline saw the wardrobe on top of me, she tried to lift it back but it was too heavy for her, so Carol and Jenny helped her to lift the wardrobe up on to its feet. Then Pauline lifted me up and decided to put me on the bed, although I wasn't hurt, and we all decided to play a joke on my parents.

Pauline knew that mum and dad would be back at any moment, so she told me to stay on the bed. Two minutes later, mum came home and the next thing I heard was my sister running towards mum calling out that I had had an accident and was laying on the bed and couldn't move! Then I heard mum running up the stairs. She burst into my room saying, "Are you all right, Julia?"

"No," I said, "I think I've hurt my back."

Mum moaned, "Oh no." Then she said, "Well, I'll have to get you to hospital."

I said "Oh mum, do I have to go?"

"Yes you do," she replied.

She went downstairs to get something; she was very worried, I knew. I thought "this joke's gone far enough", so I followed her downstairs on tip toes without her knowing. When I got downstairs I saw mum going into the back room and I kept my fingers crossed hoping that Pauline and her friends were in the room, and they were. Pauline asked mum how I was and she replied that she was going to take me to the hospital. Pauline smiled and said, "I wouldn't bother if I were you!" Then mum said, "Why not? What do I do with Julia if I don't take her to hospital?"

Pauline said, "mum – just look behind you."

Mum turned round and saw me standing in the doorway. She just didn't know what to say, so we all burst out laughing! Then we told mum what had happened – how the wardrobe had fallen on me and that Pauline had decided to make a joke out of it and I went along with her.

Mum said very firmly, "Never play a joke on me like that again!" However, she was so relieved that she joined in our laughing. It seemed quite a good idea to us but not to poor mum!

## *Chapter Eleven*
# Learning to Swim

One Sunday morning, mum took me to Eltham Swimming Baths, where we saw Roseanna and her mother. After a while, my mum and Roseanna's mum got to know each other and later on after a month or so, Roseanna's mum picked mum and me up in the car most weeks, which saved us waiting for a bus.

One Sunday morning, Roy, the swimming instructor, asked mum if he could take me into the water. Mum said that it would be all right, but the moment Roy put me into the water, I screamed and cried my eyes out. Everybody turned round and looked at me. I was terrified! mum couldn't believe her eyes and ears! She didn't know what do to for a few minutes. Then she did the only thing she could do, which was to take me out of the water and dry and dress me again. The following Sunday when mum took me to the baths, the same thing happened and this really made mum cross. Nevertheless, she persevered with me.

One Sunday, a few weeks later, when Roy was busy with someone else, Len, one of the other helpers, came over to me to take me into the water. Mum didn't take her eyes off me. She was waiting to see if I was going to cry, but I didn't! mum was wondering why I didn't make a fuss, especially as I stayed in the water for half an hour! She was very pleased with me until the next Sunday when Roy took me into the water. At once, I began to scream and cry, so Roy called Len over and then I was all right. These lessons went on for two years, and then mum thought that I wasn't going to be able to swim, so I had better give it up.

A couple of years later the Borough of Greenwich had installed at Eltham Baths a Hydraulic pool for disabled people which gave me a lot of confidence. The water was also very warm. It was like being in a bath! It was on one Sunday morning that the instructor came round to tell us about it. Roy told me that my friends, Susan and Sharon would be going. So it was arranged that Roy would pick up mum and me with Susan and Sharon on the next Wednesday.

Mum came with us to look after us and help with undressing and dressing. When Wednesday came, we were all ready by 6.15pm for Roy. On arriving at the baths, Roy went through the main entrance to open the side door to avoid the stairs. It was so warm inside that I could scarcely wait to be undressed and to get in to the water.

The pool wasn't very big. It was free standing and it was divided in two by a bar across the middle. One half was evenly shallow, about two feet deep. The other half was about four feet six inches and there was a bar all round to hold on to.

I spent quite a long time in the shallow part and then the instructor asked if I would like to go into the deeper part. I said, "Yes, but only if you don't let me go under!"

He promised that he'd hold me all the time and I asked him how I was going to get over the bar. He asked me to stand up and turn my back to the bar. Then he put his arms around my waist and lifted me over it. However, I found that once I was in the deeper part I didn't like it very much because I couldn't touch the bottom. He told me to put my head back and let my feet come up so that I floated as he was holding me. I did this each time I went to the baths over a period of six months and the instructor told me to kick with my feet and legs and turn my arms like a windmill.

Eventually, I could do this on my own with the instructor putting just one finger under my head.

Many years later, when mum had MS, she started going swimming because Roy said it would do her MS good. Her lessons were for half an hour, and she also used to enjoy floating on her back in the water. After a year or so, though, we all gave up the swimming lessons.

*Chapter Twelve*

# Practise Makes Perfect

When I was ten, I made my first attempt at handwriting. My hand wasn't steady enough to hold a pen or to hold down a sheet of paper. The following year, dad and I sat down at the table and we tried again. Dad put a pen into my hand and he held the paper down for me while I did a bit of scribbling then he said, "If you can scribble, there's no reason why you shouldn't be able to learn to write."

Dad showed me how to write the alphabet and he asked me to write over the top of the letters. I couldn't get anywhere near it! Dad said, "Keep on trying, it will come to you in time!"

I did this for six months, unsuccessfully, and I was beginning to lose patience with it. Dad said, "Look Julia, if you carry on like that you'll never be able to write. The more you practise the better you will get."

Another couple of months went by, and slowly my writing began to improve but it was never on the line and it went up and down all over the page.

We were breaking up from school for the summer holidays, which meant I had six weeks. Dad was pleased about that, but I wasn't! Dad said that now I was on holiday it meant that I could practise my writing. I must say, I was very fed up with this business of "practise makes perfect", but I knew that if I wanted to write, this was the only way to do it. In the end it really worked.

Without dad pushing me or helping me to find a way to hold my book down and to hold my pen firmly in my hand, I could not have done it. My book had to be fastened to the table or else bent over the edge of it, and my pen was held between the clenched fingers of my left hand.

All I can say is that it was worth dad nagging at me during that period. Dad also kept nagging about the way I held my pen, but he never won! He even tried to get me to write with my right hand, but he failed.

Over the years, my writing improved and I got out of the habit of bending my book. Later on, the best way for me to write was kneeling on the floor with my book on the chair or the settee so that I could rest my arm on it. This gave me more control over the jerky movements. I once did this in the bank, and everybody looked at me in such a way that I didn't know what to say. One particular day, I poked my tongue out, which was silly. Now I say, "What are you looking at?" Then, they will either leave me alone or make some rude remarks!

It was many years later that I found out my writing movement came from my wrist, rather than from my finger and thumb. Roland, a close friend of mine, asked me to sign a letter, which I did on a writing board resting on his lap. It was then he noticed my writing came from arm or wrist movements. Once I realised this, and focused more on controlling my writing from my finger and thumb, my writing did improve.

*Chapter Thirteen*

# The Dentist

I can't remember the first time I went to the dentist, but I must have been about eight. Mum told me what happened then. I used to go with mum whenever she went. Then one day I needed a filling, so I let the dentist do it and I was a good girl! The next time I visited him, I had a toothache but the dentist said that he couldn't take the tooth out, so he sent me to King's College Hospital, and that was fine. The only thing was that when they put me out, they put a black mask over my face which frightened me and gave me nightmares. After that when I had to go to the dentist, I used to play up. I would cry the night before and my parents used to get very cross with me.

When I next went to the dentist, mum got me into the dentist's waiting room. I began to cry after a few minutes and when she got me into the surgery I yelled and yelled. The nurse let mum stay, although usually parents were told to wait outside. I was seated in the chair, with mum standing at my side holding my right hand. The dentist asked me to open my mouth, but I wouldn't. He told mum that if I refused to open my mouth, there was nothing that he could do. We had to leave it until another time. Neither mum nor dad were very pleased with me.

A couple of years later I had another bad tooth. Mum wouldn't take me to her dentist. Instead, she took me to Lewisham hospital. We saw a Mr. Cooper – a nice man – tall with grey hair and a little ginger moustache. There was one thing about Mr. Cooper – he had a lot of patience with me. He told mum to bring me back in six months' time.

When the six months were up and we were due to go back I made a lot of fuss and the night before I cried so much that my parents lost their patience and got very cross. They said, "Julia, you're making a fuss about nothing."

Gradually I stopped crying and went to sleep, but the next morning I was just as bad!

We got to the hospital and went into the waiting room, but sitting there started me off crying again. Mum got cross and told me off. At last it was my turn to go in to the dentist. I behaved no better, for as soon as I was in the chair and saw all the dentist's paraphernalia around, I was worse than ever! He couldn't do anything with me and one of the nurses who was there at the time wasn't very nice, but the other one was kind. In the end the dentist said that if I let him look at my teeth, I could go and see the fish, which were in a large tropical tank in the room. I had been wanting to see them, so I did as he asked and opened my mouth. One of the nurses took me by the hand over to the fish tank and I enjoyed watching them swimming around. I can't remember for sure what they were but I think some were goldfish, although there were other types with rainbow colours and long lacy fins.

While I was looking at the fishes, Mr. Cooper was having a long chat with mum. Of course, I didn't hear what they were saying, but he gave mum some big green tablets for me to take the day before the next appointment to help calm me down.

This is what happened. The day before we went, mum gave me two of these green tablets before I went to bed. It took me a long time to swallow the first tablet so mum broke the second one in half and gave it to me. It tasted horrible and took longer than the first to go down. Even so, it didn't seem to make much difference and I was crying as much as before. In fact, I was just as bad each time I went to the dentist so finally mum and dad decided not to bother with my teeth any more at that time.

When I was thirteen, my teeth were beginning to rot and my parents were beginning to get worried about them but they didn't know what to do about it. Mum knew that I'd always make a fuss, so she decided that the next time I had to see Dr. Gann at Lewisham Hospital she would ask him if he would make an appointment with the hospital dentist. When she went to see him, Dr. Gann said he would, so that settled it. He asked mum some questions and then we went home.

A week later, we had a letter to go and see Mr. Cooper, a dentist at Lewisham Hospital, on Monday morning. I was feeling all right until I got to the waiting room and then I started crying and started fussing. Once I was inside the dental surgery itself, I felt even worse, seeing all the dentist's implements around. Now all these tools are put in cupboards except the horrible drill!

Mr. Cooper let me take mum into the surgery with me and she held my hand. Mr. Cooper said, "Julia's teeth are pretty bad and I'm not sure how to deal with them."

mum said, "Couldn't you put her to sleep while you examine her teeth – just as if she were having one taken out?" Mr. Cooper said he hadn't done an examination like that before but he'd see what he could do and would let us know.

About a month later, mum received a letter from Lewisham Hospital to see the dentist. My appointment was at nine o'clock. We left home at 8.30am and arrived at the hospital just in time but we had to wait a little while and I was already crying! About a quarter of an hour later, I was called in and I grabbed mum's arm. When they put me in the chair I was still holding mum's hand and I think she was getting in the way a bit, but as I was crying my eyes out they couldn't do much about it. The doctor gave me an injection in the wrong part of my arm, so they pulled out the needle and suck it back in the right place! And this really did make me cry! The nurse and mum didn't know what to say – not that there was anything they could do about it. It was just one of those things that happened. Anyway, the minute I was asleep, mum went back into the waiting room. I can't tell you what she was doing during the time I was in the surgery, because I was with the dentist from ten o'clock that morning until three o'clock in the afternoon.

I had eight fillings and one out. I don't know whether mum had been given a cup of tea, but I know she didn't get anything to eat. The doctors and nurses were very kind to mum. About three o'clock I started coming round. When I woke up I saw mum sitting in the chair opposite me as if she'd been sitting there the whole time. When she saw me waking up, she came over to me and held my hand. Mr. Cooper told mum that I might have a sore throat but what hurt the most was that I didn't know what to do with my mouth or where to put my tongue!

My mouth was so very sore that I didn't know whether to keep it open or shut and I couldn't even put my teeth together. I just didn't know what to do with myself. It was so terribly painful!

Soon, we were told that we were to be taken home in an ambulance. Mum helped me to get ready and said goodbye to Mr. Cooper and the nurses, but when I got up to walk, I couldn't do it, so mum carried me downstairs and put me in an armchair. She sat next to me, holding me up. We had to wait nearly an hour and a half for an ambulance. At last we arrived home; it was about five o'clock. I believe it was the first time I had been in an ambulance. The ambulance attendant carried me indoors and put me down in the back room, then left us. Dad was at home and he was getting the dinner out of the oven. Mum was glad to see this as she was starving! So was I but I couldn't eat or drink anything as my mouth was too sore. I think Nobby, our dog, ate my dinner for me! I went to bed early that night as I felt too unwell to do anything much.

The next morning when I got up, my mouth was still sore. I could only drink with a straw. Mum had to break my food into little pieces so that I could just swallow without chewing. It took me a long time before I had any confidence to feed myself again. I was too worried that I might knock my two front teeth out, because as I put my fork or spoon to my mouth, my hand would jerk and I would knock my teeth.

After about a month, my mouth was better and I could eat anything without my gums getting sore. It was lovely! There is one thing that has worried me ever since that time – that is when I bite meat off the bone or bite anything hard I have always thought that my front teeth would fall out! So far that hasn't happened! I have made one loose a couple of times and knocked a crown off before now.

One day, I was eating my dinner without any problems until I came to the pudding, which was my favourite – ice-cream. I ate a couple of mouthfuls and took the next one. I don't know how it happened, whether my hand was shaking or I wasn't opening my mouth properly, but I knocked my tooth out with the spoon and I was furious with myself. There was nothing I could do about it except pay another visit to the dentist!

I think I was a lot older then because I remember I had to go on my own, but every time I went to the dentist I had to be held down. One nurse held my head still whilst another held my hands firmly as Mr. Cooper gave me an injection in my gum! Then he waited for a few minutes to let the injection work and deaden the nerve. Then he set to work to fill the tooth. He put something around the tooth to smooth the filling down. Only then did the nurses relax their hold of me. When the dental staff had to hold my head, this made me jerk my head more because I was more aware of it. This used to hurt my head more. Anyway, when it was all over, I had to wait for a few minutes to cool off and calm down and get my colour back before they let me go home. I felt very odd as if I had a big lip.

Mum told me off one time when I was quite small and I had to have a tooth out. When we reached the hospital, Mr. Cooper was not there and another dentist did his job. I was given an anaesthetic and when I was unconscious I was taken to the operating theatre. The work of taking my tooth out was done by this dental surgeon and then I was put back on the trolley and taken to the dentist's rest room. I was left there with mum to wait until I became conscious. Unfortunately, I kept turning and twisting and mum had to hang on to the trolley to stop it moving around. It was very tiring for her and at last she asked a nurse if I could be put on a bed. The nurse said, "Yes, of course." So, between them, I was lifted on to a bed and mum was much relieved not to have to stop the trolley running away with me. After about half an hour or so, I was fine and we went home.

Now I'll tell you why I had to be held down in the chair. I was fine in the waiting room except my tummy seemed to turn over. When I was called in, I could easily sit in the chair quite straight without any trouble, but when Mr. Cooper tried to bring my head back to the headrest so that he could examine my teeth, I lost control over my head and arms and found it impossible to relax. My arms would go stiff and my head, hands and arms would start to jerk and twist, especially when he used the drill; because of this I had to be held firmly. However, I am getting better and the dentists now use different techniques. If you ask me if I knew what I was dong in the dentist's chair, I would answer "Yes, but I could not control the jerking and twisting." Perhaps it is the case of excess nervousness, because as I have got older, I understand what the dentist does and why he must do it. I am not so nervous and I can control these jerks up to a point but of course I had this habit when I was young and it took years to get out of it.

Everyone on the hospital staff admired Mr. Cooper for the time and patience he had with me, and I am very grateful to them and him. If it wasn't for mum and Mr. Cooper, I probably wouldn't have any teeth now! Mr. Cooper later retired and we had another very nice man. We got on well together. We certainly had some good laughs.

Whilst the Dental Surgery at Lewisham Hospital was being decorated, we moved to Grove Park Hospital. The dentist was there for quite a while and then he left. When this happened, I got nervous and worried, wondering what the person was going to be like. I was introduced to Amanda and she was excellent. She would explain exactly what she was going to do before she started, and whilst doing my teeth. When she felt that I was getting too tense she would stop and let me become calm and relaxed, and then carry on. We had some good chats and laughs every time I went. We tried a new idea, which was gas and air, such as they give to mothers when they give birth. I would have a little nose mask on my nose, which sometimes smelled of rubber. They used to put perfume on it to make it smell better. Sitting in the dentist's chair, I breathed in the gas and air, the dentist taking my pulse now and again. It took time, but slowly my body was so relaxed that she could do my teeth better. After the dental treatment, she turned the gas off but left the oxygen on until I was back to normal. I loved this as it was like being on a high.

One year, Amanda asked me if I would give a talk at King's College Dental School on my experiences of the dentists and about my independence, including pros and cons about living in my first home independently at Bargery Road. I said, "I would love to." The way I remembered the most important points was by using key words. This worked very well. Amanda came to collect me from Ladywell after lunch. Amanda gave her talk before me and it was interesting as she concentrated on caring for the teeth of people who were coming from residential care to live in the community. Some of my points were able to back-up or support what she had said. There was an opportunity for them to ask me questions, but, because of my deafness, Amanda had to repeat the questions to me.

I really enjoyed that afternoon because it was worthwhile. Amanda did say that I might get paid and I did. The second time I gave a lecture at King's College Dental School was very different, and a bit difficult because there were more people and most of them came from abroad. Some of them couldn't understand what I was saying. To be honest, I didn't understand them either! I remember one lady who kept on saying, "Do you really live alone?"

I replied, "Yes." She just wouldn't believe me. I am glad I gave the talk because it made them aware of some of the difficulties that disabled people have to overcome when people don't understand them.

I believe Amanda was with us for about five years, then she and her family moved up north and I missed her. When I went for my next check-up, Tamsin came in to the waiting room to introduce herself and we had a good chat before going into the surgery for my check-up. When I got to know her, she was the same as Amanda. Once again, I had to have quite a lot done to my teeth and they agreed to put me under.

I arranged for Pat B. to come and collect me to take me home, which had to be after four pm. The dentist didn't mind me staying. This time I had a really sore mouth which lasted about a week. About a week later, I wanted to write a poem for the staff at the dentist's and it went like this:

THE DENTIST
The dentist is not my favourite date,
But it's my fate and I feel faint.
Past experiences I remember,
Wish it was next December.
The staff though are very nice.
The injection put me out in a trice.
That afternoon I came to,
Extraction, fillings, crown,
What a do!
For seven days I paid a price,
A sore mouth left me silent like mice.
Would I have to live on rice?
But God knew best,
Tamsin met the test.
Kind, gentle and caring,
Like the staff, she's the best.
So this is to thank them all.
They give me the confidence to dare all!

I had been going to Grove Park Dentist Unit for over ten years, when in 1993 it was moved to the Jenner Health Centre. Grove Park Hospital has now been knocked down and flats and houses built on the grounds. Tamsin moved back to Cornwall when we moved to Jenner; Sylvia, the dental nurse I had known for years, stayed until the move had taken place before retiring. It was bad enough going to a new building, but having a new dentist as well, made me feel very nervous on my first visit.

What was worse was that my crown had broken off. I knew she wouldn't be able to put my crown back as my tooth had broken with the crown. There was a bit of my tooth left in my gum which had to come out. We agreed that I would be given a general anaesthetic, during which she would take some x-rays, do a filling, take the bit of tooth out and do some impressions for a replacement. Unlike Grove Park, it had to be done at King's College Day Surgery Centre.

This was another experience. First of all, you get a letter telling you the general rules and several forms to fill in. Christina, a dental nurse from Grove Park, gave me a lift to the Day Surgery Centre. Debbie, the dentist, told me about the operation and I was quite happy, if nervous. I had thought Christina was going to be my nurse, so it was a shock when another nurse took me to the ward and told me to get undressed. The letter had said 'wear loose clothing', but nothing about undressing. Grove Park had been friendly and informal; King's College was run on hospital lines and very impersonal. When I was told to get undressed, I felt really angry. I had not been treated like this before so I refused and just took my jacket and shoes off. It would have made me feel better if I had known this beforehand and I could have worn something easy to get on and off. The staff never told me why I should get undressed, but later my dentist told me that it was because I was disabled and there could have been a problem during surgery.

This shows a real lack of communication between the hospital staff and me as a patient. When I came round from the anaesthetic and I wanted to go to the loo, I got cross with one of the nurses because of the way she escorted me to the ladies. She, again, did not communicate with me and just pulled me along, not asking how I preferred to be helped.

I could go on and on talking about my experiences at the dentist. Once I was given too much gas and it took me over a week to get over the effects. In 2003, I was still having problems with the dentist. My dentist was in Kidbrook and again, he had a lot to learn with regard to how to deal with me. He treated me as if I was a child and was very patronising. It was a horrible atmosphere when I went there and to be honest, after all these years of dental treatment, Grove Park has been the best one of them all. This is because everyone was friendly and not locked behind closed doors. The waiting room was welcoming and you could talk to the staff, who made you feel more relaxed.

In 2004, when my original dentist was on sick leave, a Dentist called Carole took her place. She managed to make me feel so at ease, and was much more like my favourite old dentists at Grove Park. I hoped that she would stay on permanently but unfortunately she didn't. Luckily, Jo the dentist that replaced her was just as good and we got on very well together. Ross was the hygienist and Caroline was the dental nurse – I got on really well with them all and I still have them to this day.

## *Chapter Fourteen*

# Pets

Now I'm going to tell you about the animals that we've had in our family. After mum and dad were married and before Pauline and I were born, they had a lovely Alsatian dog which they called Prince. Unfortunately, as I wasn't born then, I can only tell you what mum told me over the years. One day, mum was in the kitchen making some fish cakes. Some were in the pan and the rest of the mixture was in a bowl on the table. Well, whilst mum turned to the stove to see to the fish cakes, Prince jumped on to the table and ate the rest of the mixture! I don't think mum was pleased with Prince for quite a while after that!

Another incident mum told me about was when they had some lino delivered which they had bought for the kitchen, and dad laid it down. A few hours later when mum shut Prince in the kitchen for a while he started to chew up the lino! When mum went back into the kitchen, she was so shocked to see the lino torn up, she didn't know what to do or say for a few moments! Then she went to fetch dad to come and see it. Dad was very cross and he gave Prince a whack on his back leg. The dog had gone under the table where he always went when he had done something wrong.

Prince had a habit of getting in and out of the next door neighbours' garden. Once when he was in their garden, the man next door hit him with a broom, and Prince never got over this. This changed Prince's personality and mum and dad found him too difficult to handle. In the end, they had to have Prince put down.

One year when it was mum and dad's wedding anniversary and Pauline and I were quite small, dad bought mum a Siamese cat, and we named her Lindsay Loo. We had Lindsay when she was six weeks old and we kept her until she died, when she was twelve years old. You would never believe the things we did to that cat, or what a Siamese would let us do! It was quite amazing.

The first thing that happened to Lindsay was that Pauline used to take the cat to bed with her every night. The funny thing was that Lindsay Loo would get under the bedclothes and put her head next to Pauline's head on the pillow. Pauline would put her arm around Lindsay and cuddle up to her.

A couple of months later, Pauline had a very high temperature. Mum and dad were very worried and they decided to call in the doctor. Our doctor was away so we had a locum. This locum was very nice and he didn't say "Get that cat out!" when he saw Lindsay on Pauline's bed. He just left her there. After he had examined Pauline, he told mum and dad that she had Laryngitis. He also told mum that if he had not been a doctor he would have been a breeder of Siamese cats!

Pauline taught Lindsay Loo many tricks! Lindsay Loo could turn head over tail; she lay on her back whilst Pauline helped her to do the trick. Sometimes the cat would lie in the pram like a baby!

One year, Lindsay Loo had a bad tail. All the fur had come off, and it looked quite funny! Mum decided to take her down to the vet. It was always mum who had to take sick animals to the vet, and he gave mum some mauve coloured liquid to paint on the bare patch, every day for about a week.

Mum got the medication and brought it home and she went to put it on Lindsay Loo. For the first couple of times, mum had to get someone to hold her while she did it. Unfortunately, this mauve liquid had a habit of getting on things wherever the cat had been, and I believe dad had to repaint some part of the white wall after Lindsay Loo's tail got better!

Our dog, Nobby, was a cross between a Spaniel and a Labrador and he made matters worse because for a while he used to chase the cat around the house!

Nobby was a really silly dog. Once, he got up on the chair, which was near the cooker, and accidentally hit his tail against it, and burned his tail on the flames. He turned around and then burned his ear on the flames as well.

One day, Nobby managed to steal the meat off the table in the kitchen – we never knew how he did it! He also had a habit of jumping into the fishpond, although none of the fish ever got hurt!

As Lindsay got older she could not do much for herself and her breath was bad, and one day the man whose garden backed onto ours found her hanging over the gate, and he called dad who took her, but she was dead. Dad buried her in the garden and mum was very upset. When Pauline came home from holiday, she soon asked "Where is Lindsay?" Mum had to tell her and Pauline and mum cried bitterly.

Unfortunately, as Nobby grew older, he got arthritis in his back legs so badly that the vet advised us to have him put down so dad phoned mum and told her and she burst into tears. She realised it was for the best, but she was terribly upset.

Whilst we had Lindsay Loo and Nobby we also acquired another cat. It was like this:

One year on Guy Fawkes night, when dad was taking Nobby for a walk he saw a lovely little cat who was very frightened. Dad picked it up and brought it home with Nobby. When we saw dad with the cat, mum said, "Oh, not another cat!" dad replied, "Don't be silly, I'm going to put it out in the conservatory and hope it will go home tomorrow."

The next day came but the cat did not go home. In fact several days later, he was still with us and wouldn't go home! I got round dad to let us keep him. Dad said, "Oh, I suppose we could." That really pleased me. We called him Tibby. He was most unusual to look at because it was as if he were wearing a hat and coat!

Mum used to laugh at the way I picked him up. It was really quite funny! All I did was to put my left arm behind his front legs and swing his back legs on my right arm. Sometimes he cried but he did not even once hurt me.

When I went to Charlton Park School, the lady on the bus grew very fond of Tibby. One day when I was outside waiting for the bus which was a little late, Tibby came up the road and I went to meet him. I picked him up, and as I got to my gate the school bus came. I waited for mum to come out and take Tibby from me. The bus lady said to me, "Oh Julia! What a lovely cat!"

I said, "Yes! Isn't he gorgeous!" Then mum came out and took Tibby and I said, "Goodbye," and went to school. On the way home the bus lady asked me if I could bring Tibby onto the bus the next day to show him to the children. I answered, "Yes, but it depends whether Tibby is out or not."

Anyway, the next morning Tibby was in. So when it was nearly half past eight mum put on my coat and I went to get Tibby comfortably settled in my arms. The bus lady asked if she could hold him and I said, "Yes, why not?" The children loved him and even the driver said that he was a lovely cat.

This went on for quite a long time and we had a good time with him. Then a strange thing happened. Tibby started bringing home another cat. We couldn't find out where he'd come from, but he soon began to come into our house! So as he was with Tibby, we couldn't very well shut him out, and we thought we'd better let them stay together. What a clever crafty cat to find a good home!

He was white and black so we named him Patches. Tibby and Patches went everywhere together, but about five years later they disappeared and although we searched everywhere we never saw them again. We often wondered where they went and what happened to them!

## Chapter Fifteen

# Back to Work and Changes for Mum

When I was twelve years old, mum thought she would need to do a part time job. The only one she could get at that time was in the kitchen of Hither Green Lane, Catford County Boys' School (no longer existing). Before she started, she asked dad, Pauline and me to help her to keep the house tidy and to share the housework. Of course, we agreed but it didn't turn out like that because in the end, mum did everything. When mum used to work at the school, every now and again she used to bring back a bagful of freshly cooked shortcake biscuits and I used to eat most of these!

The only reason she went to work was to have some extra money. I often wonder if it was all this hard work over the next few years which caused her to become disabled. Then I remember that you can get Multiple Sclerosis at any time but in different degrees and that it can happen to anyone of any age. Unfortunately, my mum happened to get it.

I think this is more or less the way it started. Pauline and I were on summer holidays and it was our last Friday; we were going back to school on the Monday. It was 1965 and it was usual for mum to go into work on the last Friday of the holidays to get everything ready for work on Monday morning. For example, she had to get dishes, trays and cutlery out of cupboards and drawers and see that all the plates (six hundred of them) were clean and ready for use; most importantly of all she had to go to school to collect her holiday pay. If she had not gone in she would not have been paid.

That day, it continually poured with rain and mum got soaking wet going to and from work. Then, when she came in, I remember clearly that she didn't change her coat and tights or dry her hair but she went around to the fish shop to get fish and chips for our dinner. When she came back, she was utterly soaking wet!

The other thing that happened around about the same time was this. Pauline went out with her two friends and Nan was coming to look after me, but somehow, Nan didn't arrive so I had to go to work with mum. How bored I was with my own company and with the other people. It was lucky for me that I had taken my colouring book with me, but how glad I was when mum finished work and we were able to go home.

It was in September of that year, 1965, when mum was working in the school kitchen that her legs suddenly went weak. She held on to the sink but finally she slid down on to the floor, and couldn't work any more. Barbara and Betty, who worked with mum, helped her home. Mum went to bed early, and she said that during the night she had a queer feeling in her legs. After two weeks, when her legs were no better, she decided to go to see the doctor. When Dr. Cann finished examining her he said that he couldn't do much for her but he gave her some tablets and told her to take them three times a day after meals. When mum asked him if she could go back to work, the doctor said, "I don't see why not if you can manage it and don't over do it." So mum went back to work, but she had to take tablets every day.

Two years later in 1967, Dr. Cann retired and a new doctor took over the practice. His name was Dr. Mack. I think that mum went to the surgery to get some more tablets and when Dr. Mack examined her he told her to go down to Lewisham Hospital to have her complaint investigated and he gave her a letter for the specialist. Mum, I am pleased to say, thought that this was a good idea. She hoped that, with new ideas and perhaps different treatment, maybe she would get better. However, if she had remembered what Dr. Cann had told her, which was that even if he had sent her to hospital, he did not think that anything more could be done to cure her, she might have decided not to go.

She was taken into Lewisham Hospital and given test after test. She had injections in her spine (lumber puncture). These were done so that the fluid that was taken out could be tested. Mum had to lie flat on her back otherwise she got terrible headaches.

Whilst she was in hospital, dad, Pauline and I had to work out a plan of action at home. During this time, I played up once or twice because I didn't get all the attention that mum used to give me and one thing I do remember is that dad had to help me to dress, etc., and then when he was ready for work, he took me to Mrs Ruby who was an attendant at school and who lived in the next road. She had to be at school, which was Charlton Park School, at about nine o'clock, so our bus driver dropped her off on the way and then we went on to Woolwich to pick up other children, getting to school at about 9.20 am. Coming home, the bus dropped me at a neighbour's house, Mrs Meadows. Pauline was all right because she could look after herself.

I used to get cross and lose my temper with Pauline because I couldn't get my own way as I did with mum, and Pauline tried to make me do things for myself. I didn't realised that what she was doing was really for my own good, and the best thing that she could have done. Now, I am grateful to her because this was the first time that I began to realise that if I tried hard I could learn to do things for myself. This didn't happen just like that – it took a very long time and patience and effort.

After all her tests, mum was told that nothing more could be done except to carry on with the tablets and a nurse would come to our home once a month to give her an injection. She would come four times and mum would have a check up at the hospital.

I think mum was glad to be home with all the tests over and I'm sure that we were pleased to see mum back home again, and I was delighted!

I think mum went back to work for a while as I remember her waiting for the District Nurse to come and give her injection before she went off to work. However, after being back at work some while, mum had to give it up because it was getting too much for her. I think it was when she went back to Lewisham Hospital for a check up that the doctor suggested that she should go to see a specialist at the National Hospital at Queen Square. Mum wasn't too keen, but she said yes. He made the appointment for her, and she went a couple of weeks later, after she had been sent a letter and an appointment card. Dad had half a day off work to take mum to the hospital. One thing dad disliked about hospitals was all the hanging about! He thought that if your appointment was at 10 o'clock then you should see the doctor at 10 o'clock! However, I think they arrange to see all the new patients first, say between 9 – 11am and then they start seeing the old patients, but I think they put too many appointments for the same time, say ten o'clock, and then when eleven o'clock appointments turn up the patients have to wait such a long time because the doctor still has so many of the ten o'clock appointments to attend to.

Dad allowed plenty of time to get to the hospital but he wouldn't leave the car outside the main building. He helped mum out of the car and whilst she was walking up the steps he went to park the car. It took ten minutes to find a parking space and five minutes' walk to get back at the hospital. Mum wondered where he was. Then they had to wait twenty minutes before they saw the doctor. When he had finished examining her, he asked if she would mind going in for a while. Mum said she didn't mind because she thought that they might be able to get her legs working well again.

A couple of months later, mum had a letter from the National Hospital Queen's Square to say that they were ready for her. Whilst she was there, she was given many different tests and a special injection where a fluid was injected into her spine and the table which she was lying on moved up and down in a tilting fashion and from side to side. Again, after this test, mum had to lie flat on her back, otherwise she would have had a bad headache. Even so, I believe she did get a headache.

Following on from these tests, mum was told that she had Multiple Sclerosis and the consultant said that nothing more could be done for her, except that her injections (vitamin B12) would be increased from once each month to once a week. She was also told to carry on with the tablets as they were doing her some good. After three weeks, mum was allowed to come home and we were all very pleased.

When mum was in hospital, dad, Pauline and I began to wonder if she would ever be well again as we knew the illness was serious. This made me think again about myself and how I had been behaving. I realised that I must try to stand on my own two feet, even more than before and to do things myself and NOT to wait for someone to do them for me. As it took me a long time to do some things, it was very easy to let mum do it for me. We knew that our family life would change and be different from now on.

Our family doctor arranged for a district nurse to come in every Tuesday to give mum her injections. Some nurses were kinder and more gentle than others. There are two things that I remember about these nurses. Some nurses used to break the needle after giving mum the injection, which meant that I couldn't play with the syringes. Some just pulled off the needle, but they all wrapped up the syringe and the needle in paper to be thrown away. However, when the nurse had gone, I used to take the syringe out and put it in my box with the other ones I had collected! I was able to play jokes on people by filling up the syringe with water and squirting it over them! The first time I realised that I could have fun with the syringe was when I'd had a blood test and after the doctor had taken some blood, he took off the needle and gave me the syringe which I played with for a very long time as it was a large one!

Once, one of the nurses, who was very kind to me, gave me her pen which was very different from other pens because it had a pulse-timer in it. It looked like an egg-timer. The nurse showed me how to use it, and I practised with it on mum. It was good fun.

I remember when mum had a nasty accident in 1969. She was on her own as Pauline and dad were at work and I was at school. She had been having a rest in the back room as she felt tired when the door bell rang. Mum thought "Oh, I can't go to the door just now."

But the bell went on ringing, so at last she struggled along the hall to open the door. As she did so, she fell down and hurt her arm on the wooden milk bottle holder which I had made at school. She managed to open the door and see the insurance man. Then she crawled to the stairs with her mouth bleeding. The insurance man asked her if she needed some help and mum said "Get my neighbour, Mrs. Meadows from No. 41, and ask her to spare me ten minutes."

Luckily, Mrs. Meadows came back with the insurance man, who left her to cope with mum. Mrs. Meadows told mum that people couldn't get an ambulance unless you phoned through your doctor, but mum knew that all you needed to do was dial 999 and ask for ambulance service, but Mrs Meadows was convinced about phoning the doctor first. So they did this, but there was no answer. Mrs Meadows gave mum the phone so that she could phone dad and ask him to come home. When he arrived he phoned the doctor, who told him to ring for an ambulance! Dad did this and then he and mum spent several hours in hospital. Dad was "hanging about" in the waiting room. Dad had asked Mrs. Meadows if she would wait in our house to let me in when I came home from school and Mrs. Meadows said that she would do this.

I can't quite remember what happened next, but I do remember the ambulance men bringing mum in, in a wheelchair – an ambulance wheelchair which is carried in the ambulance nowadays. The man lifted mum out of it and put her into an armchair and I saw that she had her arm in a sling and her face was swollen. It looked as if someone had punched her in the mouth. She didn't look like herself and I couldn't help laughing although she looked really awful. Gradually as the days went by, she improved but her upper arm never completely got better. She had to go to hospital twice a week for exercises. This went on for a long time, and she still used to get pain in her shoulder. Because of this accident, she was put right off using her legs and it took a very long time for mum to get back any confidence in walking and getting back to the way she was before the accident.

## Chapter Sixteen
# Learning to Cope

Let me tell you how mum learned to cope with her injured arm when she worked at home or when she went out.

Mum had a shopping basket on wheels and she would never go out without it, even if it was just to go round the corner to buy one item. This wheeled basket gave her support and helped her to keep her balance.

If mum did not have her wheeled basket to hand and she felt she might be falling over, she would grab at anything near her and it was not always safe. Sometimes, if she leaned on the back of a chair it would tip over with her in it, making a terrible clatter and noise. When she leaned on the side of a table she thought she would be safe but it often tipped up and she and the table would fall together. At first, I was scared and nervous when I heard the crashes but I got used to it, but dad would get cross and almost seemed to think she need not have fallen.

When dad asked her what she was doing on the floor, mum would say, "I didn't do it on purpose or for fun!" I think maybe dad was concerned about her falling, but he couldn't help sounding cross. Mum did not always want to be helped up. Unfortunately, when mum got to the stage when she wanted dad to help her, dad would not offer because of the fact that in the past she would have usually refused help.

In our bathroom, we had a washbasin which dad put in, as he was good at doing things like that. Every time mum had a wash or cleaned her teeth, she would lean with one hand on the basin, which in time pulled it away from the wall. It later had to be re-fixed and re-plastered twice. When the washbowl was waiting to be repaired, dad would ask, "Is it worth it?"

After her accident in the hall mum had to rely even more on the furniture around her; but there was one thing she could not do again – she could no longer go for a walk round the corner with her basket and that really did upset her more than anything.

After the accident, when she had been home two days she had to go back into hospital for two weeks, but I don't remember why. Then she came home for a month and had to go back to hospital twice a week for six weeks to have her shoulder exercised. However, it seemed that her shoulder did not get better because she had fractured it and there was no more the hospital could do.

It was some time before mum could walk again and then only with a four pronged walking stick. When her shoulder improved a bit, she was put on elbow crutches and she walked quite well but steps were difficult to negotiate and someone had to lift her foot for her.

When we went out in the car she could not sit for longer than an hour because her legs went so stiff that she couldn't move them at all. She found that if she gave her knees a good rub just before getting out of the car she could manage to move her legs more easily.

Mum wanted to be well again and although she knew that she had Multiple Sclerosis, she couldn't accept it and she was not patient with herself. I found this attitude very surprising as she had so much patience with me. I thought that having a disabled person in the family would have encouraged her, but it seemed to make her depressed about herself. Perhaps she lost patience with herself because she felt the responsibility of being a wife and mother. Dad didn't seem able to accept mum's disability either and he didn't go out of his way to make things easier for her or to help her, except when she specifically asked him to do something for her.

Mum's doctor told her that because she had MS in later life, it was slower to progress. If she had got it when she was a lot younger it would have progressed a lot more quickly.

When Pauline and I were quite young, mum and dad belonged to an Old Time Dancing club. They went every Thursday evening with Auntie Eva and Uncle Fred. This is how they worked out the baby sitting – Uncle and Auntie brought their two sons around to look after us – they were older than we were. After we had said "good-bye" to them, our cousins, Eric and David, would sometimes play games with us, but most of the time we watched T.V.

There were three programmes which I can remember enjoying very much. They were: "The Man from UNCLE", "Top of the Pops", "Emergency Ward Ten" and a programme about nuns (which I really loved to watch).

At about 9 o'clock, David would say, "Time to go to bed!" Sometimes, Pauline and I would try to get round him to let us stay up. Sometimes it worked and sometimes it didn't! I think after we were in bed, Eric and David made themselves a cup of coffee while they watched T.V. and waited for their parents to come round. Then my cousins and my aunt and uncle went home. That was how we used to spend our Thursday evenings.

This went on for quite a few years, as dad didn't have his car then and sometimes mum and dad went dancing on a Saturday night on special occasions. We liked this because then we went to my aunt's house and had a lot of fun. The parents came home about midnight and I know I was more sleepy than Pauline by that time. As we got older, we were able to cope on our own.

One day a year or two later, mum was going to put the clean curtains back on the rail, but before she could do this, she had to think of a way to reach the rail. We had an armchair right near that window, so she decided to stand on this. As she was reaching up, one of her feet went right through the bottom of the armchair. It took quite a long time for her to get her foot out of the chair, and the foot was painful for the next few days.

When the District Nurse came to give her her regular injection, she told the nurse about her foot and the nurse decided to have a look at it. When she saw it she told mum to go to see the doctor, which she did after a lot of argument. The doctor couldn't do much about it except to do it up in a crepe bandage and hope for the best, telling her to come back if it didn't get better. After about two months her foot did get better. I'm not sure whether mum visited the hospital with her injured foot. Mind you, she learnt her lesson as she never stood on any more armchairs and that of course included the settee!

When I was 23 years old, mum had been disabled for eleven years, but as the years went by, her legs continued to get steadily worse.

There is nothing more I can say about her disability, and the doctor couldn't do any more either, so that meant mum had to learn to accept the fact that she was not going to be able to do things as she had done before.

There was one thing that particularly annoyed her, and that was her tiredness and when we wouldn't do what she wanted us to do within that minute. Because of this she would just get up and do it herself. Sometimes, she used to fall down, or we could see her knees were giving up. Then she would collapse on her knees. Sometimes, it took her a long time to get up from the floor because she couldn't get up like you and I can. Mum had to crawl over to the nearest chair and climb on to the chair and get up that way. If dad was there, he would pick her up just like that! If dad was in another room she would never call him unless she was really stuck. Sometimes, dad didn't always hear her calling, as over the years he was getting deaf. Sometimes, dad would tell her off for falling down! Why, I don't know, but believe me there were times when I got really frightened of my dad! Maybe it's the way he said things.

I had better explain why I didn't help mum to do the work in the house, although if I really had to do it, then I would have. When I used to tidy up, I used to have a habit of putting everything away. It didn't matter what it was because if I thought it was rubbish then in the bin it went. I believe I picked this up from my sister when she was living at home, as she used to do this quite often. I could do the tidying up but there were lots of things involved in housework which I couldn't do, like hoovering, because I just don't have the strength in my arms to push. Now, what has all this got to do with mum? A lot! – if I did do everything she asked me to do, within my capability, she would start to rely on me and I can assure you that mum would have gone down and down until she couldn't do anything any more, and I did not want this to happen. I wanted her to do as much as she could, so as to stop her from getting worse, more quickly. Anyway, mum was too independent to allow it.

It wasn't until five years later, when I was on a course that I found out that I was right about making mum do most of the work. Nearly all my relatives, including my sister, thought that I should do more to help mum (yes, with the tidying up because I can be very untidy from time to time). Multiple Sclerosis is not only to do with nerves, but also to do with muscles. I am sorry to say this but it is true that you have got to be cruel to be kind.

There are three mistakes I think mum made. Unfortunately, she didn't realise at the time and neither did I, until I started the course called "The Handicapped Person in the Community", with the Open University. The first mistake was when she could no longer get out or walk on her own. Mum tended to shut herself in from the outside world. She was very happy when anyone came to visit her (especially when she first gave up work) but as time went by, visitors stopped coming.

After a couple of years, mum had to have a wheelchair because she couldn't walk very far with her crutches, which were the old straight kind and were uncomfortable. Every now and then, dad would offer to take her down the road in the car and push her around the shops in her wheelchair. Unfortunately, she didn't want to go. This went on for about two or three years. After that, dad didn't really bother to ask her any more, but they did go out now and again for a short car ride. Sometimes, on Saturday evenings, they would go to a pub in Farnborough and occasionally I would go with them. We would never go inside the pub, but always stayed in the car while dad went in and got the drinks. I believe this is the pub they used to go to when they were young.

Sometimes on Sundays they used to spend a couple of hours in Greenwich Park. I didn't go to Greenwich with them very often because I used to get bored. Now this is where the first mistake came in. If mum had gone out nearly every time she was asked, it would have brought them together more, instead of pushing them apart.

The second mistake she made was that when she became disabled she did not have any patience with herself. I thought we were going to help each other with all sorts of things, but unfortunately it didn't work out that way! We both went our own ways, which was quite difficult at times. Sometimes, we would argue over silly things. For instance, I would say that It's better to be disabled in your legs because you still have got a good pair of hands and it doesn't really stop you from doing things. Ok, it stops you from getting from A to B and doing the shopping, but there are always ways of getting about.

One thing mum said, and I really agree with this one, is that it is better to be born disabled than having it happen later in life because you don't know any different if you are born with a disability.

We used to argue about the way we did things. Sometimes, mum used to say to me, "Why don't you do it my way?"

I used to reply, "I find it easier doing it my way." Even so, sometimes, my way of doing things was more difficult, but if I found it easier doing it that way, I would keep it that way unless I found a better way for me. I would not let people find a way for me, and expect me to do it their way just like that. I would think about it first to make up my mind whether it might be easier or not for me. If I was not sure then I would have a go, but if I knew damn well it was not going to make it easier, then I wouldn't bother!

The handle on our front room door was a knob that you had to turn. To turn that, I had to get to the side of it and turn it down by using my whole arm, not just my hand.

What I am going to tell you about now is something I used to do when I was a little girl, and my own mum did it, and I can assure you that mum didn't realise what she was saying to me at the time. She knew that there was nothing she could have done about it. It helped her to understand me, but unfortunately she could not grow out of it. From the age of five I have had the habit of dragging one of my feet along the pavement and sometimes I used to fall over. Then mum used to say to me, "For God's sake lift up your feet when you walk!"

I would say "Oh, mum I can't help it." and she would say, "Yes you can help it!"

As time went by, I gradually grew out of it, but now and again my foot still went over sometimes and down I would go.

When mum did it, it was slightly different because she didn't only drag her feet but they also got stuck to the floor or carpet, etc., and she just couldn't move them, so we used to say "Lift your feet up then you might get somewhere!"

Mum would say, "I can't move them," which was true – she couldn't until after a few moments! Now you can see what I mean; we had a sort of change over. The other thing she did was to get one foot stuck behind the other one and she just couldn't move that leg, especially while she was going up the stairs. Sometimes she didn't even realise that she was doing it until we told her to move the other foot out of the way.

One year, mum went back to the hospital to have her normal check up at the National Hospital. I suppose she was feeling depressed, knowing she wasn't going to get any better. Well, I'm sure you know what it's like to suffer from an illness. You might have been one of those lucky ones who got better or maybe you have been just like mum, who had been able-bodied and then suddenly went down with an illness. I don't know what it is like to be able bodied. I can only imagine how lovely it must be to be able to do anything without concentrating and jerking. I have to think how I am going to do something and what accidents could happen while I am doing whatever I am doing.

Let me get back to what happened to mum. As usual, the doctor asked mum the same old questions, to which she gave the same old answers, but when it came to mum's turn to ask questions, she nearly always forgot to ask them, even when she had written them down.

The doctor thought that it might be a good idea for mum to get away for a rest. She wasn't very pleased about this idea, because she knew what it meant, but then dad agreed that it might do her good. There was nothing she could do about it except agree to go! So the doctor said that he would arrange for mum to spend a couple of weeks at Finchley Hosptial; then he said that he would see her again in six months' time.

Finchley Hospital came under the National Hospital Queen's Square. I suppose you could say that it was a convalescent home, but I'm not sure because of what they did there. It didn't look very much as you walked down the driveway. It was next to Finchley Underground Station. When you came out at the end of the driveway, you could see a little bit of the house, but really you saw nothing but trees around the whole grounds, with a lovely garden; the house was more or less on the right of the site.

The house was quite big once you got inside: There were two floors. The ground floor was where the patients lived, and the nurses lived upstairs. At one end were the men's wards, and the ladies' wards were at the other end. In between these two wards there was quite a long corridor, but on either side there was a kitchen, a dining room with a T.V. set in it, bathrooms, toilets, telephones for the patients, an office for the nurses to do their paperwork, an occupational therapy unit, a lounge and a staircase leading up to the nurses' home. During the 1960s, or it could have been at the beginning of the 1970s, they had a Sun Lounge built on to the ward looking out into the garden. It looked really nice during the summer. Inside the sun lounge there was a coffee table with comfortable chairs and lovely flowers all round the room. It got really hot in there during the summer.

The first time mum went in there was in 1971. Dad took her to the National Hospital in the morning and I believe it was during the afternoon or the next morning their ambulance would take the patients on to Finchley Hospital. She didn't know what to expect but on the first day she really did enjoy herself because she didn't do much. The next day she had to get up at six o'clock and have a bath, which the patients had every other day. At eight o'clock it was breakfast time. They had a cooked breakfast and then they started work at nine o'clock (this work is explained in the following paragraphs).

At ten o'clock there was a coffee break, then back to work at 10.15 until 12 noon, when they had their dinner – which was a cooked meal. From 1.30pm until 4pm work again. At 4pm – tea break. Then at 4.15pm I believe they did some more work for about an hour. After all that, they could do what they liked until 6pm, when it was time for supper. After supper, they had from tea time until 8pm free, and then they had a hot drink. Between 9pm and 10pm they began to get ready for bed.

On Thursdays, mum had to go for Physiotherapy exercises, which included crawling, sit-ups and press-ups. In the afternoon, she went back for walking exercises. One nice day, the physiotherapist took her into the grounds but walked her too far and her legs gave way and she fell down. She had to be brought back into the hospital in a wheelchair. Mum was very upset that this happened and she would not do it again.

Mum took pottery, woodwork, typing and cookery as her activities. One day in the woodwork class she decided to make a rush-topped stool. She had to glue the parts together, weave the top, sandpaper, paint and varnish it. The result was good, so she brought it home and it was kept at home for quite a while. She also made a table lamp which was waiting for dad to wire up. I don't think dad got round to doing it and we had the lamp for over six years! It was standing on the book case, but where it is now, I couldn't say.

When mum did pottery, she made a small pot and an ash tray and we laughed when she brought them home because they were cock-eyed! She told us that she thought they were very good and at last we agreed with her! She did typing on one afternoon a week and she was very good at it. In cookery, she had to cook a meal to prove that she could cope in the kitchen. She got on very well and I think she invited the physiotherapist to share it with her.

She was in hospital for three weeks and then she came home. After six months, she returned to the National Hospital in Queen's Square for a check up, and was told that she was to carry on as normal. The doctor was quite pleased with her and said she was to return one year later.

Mum had been in Finchley Hospital two or three times and she made it clear that she wouldn't go back there again. Last time, she was too tired when she came home and this made her feel worse, as it took all the energy out of her. It took mum a good few weeks to get back to being herself again.

Mum was getting bored, so she looked for a job which she could do at home. I don't know whether her friend told her of someone to contact, or whether she found a job in the newspaper, but she found one where she had to type addresses on envelopes and labels. Sometimes she typed from telephone or index books, which she didn't always like because some print was too small. Sometimes she typed from index cards, which she preferred because the print was larger and she could work a lot quicker. She did not type in hundreds but in thousands and she was paid about £2.10 per thousand!

As time went by, the rate of pay gradually increased. If the employers wanted a job done within a week, mum had to stay up every night typing until eleven o-clock. Dad and I used to get annoyed with her and tell her to stop and get to bed. When she made mistakes she got very annoyed and often would swear about it. As more time went by, she realised she couldn't finish the job and so she sent in what she had done and left it at that. Sometimes her money was not paid at the right time, which was at the end of each month. She had to wait several days for the money.

At the beginning of 1970, she was so annoyed about the typing that she asked dad and I what we thought about her giving it up. I said that typing kept her fingers and hands exercised but it must be her decision. Dad said, "Please yourself."

Three months later she decided to give it up. Later on, she took up needlework, but just as a hobby. The borough of Lewisham ran two or three clubs for Multiple Sclerosis sufferers but mum thought that if she saw people worse than herself, she would get depressed. However, eventually she started going to a MS club, and for a time she enjoyed it. Later, the leaders who ran the club changed, and the way it was run was not so enjoyable, but she still used to go. The members of the club enjoyed bingo, singing, dancing, competitions and outings. Sometimes singing or acting groups would come and entertain the members and I knew one of the musicians. His name was Mr. Hooker. I knew him from my Music Club and I think he also went to another club that I used to belong to.

Once a year on a Saturday, the Leaders arranged for the MS club to have tea with another club in Haslemere. For four years, the drivers who took them got lost on the way and this made them late for tea. This meant that they couldn't spend long with their friends.

The other outing they had was to Chelsfield in Kent. After going on the outings several times, mum made up her mind not to go again because Haslemere was really too far for her and at Chelsfield she was unable to go to the toilets because she could not go up or down the steps easily.

*Chapter Seventeen*

# Mum and Dad

Dad was a complicated man and had so many funny ways. I don't really know how to explain them. I will give you some examples of what I mean. Dad wasn't a very jolly man, but you could have a laugh with him from time to time. He was quiet and could be shy at times. Dad used to have a temper. I think I shall start with some of the things that happened during the past.

I remember that my dad always used to say, "eat the fat on the meat – It'll grease your joints." I believed him and always used to try and eat all the fat!

Later on when I met Roland, we were eating pork chops and I said, "Eat the fat – It'll grease your joints!" He laughed his head off and told me that it was only an old wives' tale. When I told my dad, he really laughed!

I remember one year, we borrowed my Uncle's car for a week and went to Beachy Head. It was very windy up there on the day we went. In those days, the car door was held on by strong straps, instead of hinges. Mum went to open the door, and the wind blew the door and the bottom strap broke. The only way you could shut the door was to pull it shut and lock it. Poor mum had to climb over my dad's seat to get into her seat. Luckily, this was before my mum contracted MS or she would not have been able to manage it.

Another time I remember, many years later, was when my dad had his own car. To get out of the car, my mum would put her hands on the edge of the car roof to help her to get out. One day when she did this, dad accidentally shut the door and caught mum's hands before she could take them away. It cut her knuckles and was very painful. Luckily, we were coming home and not going out, so we could go straight inside and look after her.

I must tell you that dad was good at decorating and woodwork and he loved it. From time to time some funny things happened but really these things only happened because he didn't think or look what he was doing.

One day when I was young, dad was doing some painting. He had his ladder leaning against the wall and the ladder accidentally slipped. Luckily, the room door was open so he grabbed hold of the door with one hand and held the ladder with the other hand. Then he called out "help!" to mum, and she went to help him down. I don't know what happened to the paint! The funny thing was that if mum hadn't been in the house dad would have had to hold on until mum came back or he could have fallen off, which would have been terrible.

Another time when he was doing the painting, he wasn't using the wall ladder, but was using the stepladder and was on the top step. He started to come down and didn't bother looking where he was going and came flying down the wrong side of the ladder! He didn't hurt himself but he wondered where he was going!

The third time this happened was much later in life. He bought a new ladder – the type which you could have long or short. This was good in a way because when it is a short ladder, it doesn't matter which side you come down on as they are both the same!

One day, dad was doing some painting in the kitchen. He turned the ladder into a short one and locked it. Unfortunately, he couldn't have locked it properly because when he finished at the top of the ladder and he was ready to move it and come down, the ladder slipped and went flying with dad on it. We heard such a mighty bang and wondered what on earth had happened! Mum was standing in the hallway facing the kitchen, and dad was standing by the back door with one leg between the steps of the ladder, which was lying flat out across the floor. He had one hand leaning against the wall and he was holding the pot of paint in the other hand! Luckily there wasn't much paint in the pot! What a mess there would have been if that paint had gone over the floor and down the wall! When I found out what had happened, I just laughed my head off. Just at that moment mum couldn't see the funny side of it but she did later and we all had a good laugh.

Mum was always a bit worried when dad had these decorating accidents because his back was not too strong. He had a slipped disc, which had happened some years before when he had ricked his back trying to catch our dog, Nobby.

When I was very young, I was dad's favourite child. I don't know if I always was, but I like to think so! He always took my part, especially when Pauline used to pick on me! Sometimes I used to run to dad crying and dad would pick me up and make a fuss of me. Then after a little while I was all right. I suppose I was a daddy's girl during the years of childhood. I was about twenty-three when I started growing away from him.

Dad used to be very good at telling me that "practise makes perfect" and the other remark he used to make was "be patient and take your time – Don't worry about the people around you; let them wait." This was one of my biggest problems. I used to get very worried about the people around me when I had to do something, especially when I knew that they could do it a lot quicker than I could. Over the years I realised that he was right. However, there was one person who got me worried when he was around, and that was my sister's husband. He used to make me feel inferior because I was a very nervous person at that time. I also felt this way about my sister at that time.

Dad and I used to always play draughts together – a game that we played for years. Then, as time went by, we stopped playing it. At the beginning, dad taught me how to play the game and at first he kept beating me. I didn't like that very much! After some time, I began to realise that the more dad beat me the better player I would become. Between you and me it worked out very well because in the end, I could beat him quite easily. Sometimes I would cheat without him knowing and sometimes I would get caught and then we had to start a new game.

When dad gave me my pocket money, I didn't have much to buy with it, so I used to save some of it and spend the rest. As I was a bookworm, I used to buy a lot of books and chocolates. My sister used to buy a lot of makeup with her pocket money. Later on she started smoking but gave it up about eight years later when she became pregnant.

When I used to buy a book I really wanted (for example I used to be really keen on drawing books and practice writing books from Woolworths), dad used to say, "What did you buy this for? How many more are you going to buy?"

I would say, "When I want a new one, I shall get a new one!"

The reason I used to buy this kind of book was that I had more control over my pencil or pen on the rough drawing paper and I did not have to press so hard to prevent the pen slipping as it did on ordinary writing paper (as I am a heavy writer).

It wasn't until mum had been disabled for a few years that I had an idea that mum could be a bit jealous of me. Mind you, I could be wrong, but there were days when I think she really was a little jealous of me. I think it may have been that she saw me doing much more than I used to be able to do, whilst she was doing less. I then started changing towards my parents. At first, I used to say that mum wasn't my real mum because she became disabled and I couldn't understand how or why. I suppose because of this, I changed for a time towards my parents and didn't show them my love very much. I hid it away from them, but deep down inside me I loved them because of what they had done for me. I soon went back to my old self again. Between you and me, I think I loved dad more than mum at that time. The reason why I say this is because as time went by, dad had more patience with me than mum. When she used to get cross with me, dad would always take my part unless we were arguing over something; then he would tell us to "shut up!"

Sometimes when my parents argued they would get really mad with each other and very often I used to join in. Eventually, I learned not to argue with them. I just kept quiet and let them get on with it; but honestly sometimes they did get on my nerves and then I used to say, "Why don't you two get divorced?" They would answer, "Don't be daft – and what are we going to do with you?" Then I thought, "well, what have I got to do with whether they get divorced or not?" After a while, I realised that the reason was that mum and I were disabled and that made all the difference.

Another thing that annoyed me was that my parents had a habit of saying things that they didn't really mean – and sometimes didn't do what they had promised to do (especially mum). In the long run, this is not good when you have children because they learn to take what you say with a pinch of salt. An example was when my mum would tell me to tidy up my bedroom and put things away or else she would throw them away. In fact, she never did and I learned not to take her threats seriously.

After taking the Open University course, "The Handicapped Person in the Community" in 1979, I realised that dad had a lot of responsibility for mum over many years, and he was getting older and was not quite so energetic as he used to be.

As mum gradually got worse, dad found that it was necessary to change his working hours, so that he could come home at lunchtime (about 1.30pm) and give mum a sandwich and a cup of tea and then get back to work by 2 o'clock. Sometimes, he worked overtime and that meant that he didn't get home until 7 o'clock but usually he came home about 5.15pm. Mum would prepare and start the dinner. Dad would finish the cooking and then serve the meal, as mum couldn't lift anything from the oven. After dinner, dad went to sleep in the armchair and I couldn't blame him for that because I knew how tired he must have been. At one time, this sleeping habit used to annoy me because I didn't know what to do with myself. For some reason, I couldn't talk to mum very easily – so I just made the best of it – watching television or reading a book.

Now I run my own life and can do as I want, more or less, but the one habit that still annoyed mum and me was that dad would snore! However we knew there was no way to cure him. We used to wake him up or pinch his nose and tell him to stop snoring. Sometimes I would shout, "Dad, for God's sake stop snoring!"

Sometimes, dad would want to hear the news whenever it came on, even if he had heard it earlier. This often annoyed mum and me because we might be watching another programme and dad would say "I want the NEWS!"

One day when we were watching "Opportunity Knocks", a young choirboy in his costume was being interviewed. Mum spoke about his black tunic and collar frill – you see, my dad was a choirboy. Dad told me that sometimes he bought stink bombs and took them to church and set them off but never got found out. Apparently, dad was quite a naughty lad when he was young! My most common trick was to turn down my hearing aid, although I would also turn up the sound on the television.

Dad used to get up at 7.15am, come downstairs, have a wash and finish dressing. Then he would have his breakfast. Mum would come down later, after she had washed and dressed and dad would give her a cup of tea and breakfast. Then a few minutes later I would come down. Dad always had to do my shoes up for me and sometimes he had to do my trousers up and my buttons. However, by the time I was 29, I could do some of my buttons up with a button hook. This took me a lot longer, but I got there in the end!

Dad also had to do the Friday night and Saturday morning shopping and sometimes my parents had arguments over this, as there were times when dad bought things we didn't need or when we would say, "We're fed up with getting the same old food!" In later years, however, he was more careful and only bought things that we really needed.

Mum used to say, "Why can't you take me down with you in the car. I would put the basket on my lap and we could go round together and pick out the things we want!" Dad would reply, "You don't know what it's like down there. First, I've got to find somewhere to park the car, then to get the wheelchair out and try to get you into the supermarket, and this is not always easy. Also you cannot always get through the checkout unless you know which checkout is for wheelchair access, which is difficult with all the other shoppers pushing around you."

Perhaps he felt it would be an extra worry to have mum with him. This argument came up very often and we couldn't get mum to understand, although everybody else could see dad's point of view. The only way we could prove it to her would be for dad to take her down on a Friday night and let her see for herself. However I don't remember him ever taking her food shopping.

Today, of course, things have greatly improved for the disabled from the point of view of access, BUT WE STILL HAVE A LONG WAY TO GO!

During this time, dad asked mum about getting another dog, but mum blew her top and said, "No way!" However, dad managed to get round her. He saw an advertisement in the newspaper and bought the dog. It was a golden Labrador and its name was Rollo. After a while, dad began to realise that Rollo wasn't a house dog or a working dog but a breeding dog. We couldn't have the same fun with him as we did with Nobby (who had to be put down because of a bad leg). Although he was very good with mum, Rollo was very naughty with me. He used to jump on me and knock me over so dad used to give him a wallop. This would upset mum and me a lot because she was sentimental and would say "You'll have to get rid of it. I can't stand it any longer." You see, dad would get really keen on an animal, but would then gradually lose interest. I am like that too with some of the things I do.

During the time we had Rollo, dad began to suffer from vertigo. Mum and I got very worried about taking Rollo out. He was too big for me to take out. Mum couldn't take him and sometimes when it was time for Rollo's walk, dad had one of his 'turns', and the only thing we could do with Rollo was to let him out into the garden and let him run out there. However we had to keep an eye on him to make sure that he didn't walk on any plants otherwise dad would go up the wall.

At the back of our garden, years ago, dad made a rockery with a fish pond in the middle. Rollo used to love jumping in and out of the pond. Sometimes when we wanted him in a hurry, Rollo would splash the water everywhere, but the odd thing was that he never hurt one single fish in that pond. I honestly don't know how he did it!

I can remember once, Auntie Nancy (dad's sister) came over one Sunday afternoon for my mum and dad's wedding anniversary. The minute she got through the front door, Rollo jumped on her and it really frightened her. I thought it was rather funny and because I was laughing so much I was sent into the other room. I always wanted something like that to happen to her as I really didn't like her very much! When she left, we all started laughing as it was funny (but not at the time for her). I wonder what Auntie Nancy thought about it!

At first, when we went out for a long ride in the car, we took Rollo with us but unfortunately the dog did not like it. The only way we could tell was that when we were in the car – Rollo used to start crying. We decided not to take him out with us any more. Dad had to find another way of dealing with Rollo when we went out for day trips. The only idea he could come up with was to get a long rope and tie one end on to Rollo's collar and the other end on to a hook on the wall in the conservatory (so he could get out of the rain) – and leave him behind. Mum and I thought that dad did a terrible thing to Rollo – dad made the rope just long enough to reach certain parts of the garden, but not long enough to reach the flowers! Sometimes Rollo would pull on the rope so hard that it could have killed him, I used to think.

To start with, dad would only do this when we went out for long trips. Sometimes when mum got her bad days, she couldn't cope with Rollo, so she would put him into the garden, but if dad saw him walking on the flowers, he would give the dog a wallop and then put him on the rope.

As time went on, dad's vertigo gradually got worse and his giddiness and feeling of sickness became more frequent and he could not stand up. He went to the doctor, who prescribed tablets which unfortunately had no effect. It was not until he tried several different tablets that at last the doctor found some that would help him.

When dad got attacks of vertigo, he would go and lie down for an hour or two. Mum used to get annoyed and say, "When you don't feel well, you can lie down, but I have to keep on working even when I am not well!"

Mum did not like the way dad kept on changing his tablets and that sometimes made her cross because she felt he didn't persevere with his medicine. At last, he got rid of Rollo. He had him put down because he kept jumping up at me and sometimes knocking me over, and also dad couldn't take him out because his vertigo got so bad.

After two years on tablets, dad stopped having the attacks, which I was glad about, not only for my sake but for mum's, because she needed his help much more than I did.

As time went on, and I was growing up, life became more difficult because dad treated me like a child and I wanted to be independent. I would not let my parents influence me or try to stop me doing what I wished unless I knew that they were right and that I wouldn't be able to cope. However, I would still give the matter a second thought to make sure that they were right!

When Pauline decided to leave home it pleased me at first because I got more attention. On the other hand when she was there, if she thought I had a good idea then she would back me up. When she left home it became more difficult to act as an adult although Pauline and mum wanted me to behave like one. This was very awkward for me because in one way I wanted to be treated as an adult, the next minute I wanted to be treated as a child. I realised that it wasn't only that I didn't know whether I wanted to grow up or not, but also that I felt that dad was partly to blame because mum and dad would argue. Mum would usually be on my side on arguments about my independence. In a way you could say that I was "Piggy in the middle" – mum wanting me to grow up and dad wanting to keep me definitely dependent on him.

As time went on, some years later, I decided definitely that I wanted to be independent and make my own decisions. It took me a long time and a lot of hard work before I was able to convince my parents that it was possible for me to run my own life independently of them.

When dad left school, he worked in a baker's for a while. He later joined the RAF during the war, but because he could not fly he drove lorries all through Europe and down to India. After the war, he went to work in a factory called "Twinlock". He retired just at the right time before the company changed its name. He made some really good friends there, getting on well with the people he worked with.

Mum went to a convent school, which she hated! She got on well with one of the Sisters, but disliked most of the others. One of her favourite subjects was algebra, although she didn't ever say very much about her schooling. When mum left school, one of the jobs she had during the war was working as a typist at the Admiralty. Because all the girls were such quick typists, the repair man was always being called in to fix the typewriters. He used to tell the girls off for being so quick!

Somewhere along the line, mum became interested in playing the violin. She became very good at it and was asked to join an orchestra. However, she was more interested in getting married than being in an orchestra so she turned the offer down. I later thought that if mum was good enough to be offered a place in the orchestra, she could maybe have travelled all round the world.

Mum met my dad when she was 15 years old. Her mum was very strict with her and she always had to be in by 10 o'clock, which made it difficult for them to go out and enjoy themselves. Somewhere along the line they broke up for two years, but then got back together again. Mum always said that when she got married, she would never do what her mum did to her, and put restrictions on when her children could come home in the evening.

When mum and dad decided to get married, her mum was completely against it, but her father said he would give his permission if it would really make her happy,

During the war, dad had to have all his teeth out, possibly due to gum disease, and he came home one day all gummy! This really shocked my mother. Another thing my mum told me was that dad wasn't very good at writing love letters. She said she always knew exactly what was going to be in the letter before she opened it!

Ever since I can remember, my mum always told me that the best years of her life were during the war.

One time I will never forget was when Pauline, her husband, Paul, mum, dad and me went to The George restaurant in George Lane, Catford to have a meal. Towards the end of the meal, dad collapsed. He came round quite quickly and I believe that there was a doctor in the restaurant, who came over to have a look at dad. He advised him to go to the doctor's as soon as he could to get himself checked over.

Dad went from the restaurant to the hospital with Paul, to get a check up. Pauline pushed my mum home in a wheelchair and I walked with them. When we got home, Pauline had a real go at me because I did not have a key. However, we managed to get in with mum's key. After that day, I always remembered to take my door key.

Thankfully, dad was discharged and there was nothing seriously wrong with him.

My mum and dad were thinking about moving to Worthing or Eastbourne. In the end, they did find a bungalow in Worthing. It would have been ideal, but mum noticed a funny smell in one of the bedrooms which put her right off. I think there was also another problem with the flat. However, I don't think that mum and dad would have moved because I told them that I didn't want to go with them. All aspects of my life revolved around where we lived, in Lewisham.

## *Chapter Eighteen*
# Charlton Park

Before I went to Charlton Park School (a bungalow school for Physically Disabled Children), I was at Plassey Road School. One part of the school was set aside for physically disabled children, but there was not enough equipment there, so in 1966, when I was 14 years old, I was transferred with two other disabled student groups to Charlton Park School.

I remember clearly one of my first teachers in Plassey Road. Her name was Mrs Mason and she was a kind, gentle and understanding person. Somebody told us that she had poliomyelitis when she was young and this may have been why she was so understanding about our disabilities.

When I was in her class I had good and bad days. I don't mean trouble with teachers or pupils but some days I would do better than others – for example, doing a jig-saw puzzle or tying my apron. On other days my hands didn't seem to work properly and it would make me frustrated, because I wanted to do these things but I couldn't. Whenever I felt I was able, I did them perfectly, which is why I got so cross with myself and everyone else around me when I could not manage certain things. This is where Mrs Mason was so good and so patient. She seemed to know exactly what I felt, and knew that she couldn't do anything for me, so she left me in peace to gradually overcome my annoyance.

In 1966, when I was moved to the new school at Charlton Park, I found it was very different from Plassey Road School. The girls used to stay at Plassey Road, but the boys went to Lee Manor. Now Charlton Park is a mixed school.

The school was within a bungalow-type building, without steps – apart from a few at the entrance where the coaches parked to let the children on and off. It was easy for everyone to move around. There were 12 classrooms: four for the toddlers, four for the juniors and four for the seniors. As well as these twelve rooms, there were another four rooms for woodwork, cookery, typing, speech therapy, physiotherapy and a medical room. There were also two offices used by the staff and a lounge where staff would go for tea breaks. There was a small kitchen where the helpers made their tea. There was also a large dining room (I will tell you how the meals were organised later) and a heated swimming pool.

Charlton Park School had a residential unit for children aged between 5–11 years. They used to stay at the school during the week and go home at weekends.

During my first year, I was in Miss Jones's class. It was very different from Plassey, as we had a variety of lessons and a different teacher for each subject. We had such subjects as English, Mathematics, History, P.E., Science, Geography, R.E., Cookery, Woodwork and Needlework.

I used to do exercises at Plassey Road School every Monday and Thursday, for an hour with a very good physiotherapist who knew what she was doing. I hated the part when I had to get undressed! Every so often she would invite mum to see how I was getting on. Sometimes I used to like doing the exercises. That was when I didn't like school lessons, but when I liked the lesson I didn't want to do physiotherapy! When I did physio at Charlton Park, it was very, very different. For a start, there were many more children who needed exercises so that meant we had a shorter time with the four physiotherapists. When I was there, there were two from other hospitals or perhaps from schools. When you got a different physiotherapist there could be quite a bit of confusion because one could tell you to do one kind of exercise and another could tell you to do the opposite, so sometimes you finished up by not knowing who to believe for the best! I used to do just what each of them told me just to keep the peace! I thought this was the best way out.

I was told off frequently because of the way I sat on the floor. I liked to sit as if I was kneeling, but with my legs turned outwards, away from my thighs; the teachers and physiotherapists said this was not good for my legs. However, I think I may be double jointed as this position is most comfortable for me, but everybody else I know says it hurts their knees if they try to copy me! I did not enjoy the physiotherapy lessons very much at my school, or at Charlton Park.

The dining hall at Charlton Park was arranged to allow for two sittings. The juniors used to have their dinner at twelve noon, while the seniors had their play time. The seniors had their dinner at 12.30pm. Then at one o'clock, we came back to work. I remember once, when my friend and I went to the shop in the park before our dinner, we saw some squirrels and we stood watching them playing around and we followed them. Suddenly we both realised we would be late back, so we began to run. However, we were a good long way from the school and by the time we got back everyone had gone in, and we had to explain why we had come in so late. We could have been stopped from going out of school grounds for a week or more but fortunately our reason was accepted.

School meals were a bit of a challenge. I would not have gravy or custard with my meals because if I did, I would spill it down myself. Sometimes when I couldn't spoon up any more food, I would say that I didn't want any more even if I really did. It was just that I couldn't be bothered to ask the attendant to help me so I would leave it. Nobody knew the real reason. I have just written it for the first time.

I have always liked P.E. because there was a lot of running about and jumping, climbing up ladders and over the horse, with help or course. The best pieces of apparatus were the rings on the ends of the ropes. I used to love walking on the wooden bar because it wasn't very high. One day Miss Mason, our P.E. teacher, asked me to climb up the ladder, which I did. I went right up to the top, but coming down I had a slight accident. I thought that I was on the last rung, but in fact I was about six rungs up from the ground, so of course when I let go I fell straight backwards and landed on my bottom! My head went right forward and my teeth went through my bottom lip and into my left knee. Miss Mason came running over to me and told me that I was a silly girl! She helped me up and carried me down to the First Aid room, where she left me. Sister cleaned my knee and my mouth and put a plaster over my knee. After a while, I went back to the class but I did not do any more work, and I NEVER climbed the ladders again!

Another time, I can remember Miss Mason putting out certain apparatus and then we had to take turns to do the activities. When it came to my turn, after watching about four others, I would say to myself, "Good Lord! By the look of it I'm going to get stuck halfway," because there were certain things that I wasn't sure about. I used to wonder if I would be able to climb over them all right. Sometimes I used to get a feeling that I would fall over, and then I would go all hot and be unsteady on my legs for the next few minutes. Then Miss Mason would come over and give me a hand.

After quite some time, I found out that Miss Mason had been a teacher at my sister Pauline's school. When I spoke to Pauline about her she said, "Oh, I remember Miss Mason. She had a terrible habit of putting her fingers in her mouth and whistling if she had not got a whistle with her." I thought to myself, "Well, have I seen her do that at Charlton Park? I don't think so, but I may just not have noticed."

Every Monday, I used to do cookery with four or five other girls. I wasn't particularly thrilled about cookery but I had to do it. Sometimes I liked it better because on those days, if I was in a good mood, my hands would cope very well. However, if I was making something big and I had a number of ingredients to mix in a bowl, a bit at a time, I would find that my hands would get tired and the ingredients would not be well mixed. The finished dish would not be too good or tasty! I found it was difficult to hold the bowl in one hand and mix with the other. The teacher used to put a damp cloth under the bowl and this worked quite well. Then they brought out some rubber mats which I thought were just as good, but I still had to be careful because I could still knock the bowl over. When I chose what to cook, I would always go for the easiest dish, and then I would make a good job of it. Well, can you blame me?

Over the years, I have found two ways of holding a bowl. One way is to hold the bowl in my right arm but the best way is to sit on the floor and hold it in between my legs. When I am sitting in that awkward position then I have my hands free to do the mixing.

One time I can remember was when one of my friends was making some cakes and she forgot to put an ingredient in. When the cakes were cooked she took them out of the oven. She took a good look at them and they were as flat as pancakes. The teacher came over to look and said with a laugh, "Oh dear, you have forgotten to put in the baking powder!" I went over to look at the recipe and it said, "one teaspoon of baking powder." We all thought it was very funny and we laughed, but I think that she was quite upset about it.

Needlework was not my favourite subject. In fact I hated every minute of every lesson! The only things I could make were mats, and I used to get so fed up with doing them. Every time I needed a fresh coloured thread I had to ask the teacher to cut it for me and then thread my needle, tie a knot or start me off and that really did get me down. It's not the same thing when you can't do everything yourself. Maybe that's why I hated needlework!

My sister had a weaving loom, which I took into school, and I could use that very well without any help except that I pulled it rather tight at the sides and when I got near the end, my teacher had to do the last bit with a needle. This happened only about once a month and this made me feel much better because I didn't have to ask her to help me every few minutes or so. Very often I used to leave it at home on purpose, and then when I arrived at the lesson I would say that I had forgotten it and I was able to spend the afternoon reading a book. I think in the end she gave up because I did stop bringing the loom with me.

I liked mathematics very much and I enjoyed working with numbers and when I was at school I was quite good at arithmetic. Our maths teacher was very nice but he didn't really know just what I was capable of doing. Teachers sometimes concentrated on pupils who were taking their CSE examinations and leave the others who may have had various disabilities to work alone. Sometimes these pupils had more ability and knowledge than the other pupils. These disabled people may have been a little slow or needed someone to be an amanuensis, but they were capable of taking examinations if they were given more time. I am pleased to say that this has been made possible at colleges and universities today, but I am not sure about special schools in those days.

One day when I was in the maths class, I became rather tired of doing the work I had been given. The teacher had gone out of the room so I went to the book cupboard and I took out a maths book that I thought would be better than the one I was using. I took it back to my desk and got on with some exercises from it. After some minutes, the teacher came back and began to come round and mark the work we had been doing. When he came to me he marked the work which I had done for him but as he was marking it he realised that I had changed the book that he had given me to work from! Then he said, "Oh well, as you seem to be coping quite well with this book you may as well stay on it!"

Looking back, I feel that if the teacher knew that I could cope with CSE maths, then why didn't the school encourage me to do something about this knowledge I had, instead of leaving it until I left school, when it was a bit late.

I wouldn't say that I liked English a great deal, as it was not easy for me to write. I used to bend up the book to make it easier but then the poor book only seemed to last five minutes, and then I used to have to have a new book! My English teacher asked me if I would like to do my English on a typewriter. I said, "Oh, yes! It would be much easier and much quicker."

A couple of days later, I went into the English classroom and I saw a lovely little electric typewriter which was for my use. This typewriter certainly helped me, and made me much quicker so that I was able to do more English, but I was not too pleased about that! I have been told by my teachers and friends that I could be good at English if I put my mind to it and concentrated.

There were times when I'd had enough of English work, so I would type my work very slowly and make a lot of mistakes so that I was obliged to do it again. The teacher often could not understand why it was that one day I would do quite a lot of work and on another day, comparatively little. Well, I suppose it depended on what mood I was in at the time. The sort of English I can remember doing was from a book where you had to read a story and then answer the questions.

At Charlton Park School, we had to wear uniform. It was a grey skirt or pinafore, a white blouse, a royal blue cardigan and a blue, white and black tie. We had to wear black or brown shoes with socks or tights. After about a year, they decided that we didn't have to wear it anymore.

After my first year at Charlton Park, when I was nearly fifteen, some subjects were optional in our education. We had to do Maths, English, Science, Needlework, Cookery and Woodwork, but I did not have to do History, Geography, R.E. and one or two others. I was able to do more work on the typewriter. Mum and dad bought me a little Royal machine, and I learned a great deal about typing because mum taught me. After a few years, they bought me an electric typewriter – which was a lot quicker.

Mrs. Nicholson was our typing teacher and she was absolutely fantastic. She had all the patience and understanding that anyone could wish for and I worked with her during my second and third year. The school had a very good typewriter made by IBM and it was called Possum. It was decided that I should try it out and long afterwards I found out the reason for this was to see how long it would take me to learn all the letters by codes, number and colours.

I will explain all I can about using Possum: The machine was a very special one. There were four ways of using it. One way was by sucking and blowing the mouthpiece; another was by using head gear; a third way was to use the feet to control two pedals and the other way was to use two fingers of whichever hand you preferred. I used this last way and, as I am left handed, I used two fingers of my left hand.

The method I was using involved pressing two keys attached to the typewriter. One was red, which moved vertically, and the other was blue, which moved horizontally. There are fifty-two keys on a typewriter and each key on the typewriter had a different code. For example, A was two blues and two reds and then one blue again to press the key. B was three blues and five reds and then one blue to print the letter. C was three blues and three reds and one blue to print the letter.

Now, I if I made a mistake in counting, say six blues instead of four blues, I would have to press another seven blues which would be thirteen before the machine would return to start. Any mistake I might make, even the slightest, would mean that I had to return to the start.

Mrs. Nicholson gave me a lesson every day but during my first few weeks I used to get very confused with the colours and the counting. One minute I should have been counting the reds and I found myself counting the blues; for a time the more lessons I had the more confused I seemed to get. After about three months, Mrs Nicholson suggested that I did a project using the machine. I thought to myself, "It will take me years to do a project on this machine, but I suppose it won't do any harm and at least it will make it a bit more interesting." So at last I said, "Yes, I would like to do it!"

Mrs. Nicholson asked me to choose a project, so a couple of days later I told her that I had chosen Animals. That day, we got some books from the school library and some old animal magazines and we worked at it. When I was nearly half way through my project, I found that I had learnt all the codes for every key on that typewriter!

For another year, I did very well on that machine, but then I had to leave school so that was the end of my using a Possum machine! The project on animals I took home. Since that time, I have used many kinds of electric typewriters varying between Possum and other makes.

During my third year at Charlton Park, we had three new teachers. I liked them but one or two tried to change my way of doing work. For example, the way I held my pen and book. I found it easier to do these things my way, so of course the teachers weren't too pleased and sometimes they would get quite cross with me. However, they generally realised that I couldn't do it their way, and so they left me alone.

My third year at school should have been my last, but the Education Authority thought that another year would be helpful to me and so my parents agreed to this. Well now, if you were to ask me what I thought of this, I would say that it was generally a waste of time! I only did the basic lessons like Maths and English occasionally, but apart from them I still had to do physiotherapy and speech therapy quite regularly. At this stage, at first I didn't mind at all and when I became a school librarian it was quite interesting to be working in the library. Sometimes, however, it did become boring.

Every Monday morning as soon as the school bus had dropped us off at school, I had to let one of the staff know that I was there. Then I would go into the dining hall to pick up the staff dinner book from the cook. Sometimes the cook would tell me to be quick, but I would reply, "Well, it's not my fault if I don't know where to find the teachers!" As I was going round to the staff I used to read the book to see what we were having for dinner that week and I used to try to remember what day was my favourite meal. Often, I would stop and have a little chat with any of my friends who happened to pass by, and this would make me late back to the kitchen of course!

Sometimes on a Monday morning, the cooks would make some very tasty biscuits (like the ones that mum brought back from school) and would give me some when I took back the staff dinner book. When I finished the biscuits that cook gave me, I had to go back to my class to do some lessons.

There was another job that I did sometimes on a Friday, which was helping the medical Sister with the health and medical session. The Sister would give me a list of names and times and I would collect the children, a few at a time. Some parents were not able to attend, perhaps because they were working or looking after other children. If the parent was there, I would leave the child with them, and I would give the boy or girl a dressing gown to wear. I looked after those whose parents were not able to come. If I could manage to undress them I did it, otherwise I would leave it to the sister. Sometimes there would be a child crying and I would say, "Take something out of the toy box or read a book."

Sometimes I would play with them but if the child was very small I would lift them up on to my lap. Sometimes they were heavy or they would not stop crying and then it was hard work. Looking back, I think they gave me these jobs because they thought that I didn't have the brains for education, because they didn't fully understand Cerebral Palsy. I would have quite liked to have worked in a library when I left school, but my real ambition at the time was to do nursing. Because I was good at looking after people, perhaps this is why they encouraged me to look after the little ones.

I remember one term, the school doctor was giving me some medicine to build me up. One day after dinner my friend and I went down to Sister together. I went for my medicine and my friend went for her tablets. I think I was in front of my friend. Instead of getting my medicine, Sister gave me the tablets, which I duly took! When she realised what she had done, she gave my friend her dose of tablets but told me to stay with her for a minute or two to make sure I didn't have a reaction to my friend's tablets! I was laughing but I said to myself, "Oh, you are a stupid thing!" After a few minutes she gave me my medicine. The tablets didn't seem to do any harm, so I was glad about that!

I told you that mum taught me to talk, but remember, I could only talk in my own way. As I got older, this was to become a bad habit – I talked too quickly sometimes!

The speech therapists were giving me lots of help and they would tell me if I was saying the word correctly or not, or show me how to say it properly. I could only improve my speech by wearing my hearing aid, and by practising regularly. I have continuously improved and now I speak much more clearly – although I do mumble now and again. Another thing is that I need to speak a bit louder – it is difficult to tell how loud you are speaking when you are wearing a hearing aid.

I had another slight problem, which was that I couldn't wear my glasses with my hearing aid because the arms were too thick and pushed my hearing aid out. When I told mum she said, "Oh No! We get over one problem and then get another! Let me have a look!"

She took off my glasses and hearing-aid and saw that my ear was red and sore. We decided to leave the hearing aid and glasses off for a while. Mum wrote a letter to my teacher explaining why I would not be wearing my hearing aid and glasses for a few days. Although my teacher said, "That will be all right," I don't think she was very pleased but there was nothing she could do about it!

Although after a week I was able to wear my hearing aid and glasses, my ear soon started hurting again. This time I decided to leave my glasses off altogether and mum and I had an argument about it. Then mum took up my appointment card to find out when I was due to go to the Eye Hospital. It was not for four months, so she decided that perhaps it wouldn't do me any harm to stop wearing my glasses until then.

When mum and I went to the hospital for my eye test, the doctor examined my eyes and asked mum some questions. Mum told him about the problem with my hearing aid. He asked to see my glasses and mum took them out of her bag and gave them to him. He held them up and examined them and said "They're not very strong, so she may leave them off altogether." Mum wrote a letter to the teacher, explaining that the doctor said that I need not wear my glasses any more. So there was no more trouble.

I was very glad about this because I knew I had to leave one or the other off, and not wearing my glasses made me feel much better.

During this time, I sometimes got a pain in my hip that came and went according to how I was sitting or standing. For several weeks Sister Verity rubbed ointment into my hip but it didn't improve. I was sent to the school doctor, who decided to write a letter to my parents suggesting that I should be taken to the doctor. I was supposed, of course, to give the letter to mum. Instead I opened it, read it and tore it up. After a few weeks the sister asked the bus attendant what mum had done about the letter. Of course mum had no idea what it was all about, so when she found out what I had done, she was cross with me. Mum knew why I used to get the pain – that it was due to the way I walked or stood or sat, because my back was only straight when I was lying down. She knew it was of no use to go to the doctor, but that I must try to stand and walk as straight as possible.

Miss Mason took me to swimming lessons in the school pool and she made me do the proper swimming exercises. Within three months, and by the time I was nearly fifteen, I was swimming! Then Miss Mason asked me if I would like to go to Plumstead Baths on Friday morning and I said, "Yes I would please." One Friday she told me that if I swam the length of the baths, which was thirty three yards without stopping, I would get a certificate. I did it of course! However, somehow or another I did not receive my certificate! Shame on her!

Miss Mason had a terrible habit of swimming behind me and suddenly picking me up, throwing me up in the air and letting me fall back into the water. I enjoyed this except when she grabbed me in tender places when I would shout and scream.

During this time, I went back to Eltham baths and now that I could swim I went four times a week. Ian, a helper who taught me when I was very young, came one Sunday morning and I showed him that I could swim a length. He called Roy and told him but Roy didn't believe it, so I showed them both and they were very surprised and pleased. Roy put my name down for next year's gala to swim in the twenty yards race.

During the year, I practised very hard and a few weeks before the race, I was timed. On the day, someone swam behind me to keep me straight. Because I had one arm stronger than the other, I tended to swim towards the strongest side. I am happy to say that I came first in the race. Then I swam the final and came second. Every one was pleased, especially mum, because she thought that I wouldn't make it! At the end of the gala when the prizes were given out, I won a silver medal for that race. After a little while, my name was called out again and this time I was presented with a cup for effort throughout the year. I felt very pleased with myself.

This really proved to me that with the hard work I had put in, I had been able to achieve something that I had never thought I would have been capable of doing.

Every year, the Girl Guides Association held swimming galas throughout the country. Our gala was always held on a Friday evening in September. My Guide Captain asked me if I would like to take part and, as by this time I was quite a good swimmer, I agreed. However, I wanted to know how long the bath was and how many lengths I had to swim. As the captain did not know, I suggested that it would be best if I just swam in the one-length race. The captain was pleased that I wanted to swim in the gala.

On the day of the gala, mum and my friend, Roseanna, came with me. When we got to Ladywell Baths, I took one look at the length of the bath and exclaimed, "Good Heavens! I don't think I can manage to swim fast for that length! It will take me a long time, but I will have to do it now that I'm here."

Roseanna and I went to get changed but when we came back to the group, we were told that we had quite a long time before our race came up. So we decided to sit on a bench at the side to watch the other races. All the time we sat there, my tummy was full of butterflies as I thought about the race! I said to myself, "How am I going to swim that length? Where am I going to get my energy from?"

At last, Roseanna and I were told to come to the starting point. There were only three of us as the fourth one had dropped out. I was near the bar and someone was swimming behind me to keep me straight and to see that nothing went wrong. I was feeling a bit sick, but I wasn't going to drop out now. I got myself into the water and we got on our marks. The whistle blew and off we went swimming on our backs. I kept my head well back so that I couldn't hear what was going on around me. The water stopped me hearing. I was just over half way when I lifted my head up out of the water and all I could hear were shouts of people cheering us, so I put my head back in the water but I felt very tired. I felt as if I couldn't keep it up and wanted to stop, but I just had to go on. At last, I reached the end of the bath, but didn't have the strength to turn over and get hold of the bar. Instead of that, I brought my head forward and I went down to the bottom of the pool! The lady swimming behind me had to kneel down and get hold of my arms to pull me out of the water. Everyone clapped their hands and cheered, but all I wanted to do was to go to sleep! mum had to dry and dress me.

At the end of the gala, when my name was called out and as I was walking towards the table, everybody clapped again. "Oh no! Not again," I thought, because I didn't win. But then I remembered that as there were only three of us in the race – I must have come third! I got a certificate, but I knew I could never do it again. I felt rather pleased with myself that I had done it and I hadn't given up. It certainly will take a lot of pushing to get me to do that again!

When I left school, I gave up swimming for a long time and then started to go to New Cross Baths. In later years I used to go swimming with Peggy from the Guides. Then there was a gap of about 20 years, until I began to go swimming with Jo, my personal assistant, to the baths at Greenwich, which I enjoyed. We then went to the one at Waterfront in Woolwich. Jo also took me to the gym. At first we went to the one in Eltham, but then I went to the gym at the Waterfront, which was more convenient as it had a good car park on the site. When I was at the gym, I went on two different bicycles, a leg weight machine, and an arm 'bicycle' machine.

From the year 2000, Charlton Park School changed its name to Charlton School. They added a new building to it, and it completely changed from the time when I was there. It is no longer a school for physical disability.

## *Chapter Nineteen*
# Valium

During my last year at school, I had an appointment with the careers officer from the Employment Agency. Because mum had contracted Multiple Sclerosis four years before, she was beginning to find her leg muscles were deteriorating and walking was becoming more difficult. We had to alter the time of my interview to take this into account and so mum could come to school with me early one morning on the school bus.

The careers officer discussed the job possibilities, and asked mum if I went out on my own. Mum said that I did not and that we hadn't even thought about anything like that.

Later, at one of the school meetings, Miss Mason talked to mum about me going out alone, and mum said that she would be worried in case I fell down and could not get up. However, after she thought about it, she said, "I could let Julia go out and post a letter for me, as the pillar box is not far from our house and there are no busy roads to cross."

Miss Mason thought that this would be a start. So, for a time, this is what I did. Then one day, Roseanna asked me to go out with her. When I asked mum she said, "Yes, why not?" At first, we only went to Catford. But gradually we went further from home. After about 2 or 3 years, I was going anywhere I pleased on my own.

As I helped Sister Allen with the medical examinations list, and the secretary, Mrs King, with the dinner register, and was also used to working in the library, I told the careers officer that I would like to have a job in a hospital, working with people. Actually I would have liked to have been a nurse but I knew this was impossible. The careers officer had suggested that I went into a factory but dad said, "There's no way will I allow that!"

As dad was already working for Twinlock, he knew all about factory work. Mum and dad suggested that I could do a job such as filing. I quite liked this idea, but unfortunately nothing came out of this interview.

A year or two before I left Charlton Park, I had an appointment to see my doctor at Guy's Hospital, Dr. MacKeith. Unfortunately, he was not there on the day, so we saw an American doctor. He did the usual things that my doctor did, but he put me on drugs. Mum wasn't very pleased with this, but there was nothing she could do. She asked him, "What will these tablets do for my daughter?" He told mum that the tablets would help me to relax and I might find it easier to do more. Mum said, "We will give them a try then."

The American doctor told mum that he would like to see us again in a year's time. The tablets were called Valium, and each tablet contained five milligrams. He told mum to give me one three times a day after meals, so that meant I would be taking 15 milligrams a day!

Within two weeks, I was falling asleep at any time. I didn't know what I was doing or saying because I was too tired to think. Mum was getting quite worried about this so she made an appointment to see Dr. Gann at Lewisham Hospital. Unfortunately, Dr. Gann was in Africa, so we had another doctor. Mum told him about the tablets which the American doctor had given me at Guy's. He told mum to leave out the midday one, and I was to take two a day. Then he said, "I will make you an appointment to see Dr. Gann when he comes back."

I was a little less drowsy, but not really as wide awake as I should have been. About a week later, we had an appointment to see Dr. Gann and this time we did see him. When he read the report he said to mum, "What the hell is she doing on these tablets?" Mum answered quite sharply, "Well, I didn't put her on them!"

He said "Who did?" Mum told him that the American doctor at Guy's Hospital prescribed them for her. Dr. Gann said, "They have NO right to put her on drugs." He told mum not to give me any more and said, "I will see you in six months' time." As I hadn't been taking vallium for very long, I soon recovered and got back to my old self.

Six months later, back to Lewisham Hospital we went for a check up. I was first weighed and my weight was six stones and seven pounds. My height was four foot eleven inches. Dr. Gann asked me a few questions about myself and then he asked mum how old I was. Mum said to me, "Julia, tell the doctor how old you are." I said, "I'm fifteen."

Dr. Gann said, "Gracious, she should be bigger than that."

mum said, "Yes, I know that, and I've been telling you that over these last few years."

"Well," he said, "I didn't realise she was that age."

Mum was getting a bit cross by this time. Then Dr. Gann asked about my periods, and mum told him that I hadn't started yet. (This did not worry me; I used to say how lucky I was!) However, Dr. Gann was worried and told mum to take me for a blood test and that he would see me in six months.

When we went back after that time, Dr. Gann told mum that I was anaemic but it was nothing to worry about because as I had been born two months early, I was three years behind my age, so mum need not worry about my periods, as some girls don't start them until they are eighteen. So our minds were at rest. I was given some medicine to take for the anaemia, and Dr. Gann said, "I will see you in six months' time." That was his favourite saying.

On our next appointment, I had to see Dr. Gann at Lewisham Hospital at 9.45am. We arrived early and I was weighed and measured and then, as usual, we returned to the waiting area until we were called to go in to Dr. Gann. Time went by; and patients were going in and coming out. 10 o'clock went by, 10.30am, 11.00am and then at 12 noon we saw Dr. Gann come out and go through the door. Mum thought that he was coming back and spoke to the sister, who said, "No, he's not coming back. He's finished!"

Mum exploded with anger. "We've been waiting since 9.30am. It is quite disgraceful to keep us waiting all morning and then calmly tell us that Dr. Gann has finished for the day!" The Sister apologised, but mum was right to be annoyed. The Sister wanted us to see another doctor. When we went in, mum said to him, "It is no use you looking at Julia's records because you know nothing about her!"

The doctor agreed but looked at my records. Mum said, "Good day, doctor", and mum grabbed me sharply and we walked out. He had given us the appointment slip but mum said afterwards that she was so angry she felt like ripping it up. However, as we were going out, she had second thoughts so we went back and made another appointment, luckily for the following Friday.

We arrived at about 8.50am, and I was being weighed when the nurse came out and said, "The doctor is waiting for you." Mum thought, "Well, it would not hurt him to wait a few minutes, seeing how long we waited last week!" Anyway, as soon as I was dressed, we went in to Dr. Gann's room. The doctor apologised about not seeing us, but mum showed by her manner that she felt the whole business of last week was most unsatisfactory. Dr. Gann was satisfied with my progress and told us to make an appointment for the next year.

Sadly, by the next time I had to go to the hospital, mum couldn't take me any more, so that meant that dad had to take me. He wasn't very pleased with that but there was nothing he could do about it.

My appointment was for ten o'clock. We got there at 9.45am. When 10 o'clock came, dad got a bit cross because we hadn't seen the doctor. At 10.30am we were still waiting. Dad really did get mad. He told the Sister off. 10 minutes later, my name was called. That really pleased dad. Dr. Gann asked dad the usual questions, as he did with mum. Then he asked dad about my periods. I still hadn't started them, so Dr. Gann said, "We'll leave it for one more year."

At this same time, when I was seventeen, I had another appointment for Guy's Hospital for my usual check up. The doctor was so pleased with me that he discharged me. Dad said, "Thank God for that. We've got one hospital out of the way!"

When I left school, we went to see Dr. Gann again at Lewisham. He asked the usual questions and I told him I had started my periods. He asked whether I went to work and dad said that I was going to Trinity Day Centre. Then he asked if I was going out with boys and I said I was. Dr. Gann asked dad if he wanted me to go on the pill? "No," said Dad, "Julia knows what is right and what is wrong."

Dad asked Dr. Gann if he still wanted to see me because dad wasn't keen on dragging all the way up to the hospital. Dr. Gann asked "Why?"

Dad said, "Well, you don't examine Julia, you only ask her a lot of questions."

Dr. Gann said he would discharge me if I felt this was all right. As I said I did, he discharged me from the hospital. No more hospitals!!! I felt so pleased because I felt that the time that my mum, dad and I spent attending hospitals was just a waste of time.

## Chapter Twenty
# Reflecting Back

When pupils left Charlton Park School, at seventeen years of age, there was always a ceremony in front of the school where those leaving were given a Leavers' Prize. My prize was an Oxford Dictionary and I was very pleased with it. I used it regularly for many years. I left Charlton Park at the end of the Spring Term just before Easter, and I was at home for about two weeks.

Looking back on my schooling, I feel that I wasn't really encouraged enough or pushed hard enough to do more, because of my disability. The schools did not understand enough about cerebral palsy at that time. With the technology that they have today, such as computers, I would have probably had a better education and things could have been a lot easier. For example, in the 11 plus exam, if I had been able to dictate the answers and a teacher mark the box for me, I would have had as equal a chance as anybody else. Instead, however, I had to mark my own answers and my writing was too big to be recognised properly, so I didn't get anywhere.

In my eyes, if I had gone to a mainstream school, I still don't think I would have been able to cope because of my writing and the length of time it would have taken me to do things. I would still be well behind unless I had a full time assistant, which would not have been an option at that time. Even now, it would probably depend on where you live as to what resources are available to you and what support you can get from the Education Authority. The other area they would look at is the degree of the child's disability.

I think that today, schools are slowly making progress but we have still got a long way to go.

*Chapter Twenty One*

# Clubs

I believed I joined Music Club as I knew some of my friends belonged to it. I also knew that one of the Borough drivers (Bert) was a member. When a new member first joins they are taught how to play a recorder unless they can read music or can play another instrument; then they can join any group they wish. Although I did music at school I was not taught how to read music. I played a simple instrument which now I feel was good exercise for my breathing and fingers.

I couldn't read music at first so I joined the recorder group. This was very difficult for me. Firstly, I couldn't hold the recorder properly and secondly, I couldn't use both hands to play the notes. The teacher tried to teach me to play with one hand but it didn't work. I had an idea but I never tried it out. It was to have something round my neck with two pins which would be connected to the recorder to hold it in place while my fingers covered the holes to make the notes. I had to laugh when they asked me to blow a trumpet. I said, "You're joking, I certainly haven't got enough wind to blow that thing!"

Anyway, I was proved right so they decided that I could play a xylophone. This was all right but I could never be sure that I hit the right key because of the jerks I get in my hand and also I can be slow at times. I learnt to read music and that was good enough.

I believe it was twice a year when all the clubs got together to put on a concert. A couple of weeks or a month before the concert, we would go away for a weekend to practise. I don't think I shall ever forget it. There were bunk beds, and the little ones would be on the bottom bunks and the older ones would be on the upper bunks. At first, I just didn't know how I was going to climb! It certainly was a laugh! I had a helper on each side of the bunk. One, trying to push me up and one in front of me was trying to lift me and push me on the bed at the same time. When I was finally on the bed I was too scared to try and move or turn over. It was the most uncomfortable sleep I had had for a long time!

When we performed our concerts I would never play an instrument but would join the choir for I do enjoy singing from time to time. I also believe we were on television one year. We had to wear a uniform which was a red skirt, white blouse, white socks or brown tights and black or brown shoes. I used to like wearing this uniform as it never really looked like a uniform.

I honestly can't say how long I stayed as a member of the club, as I found it was so difficult for me to play an instrument. It made me feel frustrated at times and I believe this was one reason for my leaving the club.

## THE BICYCLE CLUB

I can't remember when this club started or how I became a member or how long I was a member. I'm not sure whether the people who ran the music club were involved with the bicycle club. It was held in one of the Church Halls and all we did was to ride a bike but with a big difference! We had a three-wheeler with normal foot pedals but instead of having handle bars there were pedals which meant that you had to turn the hand peddles and feet pedals at the same time! I really did enjoy this because I knew it was an excellent exercise. The number of times I fell off, just because I couldn't get my hands and feet to turn the pedals at the same time! I could have brought a bike home with me to practice on but I didn't as I was too afraid of the accidents I might have on it and I wondered what dad might have thought.

## THE SPASTIC SOCIETY CLUB

I was a member of this club for a long time with my friend Rosanna. It was well organised and quite a good one. Every week the organisers tried to put on something different. We would go out from time to time and during my last few years we used to visit another club. There was only one thing I hated about the club at that time and that was when we went to the seaside for a day each year. We had to take an adult with us. This was difficult for me as mum couldn't come because of her MS.

Sometimes I would join in with one of the other members' family but this wasn't the same as having your own relations. One year, on a seaside trip I remember Rosanna and I wanted to go together, but the club wouldn't let us. Eventually, I managed to get my sister to come with us. Pauline didn't really want to come but we had an enjoyable day. They held some excellent parties at times and these were great fun. Eventually I stopped going because of my blindness and deafness. I did not feel like an active member of the club. I felt 'left out' most of the time.

The Spastics Society is now known as SCOPE. The funny thing is, when I telephone to cancel transport with SCOPE today, the person who answers the telephone still refers to this as a Spastic Society service.

# THE PENNY FARTHING CLUB

I joined this club when I was a member of Trinity Day Centre. I believe the club started in the late 60's and it closed in 1987. The club had disabled and able bodied members, and it was run by Task Force which was a voluntary Organisation. It was held in St. Michael's Church Hall in Sydenham. Unfortunately, the hall was not very convenient as it was very difficult for wheelchairs to get into either the kitchen or the toilet. Also, there was only one toilet for everyone to use. We played table tennis and board games, listened to records or went out for walks or just had conversations with other members.

The chairperson was Peter who used to get quite panicky and worried if anything did not go according to his ideas. Kitty and I used to tease Peter by playing jokes on him. One was that we would take a packet of sweets and keep it for perhaps half-an-hour and not pay for it and then we would put it back into the shop and Peter would get upset thinking that we'd taken the sweets and were not paying for them – but we'd say, when he asked us for the money, "We're not buying them, you can have them back!"

Another trick was that we'd say that we were going out for a walk and would be back in ten minutes. We would not return for perhaps half-an-hour and Peter would be absolutely panicking wondering if anything had happened to us – in fact we were just around the corner having a pleasant chat!

I got friendly with two able bodied members (Russell and Trish) who had good ideas for improving the club. We held an open meeting and discussed possible improvements. The outcome of the meeting was an election for a committee and a chairperson to run the club with the new ideas. I was very pleased when I won the election and became the chairperson. Unfortunately, Peter was upset that he was no longer in charge so he walked out of the club and didn't come back.

One of the activities that I arranged was a monthly cinema visit to the A.B.C. cinema in Catford. I always phoned, first the cinema manager to ask when we could come and what was on, and the Social Services Transport department in Eros House (as it was then). We continued to visit the A.B.C. Cinema in Catford now and again, and we used to visit a pub in Kent called the Portobello – it took us an hour to get there. Unfortunately we had to stop our visits, firstly because of the distance and secondly I think the landlord and other customers did not really like us going there.

Every year, I used to organise for the club to have a day's outing to the seaside – somewhere like Margate or Hastings. I used to get some helpers from the Day Centre, and I think my sister came with us one year. Once we had arrived, I would give each member £2 so that they could buy a meal to save me organising or booking a table. This was better because they could eat anywhere they liked. This worked really well.

We did have a few good parties at Christmas and Valentine's Day. Some of the drivers entered into spirit of it. Tony and Brian really did get the parties going.

Round the corner from the club, about a ten minute walk, there used to be a fish and chip shop. The club used to allow us members to go there on our own, whenever we wanted, as long as we came straight back.

The new committee, including myself, were keen to move the club to a better hall. After we had looked at several church halls we chose Telegraph Hill, a community centre, as our new meeting place. At the time I was in favour of the move because the Hall was bigger and better than St. Michaels and the toilets, while not fully accessible, were better. Telegraph Hill had a bar and I got the club members to agree that if they bought drinks they would bring them back into the Hall and not to stay in the bar. However after a while they began to stay in the bar. I used to bring in soft drinks and sweets which I bought at a Cash and Carry for sale during club evenings; the profits went to club funds for our outings etc. As the members stayed in the bar and bought what they wanted there, I had to stop the sale of drinks and sweets as hardly anyone was interested.

Looking back on it, I feel the move was a disaster, because the main activity of the club became drinking in the bar and the club lost a valuable source of income. I eventually resigned from the club because the members were only interested in drinking in the bar. I felt that I could do that anytime and did not need to join a club to do so. In fact I felt it wasn't a club anymore.

Eventually the club was asked to move because the centre was to be re-decorated. It moved to the Lewisham Council Staff Social Club in Beckenham. The club met in the bar and it was really just an evening out drinking. The toilets weren't accessible for wheelchairs and the club was at the end of a long, dark path, and it wasn't close to buses either. I was not surprised that the membership gradually dropped and in 1987 the club was finally disbanded. I was angry as I felt the members themselves had ruined the club. I was asked to go back to be the leader, but I wanted the club to be interested in more activities than just drinking and I felt it was important to find a meeting place that was easy to get to by public transport and which was accessible for wheelchair users.

My worse experience at the club was when I was at St. Michael's. One of the drivers came to see me and asked me to go out for a ride with him. I asked him, "Why?" and he said, "For a chat."

I left my bag at the club thinking we would have to come back for it. He drove me miles away, then he stopped and tried to kiss me. I panicked and told him to take me back to the club or I would get out of the car.

After about 10 minutes he gave up and took me back to the club. I felt I could not report him as I had no witnesses. All I could do was to learn from my experience and be very careful with the drivers unless I knew them very well and trusted them.

Looking back on it now I realise that perhaps it was unwise for me to go for a ride with him, but I was only 18 years old and had very little experience of that sort.

## SEALS SWIMMING CLUB

I joined this club when I was about 17 and it was held at the Grove Baths in New Cross. I could swim but I was sure the exercise would be very good and relaxing for me and also, as many of my friends belonged to the club, I knew that I would enjoy their companionship. I enjoyed being a member. We had fun and the competitions were good for us, as it proved that we could do something well because members were able bodied as well as disabled.

One Sunday morning I was at swimming. Everything went well until we were on our way home. Normally the drivers dropped me off before my friend Kitty. As the drivers dropped people off, I started to get a panicky feeling inside me, wondering when these drivers were going to drop me home! Soon, I was the last member on the welfare bus. I thought, "Ah! Me next", but then the driver dropped off his mate. I started to get worried and wondered what he was going to do to me? Soon we arrived at the depot. We walked to his car and I climbed in. As I was aware of what happened to me a few years ago at the Penny Farthing Club, I made it quite clear to him that I didn't want him to harm me in any way. We just drove through Eltham and we stopped. We had a good chat. He did try it on but he didn't succeed. Then I warned him that I must be home by one o'clock. No problems and he managed to get me home by one. From then on I knew I could trust him. I enjoyed this chat as I felt he treated me as a person.

I remained a member for about five years then unfortunately I had a nasty experience and left the club. One of the drivers who was on duty that Sunday morning came into the water with us and was having a game with me and because I could swim, he thought that I was a good swimmer. He took me up to the deep end and left me. Now my usual way of swimming was to start at the deep end, so that by the time I was tired and breathless I would be halfway down the bath. Then I would lift my head and my feet would touch the bottom and I would swim to the side and rest. Unfortunately, the driver did not know this so when he left me I couldn't reach the side and panicked and went under a couple of times. Somebody held a long pole for me to grab and pulled me to the side. I was so frightened by the experience I could not bring myself to go back into the water and never went swimming with the Seals again.

I was about twenty years old before I went swimming again and then it was with four able bodied friends (Peggy and Pete and their two friends) who understood my fears and disability. We went to Beckenham Baths on Thursday evenings. It is foolish for anyone to play tricks like that on inexperienced swimmers and it is true to say I really lost my confidence in the water because of that fright!

## THE YATES CLUB

Charlie Yates was a member of Trinity Day Centre, and I believe he died in 1975. His mother wanted us to do something in remembrance of Charlie. We thought it was a good idea to have a new youth club named after Charlie Yates. The club was held at Telegraph Hill on Tuesday evenings. The club was run on the same lines as the Penny Farthing Club.

Then when we had to move from Telegraph Hill, the Yates Club moved to the Ladywell Day Centre while the Penny Farthing Club moved to the Lewisham Council Staff Social Club. After a few years, Lewisham Social Services, who provided transport for the club, had to save money. It was agreed that instead of finishing at 10pm they would finish at 9.30pm to save on the drivers' overtime.

I think the club went on for about eight years. I was a member for about two years but left because it was getting much like the Penny Farthing. I know the club got banned from Ladywell Centre after certain events. First, one of the members put salt in the hot water urn as a joke and the next day, the centre staff had to clean the urn out. Second, on another evening, most of the members went down the road to the pub leaving two very disabled members alone, one of them fell out of their wheelchair and had to lay on the floor untill the others came back. The others stayed late in the pub and the drivers who had arrived at the centre to take them home had to walk down and tell them to go back to the centre.

## THE MULTIPLE SCLEROSIS CLUB

This club was held once a month at the Saville Club in Lewisham High Street. They organised a different programme each month. For example, outings, cheese and wine parties, bring and buy sales, old time musicals and social evenings. Once a year they had an Annual General Meeting. Mum missed quite a few of the AGMs as she hated them because she found them boring. Mum joined the club in the 1970s and though she enjoyed going to the Club, she did find it depressing from time to time when she noted that some of the members were getting worse. I was not a member of the club but used to go with mum until she got to know some of the club members. Then I gradually I stopped going and only went on special occasions or to see some of my friends. I can remember one Christmas, mum's club had a party which included a Christmas dinner. In the evening I was invited to have dinner with the Disabled Christian Fellowship Group. I managed to go to both. I nearly ate two Christmas dinners but I was really full up half way through the second dinner. I felt as if I couldn't eat any more for the next two days!

Twice a year they used to have a collection. Mum and I would go to Homebase in Bromley Road with the collection boxes, and we would stand on the door. We collected quite a lot of money. I also used to collect door-to-door.

One year, I collected for the SCOPE Club door-to-door, up our road. Unfortunately, the tin got too heavy and the bottom fell out. I picked most of it up and had to get home fast to get my dad to come and help me pick the rest of the money up. Someone had put a £5 note in the box. SCOPE would always let you know how much you had collected.

Today I am glad to hear they have changed the design of their tins!

While I was living in Lewisham, we held a Disabled Christian Fellowship meeting once a month on a Saturday. This used to be quite good as we would have a time of prayer and worship and then tea and a chat. We would then all go our separate ways home.

When I moved to Woolwich, I went to another Disabled Christian Fellowship group in Greenwich. I didn't enjoy this one as much and found it a bit boring. They met on a Sunday at around 5pm. They had an hour for tea, which didn't really suit me as I don't eat very much – just a cake and a glass of water. Also, because I cannot see, it was difficult to get to know people. Having said this, there were quite a few people there that I did like. After the hour's break, we went downstairs and had a church service and then went home.

At first, I used to get cabs both ways, but then they managed to find someone to take me there, and I would then get a cab back. In the end, I didn't think it was worth the cab money. Even though it was only Greenwich, the cab fare was very expensive.

We tried to get my local church to take it in turns to take me there, but this didn't work out. One Sunday, during the church service, it was announced that someone was needed to take me to the club. I was not aware that they were going to do this, and I felt really embarrassed. I didn't want to ask them again. I started to go less and less and eventually stopped altogether.

In April, 2005, they discussed the possibility of changing the name of the Disabled Christian Fellowship to Daybreak Christian Fellowship to make it sound more appealing for the new young members.

# TRAMPOLINE CLUB

When I was 25 I became interested in trampolining. I asked Katie, who was a neighbour of my parents and did a lot of voluntary work, if this was possible. Katie, who knew the right people to ask through her voluntary work, contacted the Manager of Lewisham Leisure Centre who persuaded a trampolining instructor to take me into her able bodied class. Carole, the instructor, admitted later that she was nervous about teaching me but soon found I was tougher than she thought, and could take hard falls as well as any able bodied student.

At first, I couldn't get up on the trampoline so the instructor had to lift me on. After a few months we discovered a way to climb on the trampoline on my own by using a chair or wooden bench. At my first lesson on the trampoline, Carole showed me how to stand in the middle then Carole would jump very lightly so that I could get my balance. I wasn't very successful, as I kept falling over. Then she showed me how to jump, but as I have difficulty controlling my balance and movements, I ended up flat on my face most times! In order to overcome these problems, Carole stood behind me and held me underneath my elbows and she jumped while I remained stationary; this helped me to get my balance and experience the sensation of jumping. Then she stood still and I jumped, but as Carole was heavier than me, this made the surface uneven and I fell over again! Carole decided to stand in front of me, holding me by the elbows and I rested my hands on her arms. This resulted in more space between us as we jumped, so I didn't fall as much as before! Very often, I would get tensed up and she would shake my arms to make me relax, this made me worse so we found that it was better for me to stand still. She could tell when I was relaxed – then we would start jumping again.

Gradually, after a few months, Carole held me by both hands, and then as I gained confidence, she held me by one hand. So now with one hand I could jump really high, but Carole couldn't keep control over my jumps! She decided to stand behind me, tie a tracksuit top around my waist and hold me by its two sleeves while I jumped. This didn't work very well as the surface was uneven and I felt she was too close to me.

Carole continued to stand in front and suddenly I began to jump completely on my own! Everybody cheered when they saw me and I felt really great. It was a fantastic feeling! Then Carole started teaching me how to do a seat drop, tuck jump, half turn twist, full turn twist, knee drop and a back drop. Every time it was my turn on the trampoline, Carole had to come and stand on the edge, in case I got out of control. About a year later Carole decided that I was all right on my own, unless she wanted to teach me something new.

There were a few exercises which I did have difficulty with. One was the tuck jump – I couldn't jump high enough or get my legs to go up and down while in the air before hitting the trampoline bed. If she asked me to do more than one exercise at a time, I could do them sometimes but not at others. The second difficulty was with the back drop. I couldn't always keep my arms in front of me and keep my chin on my chest. Sometimes I really hurt myself during these back drops as I didn't have enough control over my head. There was one exercise that I could never do – this was a front drop; My head would always hit the surface before my body, so Carole agreed that when I should do a front drop, we would change it to a back drop instead. Carole asked me if I would like to have a go doing a somersault? I said, "Oh! Yes, I'd love to!"

We never had such fun and the laughter was unbelievable! I believe we started by jumping up and down, with me landing on my hands and knees at the same time. The next stage was to tie a band around my waist, with a rope on each side, Carole held one side and one of the members held the other side. This was great fun as I never knew what was going to happen. Sometimes I would end up flat on my face, on the edge of the bed and sometimes I would be up in the air too long. We never gave up because I was determined to do a somersault! It was a very friendly class and I used to go with them to support the team when they entered in competitions.

Carole was a very good instructor and when she left after about three years, I was very disappointed. I knew it would be a long time before I got another instructor with the patience or the determination that Carole had, and I have not yet turned a somersault properly. Before Carole left, she put an article in the club newsletter which said that I was a tough little thing and she was delighted with all the progress I had made.

I stopped going because the new instructor had no confidence in my ability because I was disabled, and seemed to ignore me.

I found trampolining helped me in many ways. It made me realize that I could take hard knocks and the fact that in the end I was able to do seat drops, half twist, sometimes a full twist, back drops, tuck jumps and knee drops without physical support increased my confidence in my ability to learn and overcome problems. It taught me to relax which has given me more control over my physical movements and balance, which are affected by cerebral palsy.

Mixing with able bodied students and being accepted by them after a while gave me confidence, and I learnt to take good humoured teasing and having my leg pulled – and to give it back!

In 2004, I decided to rejoin the SCOPE club again, where I met up with some of my old friends from the Ladywell Day Centre. I was amazed at one particular friend, Lisa, because she had really grown up and wanted her independence and her own flat. She always used to say that it was because of me that she had the courage to go on buses on her own.

When the club went to the pictures, it made it very difficult for me because I always would be put right in the front in the cinema as I found it difficult to see but I had to lean my head back to see the screen. Also because I only had a small amount of sight in one eye, I would have been able to see much better if I had been allowed to sit at the back.

One day, we went to a pub, and again I had problems. The music was so loud that it was very difficult, with my hearing aid, to hear other people talking. I was put at a table with another member, who I did not know very well and left to get on with it. I was given a pub menu by a leader of the group, who left me to read it, even though, after being a member for around a year, she should have realised that I was not able to read it because of my poor eyesight. On the good side, I did manage to get a Bacardi and coke!

After that, I decided not to go the club any more, but because I wanted to get the telephone number of my friend, Lisa, I still continued to go for a while and left a few months later.

*Chapter Twenty Two*

# Trinity (Part One)

The manager of the Trinity Centre (a club for young disabled people run by Lewisham Borough) came to see us. She asked my parents and me if I would like to visit Trinity Centre to see if I would like to become a member. When she told me about the activities there, I said, "Yes, I would like to join." So I attended from Monday to Friday. In the morning, the members of the Centre had social workers to help us to do whatever we wished. For example, reading, arithmetic and educational games. In the afternoon we did industrial work to earn some money. The work was rather dull. For example, we would have to count screws and put them in envelopes or fit darts together, counting and packing them into boxes.

We worked for two hours each day, except Tuesdays. On Tuesday, we went to the old Ladywell Centre because a group of blind people used the Trinity Hall. When I started at Trinity, I was introduced to a member called Peter, who didn't live far from me. I agreed to meet him round the corner and we would get on the bus together as Peter knew nearly all the bus conductors and the times of the buses. Because I went along with Peter in the mornings and afternoons, the people working on the 124 buses, and some of the passengers, thought we were brother and sister. At first I didn't like the idea of being called Peter's sister. I used to get very angry about it, and although I said that he wasn't my brother, they were VERY SLOW to believe it!

Later on, I began to play jokes on Peter, and sometimes he would get quite cross with me, but I let his grumbles go in one ear and out the other! Sometimes, I used to go to Trinity another way on a 160 bus. Then, when I arrived at Trinity, Peter would come over to me and say, "I waited for you this morning. Where did you get to?" I would reply, "Oh, Peter. I went the other way!" When I said that, Peter would walk off; perhaps he was a bit annoyed. I think I did it purposefully because I wanted to be awkward, or it might have been one of those days when I wanted to be alone. I think it was also because I didn't like people thinking that Peter was my brother. Later on, Peter and I didn't bother to wait for each other; we both agreed that it was best to go our own ways.

One time when Peter and I were walking along the road to get our bus home, Peter fell over and cut his hands and grazed his knees. I said, "Peter, are you all right?" I couldn't understand what he had said, so I ran back to Trinity to get someone to come and help him. A helper went running down the road and he brought Peter back to bathe and clean his hands and knees. I waited for him and I went into the kitchen to drink a glass of water because I felt shocked and upset about Peter and out of breath with running back to Trinity to get help. When Peter felt a bit better, we both went home together.

Another incident that I shall not forget is when Peter and I went on one of our Sunday afternoon long bus rides. He used to ask me on a Friday afternoon if I would like to go with him on Sunday and I would say, "I'll have my dinner early and then I'll come." When I got home, I would ask mum what time we were going to have Sunday dinner.

Mum asked me why I wanted to know and I told her so she said, "About one o'clock."

After dinner on Sunday, I would go round the corner and meet Peter. We always got on a 124 bus with a driver and conductor that we knew, so that we could talk to them. The 124 bus took us to Bexley Hospital which was at the end of the journey. We used to go for a short walk and then get the bus back. We generally arrived back home at about half past five. I shall never forget when we were on the top of the bus at the back – I did not like some of the things Peter tried to do. We did this for a long time and we had a lot of fun but gradually as the time of my Sunday dinner got later, and also Peter and I were drifting apart from each other, we stopped these outings.

Another time I remember was when somebody at the Centre had upset Peter (he did get upset very easily). He ran out of the Centre and straight across the main road. Fortunately, it was an ambulance that came along and not a car, so it slowed down to let him cross. If it had been a car I feel sure he would have been run over. I am so thankful to say that Peter came back safely and I don't think he was foolish enough to repeat that again!

There were some young lads at the Centre – Mick, Paul, Alec and Charlie, who used to often play cards. Eventually, when I got to know them well, I would play 'Two and Eight' but not for money. Sometimes they asked me to go to the shops for them. One of the drivers asked me to go to the baker's to get some doughnuts. On the way back, one of them fell out of the bag. I quickly picked it up and shook it and put it back into the bag (not that shaking it would make any difference!) because I didn't want to go back to the shop. I didn't say anything about it to the driver. When he had eaten it, he said, "That was nice." I turned away from him and I couldn't stop laughing! He never knew what I had done!

Once a week on Tuesday when the Blind Person's Group used Trinity Hall, we went to Old Ladywell Lodge, which was an old people's home. I think Old Ladywell used to be a workhouse and was built fairly early in the nineteenth century. There were three floors containing 'A' block, 'B' block and 'C' block.

During the months that we were using Ladywell, the residents there were gradually being transferred to more modern homes for old folks. On Tuesdays the physiotherapist, Mary, came and treated us in 'C' block because there were some facilities at Ladywell. We also had some of our usual industrial work to do, for example, putting darts together, counting and packing them. We also had to get a dart sharpener from another box, get a blue label and stick it around the sharpener, and then pack the sharpeners. My job was to tear off the 'Unicorn' stickers, which showed the make of the sharpeners. This was murder, because if you did not line it up properly or tore it off too quickly, the corner would get damaged and you would waste one. The factory is no longer in Forest Hill.

At Ladywell I used to have physiotherapy but after a while I gave it up because, although I am left-handed, Mary, the physiotherapist, was trying to get me to do more with my right hand, but I was quite content being left handed. She would stroke the muscles on the upper part of my arm and then lift it. I think that if she could have had me to work on when I was much younger, and more supple and flexible, I might have been ambidextrous. Sometimes when it was my time for seeing Mary, I would go and hide and quite often she couldn't find me!

Sometimes at Ladywell I got bored, either because I wanted to get out of physiotherapy or because there was so little to do. I would go for a long walk around the grounds. As I walked around I noticed some interesting things about the building. At the bottom of some of the walls there were quite large holes, through which I could see a long way under the building. There were ventilation passageways and an animal – a cat or dog or even a fox – could crawl through. They were full of dust and thousands of spiders. I showed these holes to some of the other Trinity girls but they were scared of them and ran indoors. While we were going to Old Ladywell, I got to know some of the young men members very well. I was about eighteen and they were in their early or late twenties.

Charlie was in a wheelchair and only had one arm, and there was something wrong with his stomach. He used to take some kind of drugs. Charlie was an amusing, jolly person and he was very intelligent. People used to say that I could twist Charlie around my little finger and I suppose that was true, because I had a lot of feeling for him.

Sometimes at Old Ladywell, Charlie would call me over and ask me if I wanted to go for a walk. Sometimes I said, "Yes, but not too far." I would push him in his wheelchair into the lift and ask him, "Up or down?" Sometimes he said, "We'll go up!" Mostly he wanted to go down to the ground floor because we were on the second floor. I would push him where he wanted to go because he could only push himself backwards using his feet.

There was one place in the building where nobody else seemed to go, and Charlie liked to go there. Sometimes he would ask me to sit on his lap and we'd have a kiss and a cuddle. After a while I would say, "Charlie, let's get back to the others. You know we shouldn't be here!" Charlie used to say "Just one more kiss!" After I did this we went back to the rest of the group.

Paul was another friend. He was quite tall and fair and he was a very good natured boy, always ready to help if you needed him. Paul and I were good friends but at that time he and his girlfriend were hoping to marry. She got a job and the wedding fell through. Paul and I used to go for long walks through Ladywell grounds. When we came back we would take the lift up but go past our floor to the next floor and go into one of the rooms. There we would talk and hold each other and have a kiss or two; it was quite fun! Sometimes Paul would get annoyed with me because on the way back, if we met any of our friends, I would go red in the face. A couple of years later, he left the centre and we completely lost touch with each other.

Another friend of mine was Mick. He wasn't very tall and was rather stocky. He had quite a baby round face and was good natured and kind, and would always do anything he could to help anyone. Sadly over the years he changed.

So much happened between Mick and myself, not only at Ladywell but also at Trinity, that I must try to start at the beginning and remember as much as I can.

At first, at Old Ladywell, most of the boys would play cards all day, but occasionally, Mick would do some industrial work. What he liked doing best though was English with the social worker. After about a year, the local council stopped the social workers coming to Trinity. At first, we carried on in the same way without them, but as time went by we began to get bored because all the help we had was from the manager of Trinity and four helpers – there were about twenty four of us.

I did the same for Mick as I did for the other boys. I did the shopping for them all and eventually I would go at any time so this became a regular daily habit.

When I wasn't shopping, working or playing cards I would sit by the gas fire and read. I read books by Catherine Cookson and Lucilla Andrews. I also enjoyed mystery, murders, ghost stories and thrillers. When I first lived on my own I tended not to read such books because they could frighten me, but as time went by I found that I could read them again with no problems.

As time went on, I found myself beginning to like Mick more and more, and then I began to realise that perhaps I could love him, but I could never marry him because of our disabilities. Actually he asked me to marry him when I was twenty one and my sister thought it might work out for us, but I said, "No."

He had some funny ways that made it hard to get to know and understand him properly. For example, if he was upset he would not discuss the problem but would go away and sulk or else keep on and on about it. Something else that always annoyed me was that Mick apologised profusely, often for no reason at all.

After I had been at Trinity for about eighteen months I began to feel really fed up and bored, not only with everyone there but with doing the same thing which did not seem to be getting me anywhere. So I applied to go to Bromley workshop because I knew somebody there, and I was accepted.

*Chapter Twenty Three*

# Bromley Workshop

Bromley workshop was in Park Road, and was run by the Spastics Society, which is now known as SCOPE. It was built as an annexe to a house, and it had a small car park for about three cars.

Inside the building was a short corridor with the manager's office on the left, and down the corridor was the kitchen. Walking through the kitchen you would reach the dining room, which was very cold in winter. To get to the workshop you went through the dining room. In the workshop, there were two rows of tables with the work spread out from one end to the other. This work was brought in from the local factories; the work went in and out of the same door.

On one side was a row of sealing machines used for sealing clear plastic bags and at the back where the work was kept were two milling machines. On the side wall there was a fan heater, which unfortunately only heated a small area around itself. I managed always to work in that warm area!

Our day started at 9.30am and finished at 4pm. We had two tea breaks each of fifteen minutes: one at 10.15am and the other at 2.15pm. Dinner was at 12.15pm and it was cooked by the nuns from a nearby convent. They brought it in, in hot containers, and two voluntary helpers served it to us.

After the meal the members took it in turns in pairs to clear away and wash-up. We also did this for the morning and afternoon tea breaks. After about four months the nuns gave up cooking for the workshop and so we were obliged to bring packed lunches. This was not such a hardship as you might think. On each day of the week we had a specific set meal, and this went on for several weeks before the menu was changed. In the winter, managers and staff prepared hot soup for us, which was very welcome!

When I first started to work at Bromley workshop, dad used to give me a lift to the bus stop in Bromley Road. The time was about 8.15am and I would arrive in Bromley just after 9am. I would go window shopping, but this meant I was walking away from the workshop and going into the High Street. This is of course meant a long walk back and often it was ten o'clock before I got to the workshop. The manager did not mind because he thought I was using my bus pass, which was not valid until 9.30am!

After a couple of weeks I got to know a window cleaner and every morning we would have a little chat because I knew where he would be each day. Sometimes this pastime would make me even later than ten o'clock! When the manager asked me why I was much later than usual I would reply, "Oh! I missed my usual bus!"

After a while I had to make my own way to Bromley Road because I had been arriving in Bromley itself too early, but I still managed to talk to the window cleaner. This worked well until one day I got to work at ten thirty am.

The manager asked me, "Where have you been?"

I said, "I have been to the dentist!"

"Let me know the day before you have to go to the doctor's or the dentist next time and I will put it in my book," the manager said.

So I couldn't play that card anymore! However, I found another way round it by pretending that the bus was late again.

Some of the work we did was for the G.P.O. telephones. We put small pieces of silver coloured metal into what seemed to be blue pocket fuses, which were kept in the locked green G.P.O. telephone boxes found occasionally on the side of the pavement near a telegraph pole.

I found this work very difficult for my hands and so we were given wooden blocks with slots in them to hold the blue pockets and this made it easier for me. Some of us in turn put the silver pieces in and pressed them down. Dad gave me a tool to use which was something like a silver ball point pen to push the silver pieces down and it did the job perfectly.

I was on that job for a month but we had thousands and thousands of these blue things and they seemed never to come to an end!

After a month we had another job, which was counting different sizes of polythene bags. We did this as a line job, one counted ten small, the next six medium; the next six large; then these were checked and lastly the bags were put together and folded in half and sealed inside another bag. If we didn't pick them up and fold them carefully they would all slip out of our hands! This meant starting from scratch again.

When we had done enough, they would be packed into large boxes. I made sure that I would be counting so that I was near the heater and it was easier for me to count than to put these bags into one another.

We had a similar job counting knives, forks and spoons. Another job was wrapping and packing coffin handles. Three members each wrapped in a different style. These were packed into boxes of one hundred after they had been checked for faults. This work was very boring.

We worked twenty five hours a week and our wages were £1.50 which we received on Fridays. We had to work for 6 months and we were entitled to sick pay. We were allowed two days' sick leave and by the $3^{rd}$ day we had to send a doctor's certificate. I was off sick many times with the wretched colds I used to catch; even mum couldn't believe that the workshop could be so cold! I tell you one thing though, I would never go to the doctor's just to get a certificate for a cold.

I met an old acquaintance, Jane, at the workshop after some years. Jane also had Cerebral Palsy – I had also known her well at school. I used to "take the micky" out of her. She seemed to me to be a proper baby, and a 'daddy's girl'. When we were in the workshop I didn't have much contact with her except when I was teasing her. Her father sometimes gave me a lift home and of course I behaved differently – no teasing! Jane had attended Trinity for a very short time but she didn't agree with the way it was run. When I told her that I was going back to Trinity, she was very cross and we had some fierce arguments about it.

I believe that Jane later went to a day centre and she did voluntary work in a SCOPE shop. She later got her own place and lived independently.

I made several friends at Bromley: Joanna, with whom I got on well and whose mother used to give some of us a lift home; Robert, who was very big with a raucous voice – he used to make his own way there and back and sometimes I used to meet him in the morning which didn't please me because I was rather afraid of his temper; and Philip. Philip had been with me at Charlton Park school and he was fun and we had some good laughs. He was very good at History so eventually we started doing History in the dinner hour.

Poppy, another friend, suffered from fits but we didn't report it when they happened because people who had fits were not supposed to work in the workshop. Maybe this rule was made because of the possibility of accidents with machinery. Instead we took her into the dining room as the fits only lasted a few minutes. She and I got on well together and none of us wanted her turned away from Bromley. We used to play tricks on the others and have fun. She also helped me in many ways, for example changing my towels when I was on my periods, because in those days they only had the tie-in ones to be used with special underwear.

When doing the washing up with Paula, another friend, we would put our heads together and write a poem.

### TEA LEAVES
Tea leaves in a packet, waiting to make a pot of tea.
Many people like it, many people don't,
But when it comes the tea leaves part at the end.
Some people just throw them down the DRAIN!
Some people tell their future,
Some come true and some don't come true,
And now there will be a pot of tea waiting for me.

There was a girl there called Angela, who had her own specific job. This was to make ornamental flowers using a technique of forming petals from bended wire, and dipping these into different coloured craft paint. After the wire had been pulled out slowly, the paint had to be left until it stopped dripping and until it dried. These then looked like petals. Green tape was wound around the ends of the wire to make it look like a stem. Leaves were also added to the stems. Stems were put together to form bunches of flowers. These could be bought by us, and all the money raised either went to the workshop or to SCOPE.

Paula was a friend who I met at Bromley and I used to talk to her when I was at the new Ladywell Centre. Many years later we bumped into each other on the Sports Day we held twice a year at Ladywell (after we had left), where the local boroughs had competitions. When Paula came with her group, I would keep my eye open for her so we could have a chat.

Bromley workshop closed down in the 1980s and Paula went to another day centre where she could learn how to be an independent person. I was so pleased because this is what I believe that most disabled people should be doing if they have got the capability to be able to cope with life. Over a period of time, the competitions stopped, and the last I heard, in the 1990s, was that Paula was thinking of getting married to her boyfriend.

I had been there eight months when I decided that Bromley Workshop was no longer for me! I felt if I stayed at the workshop any longer it would not improve my standards of work or extend me and it wasn't going to get me a job. Sometimes it seemed like being in prison because at that time we were not allowed to go out in our dinner break unless we were twenty one years old. This was understandable because the staff were responsible for us from 9.30am to 4pm. The hardest thing about my decision to leave was how I was going to tell my parents. I thought about it and decided to wait until we went on holiday and see what they would have to say.

In September 1972, I went on holiday with my parents for a week. I waited until we were on our way home and then told them that I wanted to go to back to Trinity.

Mum exclaimed, "Oh no! Not after all the trouble that we took to get you a place at Bromley and now you want to go back to Trinity!"

Dad said, "Well, we shall just have to wait and see what we can do."

I could trust dad to do this and although for a while my parents argued about it, in the end I did get back to Trinity.

Bromley workshop eventually closed down a few years later.

## Chapter Twenty Four
# Trinity (Part Two)

During the second week of our holiday, dad took me back to Trinity and we saw the new manager there. Her name was Janet and she said that I could go back as I had been at Trinity long before I went to Bromley. I got on very well with this manager. I thought Trinity had changed for the better and I was really glad to be back and to be free to do what I thought was best for me.

The first thing I noticed about Trinity was that the working hours had been increased from two classes to five hours every day, whether we were doing packing, counting or education. The first job was assembling darts, as it was before I left. We had to put the two parts together (the flight and the spike) and count them into a hundred and pack them in a box. However, after a while this job was discontinued.

The second job we did at Trinity was absolutely awful; we had to fit forty eight personal file clips into a box and these boxes were really just that little bit too small. I had to check that there were two rows of twenty four clips. Nearly every time there was one short and I had to hand it back to have another clip put in. Unfortunately very often when this last one was squeezed in the whole lot popped out!

Because this job came from the firm where my dad worked, I asked him if there was a better way of packing these clips.

"Yes," he said, "Put the alternate ones in upside down." This made the packing a lot easier but they still came out. They came out by the way I checked them sometimes! A couple of months later we managed to finish the packing of these awful clips and they were sent back to the factory and we didn't get that job again!

I had been back at Trinity for six months when Janet, the manager, and I had a long talk about many things.

I told Janet that I liked typing so she said, "Would you like to go to college and learn to type well?"

I said, "Yes, I would like to do that."

So Janet arranged that I went to Downham College in Glenbow Road to learn to type. I paid £3.00 each term. Janet told the college authorities that I could only use an electric typewriter, so when I started at college on the Monday morning there was an electric typewriter waiting for me. I went to Downham College once or twice a week and got on very well with the tutor. She was a very pleasant and understanding person. Her name was Mrs. Blank but there was one thing she just didn't like and that was the electric typewriter! I never found out why!

After a few months, I had a companion to join with me, and this friend and I got on very well and we gradually got to know everyone in the class. Learning to type was one of the best things I did and I soon became quite good at it. However, I am not very good at copy-typing from people's handwriting because I am not always sure of the spelling! I can remember once when I didn't feel like typing, I had to type a letter from an example of handwriting in the typing instruction book. Unfortunately I got it quite wrong! When the tutor came round to mark my work, she said that I must re-type the letter! This didn't please me one bit! If you ever have taken a typing course you will, I am sure, know what I mean! Anyway, I put my mind to the job in hand and re-typed the work. When the tutor came back again she said "Ah! That is a great improvement!"

After I had been typing for a year, the manager (Janet) asked me if I would like to do some typing for her and I said that I would.

I began to type letters, wage slips, papers and minutes of the representative meetings for her. I worked like this for about a year and then I began to get bored with the typing. Fortunately, the manager understood why this was.

When I became bored I used to go out for long walks or bus rides without telling anyone where I was going. I didn't even tell my parents. This could have been silly because if I had had an accident or anything, it would have caused a lot of worry and trouble. If it rained, I would go to the library and sit and read a book or would go to visit a friend.

When I returned to Trinity from Bromley I met my friends again. I think Mick began to fall in love with me because he began to give me presents. I couldn't understand why he did this as I felt it wasn't necessary to give a friend lots of presents. This habit of Mick's to give me weekly gifts went on until one day I decided to do something about it. I had tried to tell him not to buy me these presents but it didn't seem to work. He had bought me a record and it was one I would have liked to have, but I did the only thing I could think of to stop him, which was to throw the record back at him. It broke in half! Mick walked out in a temper and called me names, but I'm sure he realised that I wanted to be a friend only, nothing more. After this incident, he gave me a present only now and again.

Helen was one of my best friends both at Trinity and privately. She would often help me with my personal affairs and problems. Sometimes, Helen, Joy, Mandy and I would go to the Ladies' room for a laugh and a joke and if we made too much noise, Janet the manager would come in and Helen was always the one who got the blame! We would be laughing with Mandy who was always had boyfriend problems. She would ask Helen and me to help her sort them out! Although we sometimes got fed up with her problems, we would bring Mick into the discussion in the other room or outside of course – and he sometimes helped us out.

Joy was good fun and was always ready with jokes and laughs and we'd sometimes play around and be rather a nuisance to the other members; but she moved away and I believe she is married now. Mandy was always worried about not having boyfriends, but the boys for some reason were not keen on Mandy. Maybe she tried too hard to get them! Eventually, Mandy and her mum moved nearer to Mandy's sister.

I can remember one joke I played on Helen. One day, she was wearing a dress with a zip down the front of it. Anyway, when she wasn't expecting anything I undid her zip! She was shocked and gave me a good telling off but, years later, she saw the funny side.

The first holiday I had with Trinity was at Weston-Super-Mare and we were allowed to choose our room mates. I was with Helen and Vi, and at that time Helen was on tablets which made her slow and sleepy, so she needed help getting up in the mornings. Vi and I agreed to take it in turns, but we didn't realise this meant we had to be up by five thirty in the morning to be ready for breakfast at 8.30am! Neither did we realise how long it took Helen to get ready for bed and to do her hair and wash her face! We did not get to bed before 2am in the morning! By the time Wednesday came I was so tired that I missed breakfast and stayed in bed until 11am, and then I had a problem with trying to get dressed. I needed help to fasten my bra and to do up my zip and shoes, so I arranged with Vi that she would come back to the chalet after breakfast to help me. Nevertheless, in spite of everything, I enjoyed the holiday.

At Weston-Super-Mare, Mick and I were friendly companions and we had a good time together. When we managed to be alone, I gave him a love bite and he had it for ages!

One year, while I was at Trinity Day Centre, we had a holiday in Paris. Helen, Joy, Anne and I shared a room on the ground floor, and the helpers were above us.

Anne was completely helpless in her body, but all right in her mind, so we gave her the bed by the wall and put a chair between it and the next bed. However, Anne fell out in the night with a mighty crash! Whoever woke first always woke me up, and as all the lights went out at midnight, I had to go upstairs to the next floor in the dark! It was very difficult and scary to find the way. I groped along by the wall – we had not been warned to take torches! I woke a couple of helpers to come down and get Anne back into bed. By the time this had been done it was almost time for me to get up to help Helen. I believe Helen came with me the second time when Anne fell out of the bed.

One day when we did not go out, Philip came into our room and although I told him not to shut the door because I couldn't open it (we were going to have a laugh and some fun) - he shut it! After about fifteen minutes someone knocked on the door and Philip climbed quickly out of the window. Then I realised that I couldn't open the door so I called Philip back in to open it.

I said to him, "What are you worried about? This isn't your room. I'm the one who should worry!"

You see, we had been told not to have the boys in the girls' rooms - Then he opened the door and we saw one of the helpers standing there. She had come to get something for Anne and she said, "Philip! What are you doing in Julia's room? I am most surprised that you broke the rule! Please go now."

Then she turned to me and said, "I won't report this, but don't do it again, Julia; it makes things difficult for everyone."

One day, I went down to the hotel foyer to see if there was a letter from my parents, and I also saw one addressed to Philip Martin. I thought it was for our Philip, so I took it to him. He opened it and found that it wasn't for him. I laughed my head off and Philip was upset at what he had done.

I said, "Don't be silly, you haven't done any harm. We'll get some sellotape to seal it down and hand it back!"

He did this and we heard no more about it, but he told me off for being so careless and not reading his name properly! Well, it wasn't my fault if it looked like his name!

Another time that I can remember was when Mick, Joy, Philip and I went out for a long walk and as we were walking, we began to talk about the French language and to say all the French words we knew. As we said "oui," a man walked by and heard us and thought we wanted to have a wee! We all had a good laugh about it.

Twice we went to a holiday camp in Caister. The first time, we had a comfortable chalet and it was very good. The second time however, we were put in an old type wooden chalet. It was really cold and in order to get some warmth we had to put money in a slot meter. This was very expensive for us, so the driver, Fred, came and did something to the meter so that we did not have to put any more money in! On the last night, he came back and switched it back again. The toilet was outside the chalet, and Helen had to get up to go to the loo at 1.30am every night and I used to have to go with her. This was rather a nuisance as I had to wake up at 5.30am so that I could help Helen wake up.

At first, I thought this was really fun and enjoyed the responsibility. However, every now and again, Helen would get cross with me. As the week went by, I was getting more and more tired, and things were getting worse.

One day, Helen was in the bathroom for a really long time and I told the management because I was worried about her. Eventually, Helen came out and told the manager that she was all right. After the manager left the chalet, Helen was very, very angry with me. I got angry too because I had been so worried and everyone in my chalet had been concerned about her and she did not appreciate it.

Because she got so cross with me, I ended up asking if I could change my room.

When we returned home and went back to Trinity on Monday, we were still not talking to each other, and sadly this went on for over a month until one day I said to her, "We can't go on like this; let's be friends again and forget about what happened on holiday."

At last Helen apologised for her bad behaviour and agreed with me and we renewed our friendship!

The following year, Helen refused to come to Caister for the holiday, so Vi and I shared a chalet which was bright and modern with all toilet facilities. It was more of an enjoyable holiday and Vi and I were able to go to bed when we wished and get up at a more reasonable time. I don't think I could have helped Helen again as I was getting tired and fed up with it, and felt it wasn't my job to get people up!

I knew Vi from the time she first went to Charlton Park school. She was very shy and I had to be careful not to say anything that would upset her as she took a long time to get over her moods. As we got to know each other, we became good friends. We left school at the same time and we both started together at Trinity. Vi also came to join me at Bromley workshop after I had been there a short time. However, I returned to Trinity some time before Vi.

I no longer went on holiday with the Trinity group as I saw them every day and I preferred to go on a holiday where I met new people.

While I was attending Downham College, I had my 21$^{st}$ birthday. The typing teacher rang up mum and asked her what I would like for my birthday, but mum wasn't sure and said she would ask me. I didn't want to choose anything too expensive, but what I really did want was a papermate ball-point pen. When it was almost time to go home, I was given a packet and an envelope. When I opened the package and saw the pen, I was delighted, and I went around to thank everyone. I expected to find a card in the envelope, but when I opened it I found £8.00 inside! I was so surprised and speechless. I didn't know what to say! I still have that pen today.

Mum and dad gave me a stereo set which pleased me because now I could play all the records that Mick had bought me during the past year. Mum and dad hired the hall at Trinity Church, where we had our Day Centre, and we invited my sister and her friends. All my friends who went to the Day Centre, and some of my favourite drivers, were also invited. Helen couldn't come because she was ill and missed all the other parties that were going on at that time. Anne is two weeks younger than me, so she was born on Christmas Day. Mum and Anne's mum believed that we were born in the same hospital ward. We held the party in the evening and my family provided the refreshments.

My sister, Pauline, had two girlfriends who were twins, and they used to live up our road. One of the twins decided to make me a long dress to wear at my party. I liked it but I felt you could see that it was hand made. The party started at seven thirty and went on until eleven. We enjoyed ourselves dancing, talking and eating and drinking.

When Pauline was dancing with Mick, he told her that he hoped to marry me sometime and Pauline said, "I hope it will work out for you." When she told me, I just laughed and thought "He must be joking!"

I had many new clothes and quite a large sum of money. Brian bought me a silver watch and I was very pleased with it. I had it for eleven years and I only had to have it repaired twice. Mum and dad were most surprised, but I did not tell anyone else who had given it to me, in case they became jealous.

One thing I shall never forget is that Charlie gave mum some money to buy me something, and Mick, who had given me a heart shaped necklace, got very jealous. He wanted to know how much money Charlie had given mum because he hated the idea that Charlie had given me more money than he had paid out for the necklace! I said that it was none of his business but he kept on until he got on my nerves so much that at last I told him. That seemed to satisfy him! Did I tell him a white lie? About three weeks later I decided to buy myself a ring with Charlie's money.

A good few months later, after my birthday, Charlie had to go into hospital again for a stomach operation. I used to go in to see him about twice a week. Just before the operation, I asked my sister to come shopping with me to buy a ring with the money Charlie had given me. We went to a jeweller's shop in Bromley Common.

I chose a ring – it was silver with holes cut out around it. I took it in to show him and I was very pleased that I had done so, because he died a couple of days after the operation. He must have been in his late 20s. Charlie's death upset me very much indeed because he had asked me to become engaged to him some months before and I had said, "No!" Had I known then that he was going to die, I think that I would have said, "Yes," and become engaged. Charlie was a very kind man and he was very fond of me, and people said that I could twist him around my little finger!

Now came a time that I shall remember all my life! I began to behave at times in an erratic and unreasonable way. I would walk out without telling anyone and I would go for long bus rides or maybe I would stay away from Trinity for a day or even a week without telling my parents. I would let them think I was going to the Centre, but instead I would either go to the library or get on a bus. At one time, I took some of my mother's Valium tablets, three or four a day and altogether I believe took about twenty-eight! As they made me sleepy and 'dopey', I realised I might be doing myself some harm, so I stopped taking them.

The manager, Nigel, of Trinity Centre, realised that I was not behaving normally, but he didn't question me. The following Sunday, I told dad and he rushed me to hospital and I was kept in over night for observation. As these tablets had been down my tummy for too long, they couldn't give me a stomach pump. In the morning I was allowed to go home. I did these things because I felt that I was drifting through life without purpose, and I was not sure of anything. I think I envied my sister. Could it have been the death of Charlie?

The second time I felt the same way was a couple of years later. I took nine or more of my Dad's tablets which were for his vertigo. I went swimming and when I came home I had stomach pains and felt sleepy. My parents did not take much notice as I often got pains through swallowing the water. I was ill for three days and I didn't care what happened as I was in rather a bad way. I was fed up with Trinity and with the boys there, and I felt this kind of life wouldn't get me anywhere.

After a couple of months I managed to pull myself together because I realised what harm I could have done to myself and how serious it all could have been. However, I never told mum and dad what I did. I couldn't say that I would never to it again, as I do get these low feelings. Sometimes I get a bit fed up and restless.

Looking back on it now, I probably went through this phase as I didn't know what I wanted out of life. I was a bit envious of my sister, who had a job and a boyfriend, and I felt that I couldn't get anywhere in my life, at that time. I didn't know what the future would hold for me

At this point, Mick was beginning to get on my nerves. Then Philip went away and Brian was working with Peter and his girlfriend. I began to feel left out of things. The manager suggested that I might like to go away to college. I thought this might be a good idea. We tried the Queen Elizabeth at Leatherhead, but the course was not suitable, so then we tried the Portland in Nottinghamshire. Here I was luckier – not only was the course suitable, there was also a vacancy. Dad took me to the college for a day to have an interview and do some tests. They asked what my general interests were and what I hoped to achieve. I took mental ability, maths and English tests. I also had a medical examination. I was told that I would hear whether I had been successful. After a couple of months, I had a letter to say that I could start in September. This was in 1974.

## Chapter Twenty Five
# Portland Training College

Portland Training College was in Mansfield, Nottinghamshire. The College and its grounds were off a main road. The bus stop was near the gates but there was a long walk through the grounds to the college buildings. These were made up of several separate buildings. The girls' dormitories were in one building and the boys' dormitories in another. There were several orderlies in each dormitory and one of ours was very fussy and bossy. She was very particular and although I must have been about 28 years old, she treated us as if we were children. For example, if you had had a bath but she hadn't been around, she often made you go and have another one even if you had marked it in the book!

One building was for the lectures and another was made up of offices. There was also a workshop where students could attend wood-carving lessons and learn to carve figures. For example there was a Robin Hood figure for sale.

When I arrived, there were already three girls in the room which fortunately was quite large. We had a bed and a wardrobe each and we shared the washbasin which was behind a curtain for privacy when we were washing. The toilets were along the corridor. We arrived at about 2.00pm and after we had said goodbye to our parents who had come to the college with us, we had three hours to settle in, introduce ourselves to our roommates and have a look round.

At 5.00pm we went for supper in the dining hall and I was feeling very nervous, as I ate slower than the others. I couldn't keep up – we only had half an hour for supper – so the orderlies used to take it in turns to feed me. In one way I was glad for them to do this but I also felt rather embarrassed. Unfortunately because I was being fed three times a day I grew out of the habit of feeding myself so that when I went home it took me at least a week to get back to feeding myself – it made my arm ache for several days and I had to get used of holding a knife, fork and spoon.

At 7pm on the first evening we went into another hall to introduce ourselves and to be introduced to everyone else, including the staff. Some people were very quiet, some were rather talkative but I think most of us were rather nervous and apprehensive about out future life in the college. After talking for a little while we were asked to be quiet, so that we could be told what we were expected to do and which class we'd be in and where to go. After this talk we were free for the rest of the evening, but we were expected to be in bed by eleven pm when the lights would be put out.

There were three other girls in my room, another Julie, Lynn who played the guitar and Beth. We had to be up by 7am and breakfast was at 8 o'clock. College classes started at 9am, but before that we were told to make our beds and tidy the room every day. Unfortunately I had to ask someone in my room to help me with buttons and fasteners. One of the girls in my room couldn't understand why I couldn't fasten my bra because she said she knew another girl with the same complaint as myself who could do her bra up. We argued about this and I proved to her that I just couldn't do it so she said no more about it – it took many years of struggling but now I can fasten my own bra. I also believe that God gave me the strength to be able to use my hands and fingers which is involved when fastening a bra. This was rather embarrassing as I was the oldest girl in the room, but I needn't have worried, they were all ready to help me and didn't mind at all. I thought a nurse or a orderly would have come in to help me but it was never mentioned.

The first thing that happened when we arrived in our classes was that we were tested to find what standard we were at in arithmetic and English. When we reached the right level, we could move on to whatever we wanted to do. I had reached the standard required but as I did very well in the intelligence test; I chose to do COPY typing. Unfortunately I was only there from September to Christmas as I became ill with fibrocytis and homesick and so I returned home again. However before that happened much fun and interest filled our lives!

I have already explained why I had to be fed by the orderlies; one was a certain male orderly. I would often be nervous and very quiet. I just didn't feel at ease with him. I got an uneasy feeling about him as if I couldn't trust him. There were only two orderlies that I really liked and trusted; their names were Bob and Jack. I think I liked Bob the best, maybe because he was younger and understanding, but mainly because I could have a good laugh and a joke with him. I also got on well with Bob's wife, who I believe was one of the cooks in the kitchen. Jack was also quite funny at times but he was not like Bob.

One of the women orderlies was rather bossy, but at heart I think she was a kindly person. Many students didn't like her and my friend and I did our best to keep out of her way and not upset her. We called her "Mrs Bossy" but of course not so that she could hear us. Janet was a lot younger than "Mrs Bossy". In fact she was rather like Bob in her ways and we all liked her very much. Mrs Marshall was a nice person too, in her own way, but sometimes she would get a bit awkward if we wouldn't do what she asked. There were several other orderlies but I didn't have much to do with them.

Although my mother had taught me to read, the College told me to send a tape-recorder so I could listen as well as read. To this day I don't know why! If confused me rather than helped me as I didn't always hear the sounds clearly. Also words often sound different to the way they are spelt. I'm sure that my reading didn't improve as well as we all hoped.

There were two boys in my class who were very kind and helpful and they looked after me. Their names were Robert and Eric. They put on and took off my earphones when I had to do my reading. I couldn't keep these earphones on my head because they were too big. Every time I looked down to read they would slide off. This would get on my nerves. They also got my books out and put them away for me. They made life in the class-room so much easier for me and I let them know that I appreciated what they did for me.

We had a bath every other day and I enjoyed this very much. But sometimes one or two of the orderlies would forget to write down in the book that they had given us a bath. This used to make my friend and I angry. One Sunday when Janet was on duty, she gave me my bath but she didn't make a note in the book. On Monday "Mrs Bossy" was on duty and she told Beth and me to get ready for a bath.

We said, "But we had our bath yesterday."

"Well, it's not in the book," she said.

So we pretended to get our towels and soap but when she was looking the other way we escaped from our dormitory into the main hall and we didn't go back until it was bedtime.

One weekend when the orderlies were too busy to write the names in the book we were given two baths in one day!!

One thing I often used to do when I was supposed to be in the classroom but was bored or cold, was to excuse myself and go to the ladies toilet where it was warm. There I could have a chat with anyone who came in and then when I felt lovely and warm I would go back to the classroom. Sometimes I would arrange a time to meet a friend for a chat in the toilet – just for fun and to get out of classroom. We would talk about the teachers' behaviour and their attitude to the students, and we would have a laugh and enjoy the warmth of the toilet room.

There was a girl named Ann with whom I often went shopping on a Saturday. We had many adventures usually to do with Ann's forgetfulness and sometimes carelessness! Occasionally she made me cross!

The first time I went shopping with her in Mansfield market she left her glasses on one of the stalls and we had to retrace our steps and remember every stall that we had visited. At last, after about fifteen minutes, we found them on a ladies' clothing stall on the side where Ann had put them. Then of course she remembered doing it. This delay meant we had to hurry with our shopping and we managed with luck to get back to college in time for lunch.

Another time she left her purse somewhere on a stall and I said, "You'll be lucky if you get your purse back with all the people shopping around here!"

Surprisingly, we did find the purse at last; it was on a sweet stall and even more surprisingly her money was still in it.

I said, "Ann you are lucky, but be more careful because next time you might be out of luck!"

Ann agreed that she was inclined to be careless!

Another time I remember we were in trouble and blamed for something that was not our fault at all. We had finished our shopping in good time and we went to catch the bus to get back to college. Unfortunately the bus was late; we waited nearly quarter-of-an-hour instead of our usual three or four minutes and this made us ten minutes late for lunch by the time we got back to the college dining room. Ann went to line up for her lunch and I went straight to my table. The nurse, who was to help me with my dinner, was already sitting waiting for me and she looked very cross and said, "Where have you been for the last quarter of an hour?"

I told her what had happened and she said, "Why didn't you catch an earlier bus back? I shall have to report you to the headmaster."

Later on we were called into the headmaster's office and we had to give a detailed account of what happened. Of course it was written down in the book of misdemeanours! I'm not sure whether they believed our story!

In our room, our beds were narrow and not really long enough; I think they were children's beds. Mine was very soft and sleeping on it gave me a backache. At home my bed was more comfortable because it fitted to my body shape. I reported that my back was aching, so they agreed to put a board under the mattress. This board wasn't quite wide enough, and sometimes when I turned over I rolled off on to the floor and the mattress came on top of me, and I woke up in a fright! Fortunately, one of the girls in the room also woke up because of the noise I made and went to get someone to come and pick me up. This happened several times until I decided it would be the lesser of two evils if I did without the board, so I took it away and put up with the back ache!

Back at home, my parents wanted to buy me a new bed because the one I had sagged in the middle. I said, "No, I love the bed I have because it keeps me warm!"

Mum said that it wasn't doing my back any good but it took a year for me to make up my mind and then I decided to give in, because my parents kept on about the bed not being suitable for me.

When I finally got my new bed it took me a very long time to get used to it because it didn't sag! It was firm and flat! I was afraid when I turned over I would fall out; this happened once or twice but I just had to pick myself up, remake the bed and get back into it again! Now of course my bed is fine and comfortable!

Whilst I was at college I had several boyfriends, and we would go out together at weekends. Robert was one of my friends – he was short, had dark hair and wore glasses. I liked him a lot, and we were invited by one of the orderlies, called Bob, to go to a club where he and his wife were members. We went along and really enjoyed ourselves; it was good fun. Now us girls had to be in by 11.00pm but the boys had no fixed time. That night we left the club at 10.00pm and we were back at the college by 11.00pm. and all went well!

The second time we went to the club we left at the same time, 10.00pm, but unfortunately we missed our bus. We got on another bus but after a short distance we suddenly realised that it wasn't going our way. We got off at the next stop and walked back to another bus stop and waited for the right bus. I was panicking and worrying, but Robert sensibly told me to stop worrying and calm down because there was nothing that we could do about it. Finally we arrived back at the college about 11.30pm. My dormitory was locked, so Robert banged on the door until one of the nurses came. The first thing she said was, "I'll report you for this!" The next morning, Sunday, Robert and I had to go to the office and explain to the officers there what had happened. They told us that it was all right but not to let it happen again otherwise we'd be stopped from going out.

The third time we went to the club there was a party going on. Bob came over to us and asked, "What time are you leaving to get back to college?"

We said, "No later then 10.00pm. We don't want to have any more trouble about being late!"

Bob said, "Don't worry, stay later and we'll get a mini-cab to take you back."

So we decided to stay on. The mini-cab was booked for 10.45pm but it didn't arrive on time so I began to worry. Bob said that he would ring them again but the car arrived just before 11.00pm. We were five minutes late getting back. The door was not locked but I knew the nurse on duty would be looking out for me. She had her back to me so I quickly ran to my room without her seeing me. Only the girl with her boyfriend who was outside the door, saw me. When I ran into our room, Julie, my room mate, told me to go behind the curtain and pretend to be washing and cleaning my teeth.

I said from behind the curtain, "Pass me my nightie so that I can be getting undressed!" Luckily I was already undressed when the nurse came in and she asked me where I had been. I said, "I've been in here of course!"

She replied that she hadn't seen me come in. I told her that I had been a few minutes late but as the door was unlocked I walked in! She answered that she would report me, but I exclaimed, "No, you won't because what were you supposed to be doing at eleven o'clock?"

"Locking the door!" she answered. I replied to that statement, "If you report me, I will report you for not having the door locked at 11.00 p.m!" We both got away with our misdemeanours!

One of my friends, Eric, who was in my class, was a kind, generous boy who liked helping people; he often helped me with my tape-recorder, hearing aid and generally helping me with any apparatus I had to use. He had a girl friend at college but often when he was not with her; he would be with me. At weekends he usually went home so we never arranged to do anything then. During the time I knew Eric and Robert at college, I had bad attacks of fibrocytis so that I rarely saw them at that time. I liked Eric very much and I kept in touch for quite a long time after I left the college.

Before I went to college I had painkillers and ointment for my fibrocytis; my doctor had prescribed them and I had taken them and used the ointment for three weeks. The painkillers were very helpful, but the ointment was not. I had been at college for about two months and the wretched fibrocytis came back but the college doctor would only give me ointment and no painkillers. It was so bad that I rang dad and asked him to ring the college and explain that I had always been given painkillers when I had fibrocytis. However, the doctor refused to give them to me and the pain got so bad at night that it made me cry. I believe that this could have been the reason that I was told I must leave the college, although the headmaster said that I should go to an ordinary college because my English and mathematics were up to standard.

Eric had to stay on at college for another three or four months so I decided to write to him because I realised that I liked him very much. We corresponded regularly for about three years, then he wrote and said that he was in love with me but I wasn't sure if this was really true, although I knew that I was very fond of him.

In 1979 he decided to come to London from where he lived in Yorkshire – but it didn't work out as we planed because his mother was taken ill and I was working for an Open University exam so we had too little time together. Afterwards I wished that we had been able to see more of each other and that circumstances had not come between us. After that, we did not have any contact except writing to each other which was not very often. I always sent him a Christmas card.

When I started at Portland College I felt very homesick, and would ring up mum and dad two or three times a week and ask them to take me home. It took me over two weeks to settle down but after this time I began to enjoy college life. I would have liked to have gone home for a weekend but dad said it wasn't worth it. Nevertheless, I was not happy with the way that some of the orderlies and nurses treated the students, but I thought that the teachers and lecturers were good. The Headmaster of the college was a very sympathetic and understanding man; he was easy to talk to and would discuss any problem that might arise.

As I was one of the older students, I received more money than younger students. I had about £18.00 a week and I would put £10 in the college bank and whenever I went shopping I bought clothes – 15 years later some of these blouses and jumpers still fit me. When I left college, I took home more than £60.00!

Before I finish with my life at college I would like to talk about some of my friends.

Lyn was one of my special friends as we were both interested in Mansfield Town Football Club and we often went together to football matches. She drove a three wheeler car because she was confined to a wheelchair. We got on very well together and we enjoyed doing the same things and we had lots of laughs! Even so, I had to be careful sometimes how I spoke, as she had rather a quick temper and often misunderstood my meaning. I enjoyed listening to her when she played her guitar, and she told me that by playing and practising on the guitar her right hand, which was very stiff and difficult to use, became more flexible. We agreed to write to each other but we forgot to give each other our addresses and, although another friend gave me Lyn's address, we didn't keep up the correspondence for long.

Alan was in my class and he was gentle and kind. He was an interesting person and I became quite friendly with him. He was learning to read and write as his poor health had prevented him from learning when he was very young. He was in his twenties when I knew him. Unfortunately, because the college doctor could not, or would not, prescribe his usual medication, he was obliged to leave college and go home. This made him very upset and he couldn't understand why the college had accepted him in the first place if the doctor wasn't prepared to prescribe his usual medicine.

Barry was another of my college friends with whom I used to sit during our lunch hour. We would discuss all kinds of subjects; books, records, television, religion, politics, conservation and happenings around the world. We often had opposite views especially on religion and politics but this made our conversations more interesting and we enjoyed each other's company. When I left college we wrote to each other for about two years but gradually this faded out and now we no longer correspond.

After I returned to London I was invited to spend a reunion weekend. I would have liked to have gone, but as it was so far away in Nottinghamshire my parents didn't think it was wise for me to go. I heard that nearly all my friends were there and they all enjoyed themselves, so I was sorry to have missed it.

If the doctor at Portland had given me the painkillers I needed, I think I would have stayed on there for the full 2 years. I also think it is very wrong that they forced me to read in their prescribed way, when I had already learned to read by the way my mum had taught me. This undid all my hard work and made me more confused.

Every Friday afternoon, we had to do a crossword on the board. I thought that this was a good exercise as we not only had to guess the words but it increased our vocabulary.

Overall, I don't think Portland Training College improved me very much, although it did get me away from home for a few months. This helped me to grow up a bit and become more independent.

*Chapter Twenty Six*

# Trinity (Part Three)

I went back to Trinity in January. At that time it was still in the church hall in Faversham Road, Catford. I had just finished work at college and I was very pleased to be back at the Trinity Centre.

There were two tutors at Trinity who took general education with the members and I joined in the arithmetic and English sessions, which I enjoyed from time to time (I liked maths more than English.) I also went swimming on a Tuesday.

Sometimes I went back to the Old Ladywell building, but it was being knocked down and a new day centre and a residential home were going to be built for physically disabled people by Lewisham Borough on the site. I can't remember when the Willowmere home was built for the elderly. We were told that when the new Ladywell Centre was ready we would all move into it from the Trinity Hall.

I found, when I returned to Trinity, that quite a number of the members I had known were no longer there and there were some new members and staff. One of the attendants, Ann, became very friendly with me and I was sorry when she had to retire because of her age.

Ann was kind and thoughtful to all the members; she was easy to get along with and understood the problems we faced. She treated each member as an individual with feelings and a mind of their own. I think this is very important when you are working with disabled people. It is very easy to think that a disabled person may be mentally slow. Ann often accompanied members to hospital or the dentist. She came with me to New Cross Hospital when I needed batteries for my hearing aid or to get it repaired. The first time I went with Ann she did not know the number of the bus or how to get to the hospital. I played a trick on her; I pretended that I did not know the way and after we did get the right bus I said that I didn't know where to get off. Ann was quite worried. I gave way, of course before we arrived at the bus stop where I knew we had to get off! Ann was relieved and laughed at my teasing and she was a good sport.

She often took me to the dentist and to hospital and I missed her in many ways when she left us. She only spent a few weeks with us when we went to the new Ladywell Centre to help us to settle in to the new surroundings.

One of the new Trinity members who was in a wheelchair, Alan Green, was very bright and quick in his thoughts. The other members said that he liked me, but I was rather wary of him and, although I liked him, he gave me a slight inferiority complex so I tended to avoid him when it did not seem rude to do so. There was a record out at the time in the 1970s which I believe had the title 'Juliet' and when it was played it always reminded me of him. Another record that was out at the time was 'Julie, Julie, do you love me?' Whenever this was played on the radio, the Welfare drivers used to take the mickey out of me! I do not know if Alan was born with a disability or if he had had an accident or maybe became disabled later in life, but he died about two years after I first met him.

A new attendant at Trinity, when I returned, was Richard. He was tall with darkish brown hair and a very attractive face and I liked him from our first meeting. I became very friendly with Richard and we began to go out together for a time.

I remember that once we went to a cinema in Bromley and we came out of the cinema at about 10.30pm. We waited a long time for a bus and when it came we found that it was only going to Catford Garage and we had a long walk, about thirty minutes in my case, to get home. Richard came all the way home with me to explain to my father why we were late, because I knew dad would be worried about me. However, he accepted Richard's explanation and was not cross.

I started going to Richard's house every Saturday, sometimes during the day, but I didn't realise at first what I was letting myself in for! At that time I was a virgin and had had no need to go on the Pill so I had not even thought of doing so! The first time we had sexual intercourse I did not like it. I was rather frightened and a bit panicky but Richard took precautions. Gradually I enjoyed the love making as I got more used to it.

Richard left Trinity to work in Tower View, which was the new residential home for the disabled at Ladywell. He lived in his own flat there for the time that he worked there and I used to go and visit him regularly and we often made love. This went on for quite a number of months but gradually I felt he was using me and we were drifting away from each other. I felt that we were not really meant for each other so I decided to end our relationship. He gave me a lovely big card one year saying that he owed me more than what he could give me. Eventually Richard became a fireman and married and moved to the North of England.

Once during our relationship I thought I had become pregnant (although my periods were never regular) and it was about four months before my periods returned. Richard thought I should have an abortion but I was very scared. As soon as my periods started again, and I knew it was all right, I went on the pill.

Being in my twenties I supposed I wouldn't have much right to say whether I wanted the child or not because I probably wouldn't be able to look after it. I believe that the professionals would have made the decision for me. Later in life, I would never have agreed to have an abortion. As we come from God, I feel that it is killing a human being. I also believe that God plans and controls our lives and allows things to happen to us to teach us something. Sometimes, things happen that make us feel thankful that we are not in someone else's situation. My father said that if I ever became pregnant, he would shut me out the house. I honestly don't know whether he was being serious or not.

As a disabled person I think I was fortunate to have had that sexual experience. I have met several people who think physically disabled people shouldn't and can't experience sex. I think this is rubbish because disabled or not we all have feelings.

There are times when I wish I never had sexual experiences as I feel it can spoil the relationship if I get married because I know what is involved and therefore I feel it is not something new between me and my husband as it should be.

My menstruation periods were a nuisance because I didn't know how to manage. The doctor told my parents not to worry about it - but I did! After many years of trying different pads to find the most suitable one for me to cope with, finally I found one that I could manage on my own without anyone coming to the ladies' with me.

When I first started periods I was very lucky because I had no pain. I could never say when I was going to start a period and it lasted three or four days. When I first started, mum had to help me to put the bikini knickers on and then get the pad and change it as it was fastened by press studs. Mum had to come to the toilet with me to undo the pad; then she would go out of the bathroom to let me go to the toilet. I would call her back to make me comfortable. As time went by we were fed up with doing this, so we decided to do it another way and this worked out quite well.

There was no way I could do it all by myself and it was always rather embarrassing. About five years later, press-on towels came on the market. These were just the thing for me, and meant that I didn't have to have any help when my periods started. At first I didn't like these press-on towels because they wouldn't stay where I put them, but as time went by they got better and I got used to them and now I don't know where I would be without them.

It was very difficult when I had to ask someone to help me to change my pad at work. I would never ask the attendant at Trinity or at Bromley and yet at Bromley at that time we only had one attendant and the manager. I certainly wouldn't ask the attendant to help me when I needed help, because I had a funny feeling about her, and yet I liked her and we used to get on quite well together. When I was at Trinity more or less the same thing happened, but there was one attendant who I would ask to help me and that was Ann. There was a tea lady who I would ask from time to time but apart from these two I don't think I asked any other attendant. My friend Helen would always help me if she was at Trinity on my difficult days. I think the reason I asked Ann or Peggy was that they were both married with children and I could have a good laugh with them; I think this made all the difference.

Many years later when Ladywell Centre was sorting out old records, Maurice gave me my old letter from Trinity. I was shocked to see a letter dated 1974 from a hospital Consultant. The Consultant wrote that he had been told that I had a rather low IQ. He went on to say that he did not agree with this, and thought me quite a bright girl. Since then, I have wondered who thought I had a "rather low IQ" – Trinity or Charlton Park? If it came from Trinity, I think it means that they did not know me or didn't encourage me enough to see my full potential. If the remark came from Charlton Park, it also would indicate that they didn't know me very well, or spend enough time with me to find out what I was capable of.

Wherever this information came from, I feel it showed that staff did not know me as well as I thought they did, and it raised questions as to how good they were at their job (see my chapter on Education, which disproves their low judgement of my ability). When I read this comment, I felt that it was like a 'slap in the face', and also proved that they did not support me as much as they should have.

While I was at Trinity, mum came to visit me at the centre so that she could have a go on an electric wheelchair. She loved every minute of it, except when she banged into tables and chairs! A couple of years later, Social Services did give her an electric wheelchair. However, this was not one which you could use outside; in fact it was harder to use inside over carpet. A couple of years later, she sent it back.

## *Chapter Twenty Seven*
# New Ladywell Centre

The new Ladywell Centre was purpose-built for people of all ages. From school-leaving age, anyone who had a disability of any kind could attend any week day until such time as they were too old to travel in the day-centre coach.

In April 1977 the Trinity group, about twenty people, was transferred from Faversham Road to Ladywell and we were given a large pleasant room for our own use. It was suggested by Ray, the Trinity assistant manager, that perhaps we would not have the use of it for very long, as when the number of members increased we would have to join in with them in their activities and our room would be needed for craftwork. In fact, after about two years we were moved into a smaller room. Ray and I were able to get on together very well; we seemed to understand each other. He had had some traumatic experiences in the R.A.F. during the war, which I think made him able to empathise with and help the young disabled members.

When we were asked before we left Faversham Road what activities we would like to take up, I said that I was interested in art and cookery. In the end I did art but I still used to go in and out of the Trinity room as we called it, if I was bored with the activities. I suppose I missed the companionship of people like Helen, Mick and Brian whom I had known for a long time as we were not free to go in and out of classes just to say hello to somebody. It seemed to me that there were more disadvantages than advantages in moving Trinity group to Ladywell. Trinity was close to buses, shops and the library. The small building meant it was easier for members with walking difficulties to get about, and the group gave us a great feeling of companionship and belonging. It also meant you could get individual tutoring if needed. While Ladywell offered more activities, it was a long walk from the buses and shops. The big building meant those who had difficulty in walking had to rely on wheelchairs more often to get about, and the number of members going there meant you lost the closeness of a small centre and one-to-one tutoring was unlikely.

Gradually I found the activities I was doing were not satisfying me; they seemed to be more like school and I began to stop going to them now and again. I never started the cookery class because I don't think it started until one or two years later. However, I did keep the appointments with the speech therapist and I worked hard to improve my speech. The speech therapist's name was Jean; she was sympathetic and understanding and she taught me a great deal. I got on with her very well. She was married and had two or three children and I think this helped me to talk and discuss my problems with her. She got me to sit in front of a mirror and practise speaking while trying to control facial spasms caused by my disability. I used to hate mirror work because every time I pulled a face (or as I call them, my facial spasms) I got all tensed up. As I realised how often I did it, it made me more tense and self conscious, which did not help. Visual work *was* also used during head and shoulder relaxation to help inhibit my jerks and to cut down tension.

Articulation practice was something I didn't mind doing as I felt I was learning to pronounce words properly. I had difficulty pronouncing certain sounds. For example "dog" came out as "go" or "church" as "schurch". I had trouble with four letter words and certain letter blends – words starting with 'd' and 'g' were a problem. I also had problems with one or two other blends which made a sound I could not make; for example "spoon" would come out as "poon" or "skirt" would come out as "kirt". "Ladder" would come out as "lagger". As I don't have any problems with saying daddy or dad, Jean would get me to say dad, dad, dad, dad, dog. Most times this worked quite well.

Sometimes Jean would test me on my hearing and I had to tell her whether she was saying a word correctly. I could do this very well by lip-reading, but when she told me to look the other way, nine out of ten times I would be guessing because I couldn't hear properly. I nearly always forget to put "a" on the end of the words. Many of my speech problems have not been helped by bad habits such as speaking too quickly or excitedly, which resulted in words coming out back to front. I did not concentrate enough on my articulation when speaking. This meant it was difficult for people to understand me at times. Jean made me think about my faults and I had to think more about what I was going to say. Jean would get me to read out aloud to give me confidence and to get me to improve my articulation. Sometimes I would hate this exercise because when I came to a word that I knew I was going to have difficulty with I would get embarrassed and go silly; other times I tried to jump the word to avoid having to say it. Nine out of ten times, Jean would know and she would get me to say it whether I liked it or not! Mind you, I was glad in the long run.

Another exercise I really did hate doing was reading to the tape recorder. We used to play it back to find out what I sounded like. Sometimes I would feel ashamed to hear myself speak that way. This was good because it certainly made me want to improve my articulation.

Jean and I did some cultural education together as I am very interested in Victorian and Tudor times. We visited some art galleries in London and then I did a project on Queen Victoria. I found a good deal of information with the 'Jackdaw' history pack which we used to buy.

Sometimes, when the weather was fine and warm, we would go for walks in the park. I also visited Jean at her house and I got on very well with her family. Jean was a great help when I joined the Open University. After a few years Jean left the centre, but I knew that I could always get in touch with her at any time to have a chat.

Carole came to the centre in January 1980 to be the hairdresser and she shampooed and cut my hair for me. If I think I am going to get on well with a person, I try to make opportunities to be in their company and talk with them. I felt like this about Carole and so I popped into the salon to have a chat with her. In this way we got to know each other very well and we became good friends. I would often, at that time, go along the road to get a sandwich for my lunch and one day I asked Carole if she would like me to get her a sandwich and she said yes, so this became a regular habit. One day, however, I did get upset when another person bought the sandwich for Carole. Sometimes, this happened as I was late and Carole thought that I wasn't coming in that day. From time to time I would get upset over Carole because I would take something she said the wrong way. Then after a while we would talk about it and everything would be all right again.

During 1983 Carole and I adopted each other like sisters. As she has a brother she told me that she always wanted a sister. I also played a lot of jokes on her especially with water. Sometimes when the other staff or members used play a joke on Carole, I would get the blame until I could convince Carole that I had nothing to do with it. My laughing didn't help either! When Carole went on holidays, I would get upset as I didn't know what to do with myself.

As time went by Carole began to encourage the members to take pride in their hair and so I became more involved with Carole as I often helped to shampoo the hair of members and staff and take their curlers out. I can remember washing my mum's hair and at first, I was very nervous and the water went all down her neck.

When Carole asked me to put a roller in mum's hair, this was even worse as I just couldn't get my two hands to work together but I managed to get one roller done which took me about half an hour. Carole and mum were pleased and they could see that I didn't give up easily. I certainly made it clear that I wasn't going to put rollers in people's hair very often. Each time I washed somebody's hair I got better and better. Sometimes while watching or washing their hair, I would play a joke on them. I would either make them wet by putting the shower over their face or put shampoo in their face. I used to get a lot of fun out of this.

Eventually, Carole and her husband moved to Cliffe in Kent and in June 1984 she left the Centre on maternity leave to have her first child. She had a girl called Karen who was born in July. I was invited to Karen's Christening on October 7th 1984 and I agreed that I would travel to Carole's place by bus. I told Carole that it would take anything up to two hours. Anyway, on Sunday dad gave me a lift to Lewisham Bus Station and I caught a Greenline bus to Chatham. Then, when I went to get the next bus, I found they did not run on Sundays! So the only thing I could do was to find a way to contact Carole. I had Carole's address and phone number on a piece of paper. I gave it to the inspector and asked him which was the best way? He took the paper and went into his office. When he came back he said, "Come and sit here and Carole will come and collect you within fifteen minutes." He was very helpful. When I saw Carole we both laughed as she didn't know about the buses!

Carole came back to the Centre at Easter in 1985, and we carried on as before. She left the Centre in 1986 because she was missing the baby growing up. I have visited Carole and the family from time to time. One occasion which I shall never forget was when I had made up my mind to go a different way and that was by train. I told Carole and she asked me to ring her when I arrived at the station.

What Carole didn't tell me was that I only had to dial the last six numbers and not the code number. Anyway, I arrived at Strood Station (it might have been Higham Station). I walked to the pub as Carole said there was a phone box there. When I phoned her, this woman answered, saying that I had the wrong number. I thought – funny, maybe I misdialed, so I rang again and the same woman said, "I have already told you that you have the wrong number!"

I just couldn't understand what I was doing wrong. I gave it one more try and of course the same lady answered. This time she was really cross with me. I just let it go in one ear and out the other. So I thought, " Oh! dear, what do I do?" I asked a woman who was just coming out from the pub and she went back into the pub to find out for me. I even went into the Post Office and they were not much help. I went back to the telephone box and looked at the board and there it was, all I had to do was to dial the last six numbers and after all this I finally got through! Carole was very worried and wondered what on earth I had been up to. She been waiting ages for me to ring. When I told her we both laughed and she said, "Oh dear, I forgot about the phone number." It was a baking hot day and all I wanted was a lovely long cold drink!

Another time I remember travelling down to Carole's place and this time I went to Chatham bus Station. Carole said she would come and collect me. I was waiting and waiting on the Station. In the meantime she had rung the Station and asked them to look out for me and tell me that her car had broken down and that her friend, Jane, would be coming for me. Well, that inspector didn't say a word and all I could do was to wait and see what happened. Eventually, I saw Jane walking towards me and I believe that one of Jane's children or Carole's daughters had Chicken Pox or something like that. I spent a week with Carole and had a good time.

Back at the Centre, I helped Carole a lot in the salon which I enjoyed very much. When Ursula came to take over I sort of lost interest and wanted to be more involved in counselling, in order to be able to help the members and staff in the centre, and to get some practice and more experience.

After Carole and I became friends I got to know Carole's mum and dad and her Auntie and Uncle. One year Carole invited her mum to the Centre's Summer Social. Dolly (Carole's mum) came over and sat at our table for a while as she already knew Helen and me. I introduced her to my mum and we all got on very well together. From time to time I used to phone her and sometimes she would write to me.

Dolly became seriously ill during 1986; her husband had died about 2 years before. She died Christmas Day of the same year. I went to her funeral and shall always remember her as a warm and friendly person.

James, another member of staff, started in 1979 as an attendant in the print room. I always used to be in that room because I liked the instructor, Maurice. Maurice and I played lot of jokes on each other. This gave me a good opportunity to get to know James and we got on very well together. I helped James by talking about disabilities and his job. After a couple of years, James took over the Trinity Group (Special Unit) and I think he could have made a good job of it. He had all the right ideas but unfortunately it didn't work out.

When James was living in Peckham, I used to visit him on Sunday afternoons to have a laugh and a chat for a couple of hours. I became very fond of him and I was very upset and hurt, when he told me that he was a homosexual, because I was hoping to start a closer relationship with him. He told me a lot about homosexuality and how it affected him and I said that I would always be a friend to him and stand by him. The information he gave me was to be of great use in my counselling.

I tried to introduce Christ to him but I could not convince him. I do try to remember him in my prayer times.

In late 1983 James became ill with back trouble and was out sick for a very long time. In the meantime he had openly become a homosexual and got "married" to his boyfriend, which I believe didn't help him. He was eventually medically retired by the council in 1984. I believe it was 1986 that they moved to Cornwall to live. I wrote to him a couple of times and sent him Christmas and Birthday Cards by giving them to Jenny, a member of staff who visited him now and then. Jenny left the Centre in 1987 and moved to Brighton near Ursula. I wrote another letter to James and gave it to Ursula to give to Jenny for her to post it on to James! In 1989 Ursula left the Centre which meant that I wouldn't hear from James again. In 1992 a friend of mine told me that James and his partner had split up.

Another member of staff who was a lot of help to me was Maurice, who started in 1978. He influenced my Christian life and helped me to understand Christianity more clearly.

Maurice worked in the Print room and most of the time I would be in there just to wind him up and play jokes on him. When he wasn't looking I would put some ink on my finger and then put it on Maurice's face. Sometimes if I was quick enough, Maurice wouldn't know I did it, then I would say, "Maurice, what have you got on your face?" Often he would laugh and get his own back on me when I wasn't expecting it. Now and again he would get cross with me. When he had papers laid out in order on the table ready for the next part of the job, I would take the first few sheets muddle them up and then put them back. When Maurice went to finish that job, he would suddenly realise that they had been altered. It didn't take him long to work out that it was me! In the print room there was a big black bin and sometimes Maurice would put me in it and leave me there! I didn't mind this when I was near the wall as I knew I could put my hand on that wall to balance myself. But when it was in the middle of the room I just had to stand still and not move at all as I felt very afraid that I might fall over!

Sometimes Maurice would hide my drink out of my way and there was no way I could reach it so I used to get round anybody who was tall and had long arms. Very often I would do this behind his back then say to him, "Ha! Ha! Ha!" Quite often I shut Maurice in the dark room and I believe that I did lock him in one day.

Another time, which I found funny, I will never forget. In the dark room there was a cupboard with a space from the cupboard to the ceiling. There were boxes and papers up there. One day, Maurice said to me, "If I lifted you on my shoulders, do you think you could get down a box?" I said that I thought I could, so Maurice lifted me up and, although it was very difficult for me to keep my balance, I eventually managed to reach a box. I went to get hold of it and pull it down. The next thing we knew the whole lot came down with a crash. After Maurice put me down we just looked at each other and laughed! People outside were wondering what on earth we were up to! It was a good job that I was wearing my trousers that day!

In 1982 Maurice was promoted to Liaison Officer at the Centre. I was upset because I couldn't talk to him so easily as he now worked in the main office. In 1984 Maurice left the centre to go on a two year course for the C.S.S. which was run by Bromley College. I knew that when he came back, things would never be the same because he would be more involved in management and would not have time for me.

In 1986 he returned to the centre and was promoted to Assistant Manager responsible for rehabilitation. At first I felt he was different in his attitude and behaviour, but after about 9 months he was the same old Maurice. The trouble was that I couldn't play half as many jokes on him as I did when he used to be printing instructor! In 1988 Maurice became my Key worker. I was very pleased about this but I felt that I couldn't tell him everything I had on my mind when I was worried about something.

George was the caretaker at the Centre and he was a bit like Maurice as I did get a lot of fun out of him. Again, we played jokes on each other. One of the jokes was that I would pretend that somebody wanted him. When George found the person and asked him, they would say, "No, I didn't tell Julia to get you."

Sometimes he could hear me laughing in the background and he made sure that he got his own back on me. He made me all wet a couple of times by throwing a cup of water over me or squirting me with water from the garden hose. Nine out of ten times, I would get the worst of it.

One year in the winter, George offered to give me a lift to Brownhill Road Boys' School to save me walking through the park in the dark. I was very happy with this idea, but I had to hide from 4 o'clock till 4.45pm., which was when George finished work.

After I left the centre in the afternoon, I would sometimes go and visit someone in Tower View – a residential home for young people with disabilities, but most of the time I would sit in George's car. This went on for about two months. Then George got told off by the deputy manager. Then we both got told off. At first, we didn't take much notice but in the end George had to stop giving me a lift. I thought he would have got away with it as he was looking after my welfare. The centre said I wasn't insured after 4pm. Eventually I got to know his wife as George would bring her to our parties from time to time. When George retired I went to visit him where he lived in Dartford, and we phoned each other up now and then.

Esther, who was an attendant at the Centre, became very friendly towards me. She helped me in many ways. Once on New Year's Day she came with me to the dentist and her husband came to pick us up afterwards and took us back to their house. Esther was so kind to me, and I thought because she was a big comfortable looking lady, she was like a granny so I began to call her "Granny". She didn't mind at all; in fact I think she rather liked it. Later on, I learned that Esther's husband worked for Lewisham Social Services as a Welfare driver. He was very kind so I began to call him Granddad! I also played jokes and tricks on him. Unfortunately, Esther became ill and had to give up her work and so I only saw her from time to time.

Several years before we moved to the new Ladywell Centre, I had a very helpful Social Worker with whom I was very friendly. One day. I suggested to mum that she might join the Ladywell members, but mum said, "No, I don't want to go there." However, my Social Worker, Josephine, came and talked to her and suggested that she went to have a look around. She was so persuasive that mum agreed to go and look. What she saw she liked and so she said she would like to join the Handicraft group.

Later in 1987, mum joined the doll-making class and she enjoyed making porcelain dolls very much indeed. She used to go twice a week on Tuesday and Friday (and she also went in to have her hair and feet done). She did some beautiful work and won prizes for her patchwork quilts. She also won many other prizes for her handicraft work. She won first place for needlework and embroidery and also two second prizes: one for needlework and the other for needlework and embroidery. She also won a third prize for patchwork and handicraft. All these prizes she won with the Lewisham Age Concern group. She made me a beautiful, large teddy bear about 2ft 2" tall because one day I said I had never had a big teddy bear and I had always wanted one when I was small.

In 1988 the local Multiple Sclerosis Club in Lewisham had its own competition and mum decided to enter her pineapple patchwork cushion and it won the overall prize!

For the first five years of the new Ladywell Centre, the staff put on a pantomime at Christmas time. It was always very good and very funny and nearly all the managerial staff were in it. They worked there for several weeks before Christmas and the pantomime was really worth watching. The staff performed in the pantomime over two days so that we could all see it. We watched it after our Christmas dinner.

Over the years a drama group had been formed, run by the tutor and the members, and the pantomime became their responsibility. Although it was quite well done it was unavoidably slow and sometimes the audience were not able to follow the words that were spoken. One year I was the princess in Aladdin and although I enjoyed doing the part I found it was not as exciting as I had hoped.

During the 1970s, the Ladywell Centre invited Princess Anne to come and visit us to talk to some of the members and have tea with us. What a palarva that was! All the staff had to learn how to greet her and the whole centre was repainted and decorated. She did accept our invitation and in the end it turned out to be a really good occasion. She appeared to be very interested in what went on at the Day Centre and spoke with some of the members.

Once, we had a strike at the Centre which disrupted everything. Quite a number of members could not get in so that only about two dozen people managed to get there, either by public transport or private car. In spite of the upset, I quite enjoyed the time of the strike because the manager and his deputy cooked the lunch and the members cleared up, made morning coffee and afternoon tea and generally carried on as normally as possible.

Kieran was a member of staff who worked at the centre for about two years. (1988-90). He was Irish, good looking and very much a gentleman. He was a proper man. At first I didn't take much notice of him but as we started talking I grew to like him. We often had a good chat and a laugh. Then one weekend he asked me if I would look after his gold fish for the weekend while he was away. I said that I would. At the time, I was living at Bargery Road. He brought the fish round and stayed for coffee. After about six months, Kieran gave me the gold fish who was called Fred, as it was going backwards and forwards from his place to my place. The only problem I had was that I couldn't clean the bowl out, so Maureen or Sylvia (the home helps) did this for me.

One day I had to do it myself and I thought I'd lost him but I hadn't. He was in the sink and I had a terrible job picking him up. I finally did it by putting the plug in the sink and turning the water on to fill the sink up. I caught the fish in a cup and put him back in the bowl. To clean the water in the fish bowl, I placed the bowl in the sink, with Fred in it, and ran the water into the bowl until it ran clear – making sure Fred didn't get washed over the top. Fred came with me to Verdant Lane but died about a year later. Kieran came for a meal a couple of times and he cooked me a meal. He went to the pictures with me and we saw 'One Flew Over The Cuckoo's Nest'.

As Kieran was becoming more friendly there were two attendants at the centre who became very nosey about our friendship, but I ignored them. They wanted to know what I had that they didn't have, because they fancied him! I told them that I didn't know. Roland thought they were envious because one of them definitely fancied Kieran.

The centre summer outing to Brighton that year was good fun because Val agreed that Kieran could push my mum. It was fantastic, we had a lot of fun; both of us got wet paddling in the sea and splashing about. He was excellent with mum as we went round these little shops. Mum wanted to go in the handicraft shop but was convinced that we wouldn't get the wheelchair in but Kieran moved all the baskets around the doorway and pushed mum in. Mum was surprised but Kieran was like that – he would have a good try before saying it could not be done.

Kieran went back to Ireland to look after his mum. We had become good friends and he had a girl friend in Ireland who he is now married to. As his sister was working and living in London, Kieran asked me if I would meet his sister. So we fixed a date and we met in the David Copperfield pub in Catford and we got on very well together. She gave me a lovely book about Ireland. We were supposed to meet up again but never got round to it.

Kieran invited me to Ireland to stay for a long weekend. Really and truly, I should have found out whether I was in a hotel or with his family. Otherwise I would have taken more money with me than I did, but everything went OK. Roland came with me to book the flight with Aer Lingus and explained to the travel agent that I was partially deaf and disabled. Everything was booked and all I had to do was to write to Kieran, saying what time I would be arriving and make sure he was going to collect me.

At Heathrow the Aer Lingus stewardess who met me was excellent. She didn't ask Roland the questions, she looked at me and gave me the time to answer her questions. There couldn't be anybody better than she.

I had no problem at the airport as they really did take good care of me. I had a meal on the plane which was a bit difficult but I managed with a little help from the person who sat next to me. At Cork airport, the staff took good care of me and stayed with me until Kieran came to meet me. He took me to a guest house and I was very concerned about the money side but I needn't have worried because it worked out very well in the end. I think I stayed in the guest house for two nights, then spent a night with his Godmother and then one night with his mother.

The first evening we went to a pub and had a drink and later we went to have a meal. Paula, his wife, came with us. As time went by I found myself becoming more uncomfortable with Paula because she admitted she found it hard at first to get on with people who had a disability. Later it became clear that Paula did not appreciate that I only needed help with certain things, that I would ask for help if it was needed and the rest of the time I could cope. It was very sad because I got on so well with Kieran but knew I couldn't change the way Paula thought about disablement.

Kieran and Paula took me to some lovely places. The evening I stayed at his Godmother's house the most was embarrassing because Kieran and Paula promised to collect me at about six and but didn't turn up until eight. His Godmother kept on at me to tell him off which upset me because she was right in one way but on the other hand I was his guest. When Kieran came she had a real go at him and Paula – who she especially blamed for the delay. Apart from this I had a lovely time in Ireland. I said good-bye to the people I met and Kieran saw me to the airport and brought me a friendship ring. I vowed that if I ever went back to Ireland to see Kieran and Paula, I would make sure I booked myself into a hotel!

About two and a half years later the friendship ring started hurting me and Maurice came to the hospital with me to have the ring cut off. He took me but said he wouldn't come in. In the end he did, and you know what it's like when you are kept waiting, you need company. The ring had to be cut off because my skin was growing over it. Maurice was surprised to see how quickly I was treated.

One or two of my friends that I really got on with were Vince and Bob. Vince was very good looking and had M.S., I think. He was married and so I did not want to get too close to him, but we always had a good laugh.

Bob, on the other hand, was different. He used to go to the M.S. club for a while, when he lived in Tower View (a home next door to Ladywell Day Centre) which is not there any more. I used to spend quite a lot of time with him and we would go to the pub at the end of the road.

One thing I didn't like about Bob was that he had a beard. After we had been to the pub, he always wanted me to kiss him. I used to say, "No way! Not with your wet beard."

Unfortunately, he had progressive M.S. and he passed away a few years later.

## *Chapter Twenty Eight*
# Pauline's Marriage

This chapter is about Pauline and her husband, Paul. I have decided not to write anything personal about Paul, but instead to concentrate on my relationship with him when he became my brother-in-law; my feelings, my ups and downs and how I coped with Paul and my sister.

The first time I met Paul I didn't know what to think, as he was quite shy but friendly. He was tall, good looking and well built. Paul didn't talk very much. I felt quite wary of him as he could made me feel inferior and small. I had an awful feeling that he was very pushy and I felt that I would have to face some difficult times with him. I really didn't like him and I hoped that Paul wasn't the one Pauline wanted to marry. Yet I knew there was nothing I could do as it was Pauline's life not mine!

However, over a period of time I began to learn that Paul had a lot of patience. One day I was doing a bit of maths. There was a question that I didn't understand. Paul was interested and wanted to help me by showing me how to work it out. He patiently kept on showing me until I was confident to do it by myself. This made me feel more at ease with him, though I still thought twice before asking him to help me with anything. I still felt uncomfortable in one way or another.

I believe it was in 1979 when Paul and Pauline decided to get married. At first they were going to get married in a registry office. I didn't really like this idea. Pauline asked me if I would go with her to make some enquiries. Pauline and I went to the registry office in Lewisham High Street. Pauline went in to enquire while I sat in the waiting room. She was only in there for five minutes and then she came back. As she came out from the office to meet me, the lady who was sitting next to me asked,

"Is that your mum?"

I replied, "No, that's my sister!"

Pauline didn't look too happy about being taken as my mum so we didn't say very much.

I said to her, "It won't last ten minutes if you get married in here."

Pauline agreed and we went to off do our normal shopping.

Paul and Pauline decided to have a white wedding at St. Andrew's Church in Torridon Road, Catford on April Ist, 1979, with top hats, car and everything else. I was 26 years old at the time, and went with Pauline to help her choose her wedding dress.

I never realised how difficult it was going to be! We went from one shop to another. Some shop assistants were pushy and I remember one shop we visited where they just wouldn't leave you alone to have a look. In the end, Pauline and I only escaped by saying we needed to go to the loo. Finally, after three hours of looking, we managed to find a shop where the staff were very helpful and left you alone to decide. This was lovely. Pauline picked a beautiful cream silk wedding dress with pink, white and blue ribbons which hanged from below the bust. I thought it was the best I had ever seen. This was the one.

At last the big day arrived! I was upset I wasn't a bridesmaid but I never mentioned my disappointment. She had a page boy and a bridesmaid. We invited the hairdresser from The Ladywell Centre, Roger, to come and do mum's, Pauline's and my hair. He made a good job of it.

Pauline was a bit concerned about the veil because it took quite some time to get it right. I was wearing a black pinafore dress, grey blouse, black shoes and a jacket. Pauline didn't forget about wearing something old, something new, something borrowed and something blue. They even had one of those great multi-coloured umbrellas. Dad looked really smart in his top hat and tails! Everything went smoothly and we had a good time. Mum was able to stand on elbow crutches, with help, to have the photos taken.

Before they got married, Paul and Pauline were living in Colchester. After their marriage, they bought a house in Wembley. It needed a lot of work doing to it, so they had to live with us! I really hated this as I felt left out and unhappy because their conversation was sometimes above my level and because of my partial deafness, this meant I could not always follow the conversation. They moved in to my sister's bedroom (which was bigger than mine and which I had moved in to). This meant that I had to move back into my old, little, bedroom.

The only time they had to work on their new house was the weekends. Most weekends, dad would go with them to help them as he was a good handyman. This is where a lot of changes took place.

On Saturdays and Sundays, we used to have our dinner at one o'clock. However, because of Paul land Pauline being out during the daytime, we had to have dinner during the evening. Sometimes it was gone 9pm and other times about 7pm. Mum and I used to get fed up and cross. We just had to put up with it as we knew it had to be done. When we were all in the house at meal times, or during the evenings watching the television, this was the time when I got very nervous because I never knew what Paul or Pauline were going to say or talk about. Eight out of ten times, Paul would correct my speech and my wording. I knew he meant well but I had been all through this at school and at the centres. I knew all about my problems with my speech and I also knew how to cope and overcome them but I had to do it in my own time. People keeping on to me about it just made my speech worse as it put me under pressure. He even did this to mum as well!

Another favourite topic of Paul and Pauline was my independence. They felt that I should be more independent and do more for myself. I felt that they underestimated the problems I would face. I told them it needed a lot of working out. For example, in the kitchen everything would have to be at the right level for me to be to handle things and I would have to work out a safe way to cook as I found it difficult to pick things up. All I could say was that when I was confident that I would be able to cope with the problems of living on my own, I would do something about it. These discussions hurt and angered me because, though I would have loved to have been independent, I felt I was not yet ready to cope with the problems this would entail.

I can remember one occasion when Paul really did upset me over something. I just burst into tears and stormed upstairs to my room and banged the door. I was still crying when Paul came up to apologise, but I don't forgive that easily. I really didn't realise how upset Paul was until mum told me. As time went by I slowly forgave him and he never upset me again so much, as he became more tactful in the way he talked to me.

Another thing I hated was when I had to do the washing up. This was very difficult for me as I didn't have the elbow power to get the grease off the plates and saucepans etc. Most of them had to be washed again by Pauline. Sometimes, I would be so upset about it that mum or dad would come and do it for me without telling Pauline – as she would tell me off.

Now I'm living on my own I have found a way round it. Whenever, I'm cooking something greasy, chicken for example, I will serve it up and then, while I'm waiting for it to cool down, I'd go and wash the greasy things immediately. The grease comes off quite easily. Then after I had have finished eating my dinner, I wash my plate and cutlery.

Occasionally, Paul would try to get me to light the gas cooker with a match but I absolutely refused because I knew I couldn't do it. My cerebral palsy means that I have to concentrate when I use my hands. It is difficult for me to use both hands together, although this depends on what I'm doing. If, for example, I am cooking then I can hold the bowl in my right arm and stir with my left hand. However, I can't hold a piece of paper still on the table with one hand and write with the other, because the concentration required to write means that I cannot control the hand holding the paper. I didn't have to worry too much about lighting the cooker because dad brought a battery lighter for the cooker and after lot of practice I could use it very well.

Pauline and Paul brought four Siamese kittens with them when they came to live with us. The mother of the kittens had to be put down because she became very fierce and violent. The kittens were fed by Pauline and Paul who took turns to feed them using a baby's bottle. They were pretty and cuddly creatures but they had the habit of eating any wool they found so everything had to be safely put away out of their reach! One night dad forgot and left his cardigan on the back of the chair. In the morning when we came down there was a great big hole in the back of the cardigan where they had chewed it. I think Pauline had to buy a new one! Pauline brought mum a very nice cardigan and would you believe it? It was left out accidentally and the cats chewed the cuffs! All mum could do was to make the sleeves shorter! At Christmas I bought dad and my boyfriend at that time a jumper each. My mum wrapped them up for me and I put them in a plastic carrier bag, along with other presents I had bought, and left them in the front room near the Christmas tree. On Christmas morning I gave out my presents. When I gave my boyfriend his present he found several holes in it. When we looked at the wrapping, it appeared the kittens had got at the jumper through gaps in the wrapping! Yet my dad's present, which had been on top, was totally untouched! It was quite a time before I could replace my boyfriend's jumper.

Another time, I left one of my jackets on the banister and forgot about it. Some days later I wanted to wear it but when I found it and put it on there was a big hole in the left sleeve. I was angry and felt Pauline should get it repaired as it was her cats that did it. But mum and Pauline claimed it was my fault for leaving it where the cats could get at it. After a long time we compromised with Pauline paying half the cost of repairing it. The repair was very expensive. Honestly, cats can be such a nuisance! About a year later Pauline decided to sell two of the kittens – I think because of the expense of looking after the four of them. She kept two of them – Simon and Camelia. They both lived to a good old age.

Paul kept on at me about buying a computer, saying that I could benefit from using one. After a few months, I said to my dad,

"Come on, let's go and buy a computer." In the end we did and it was called a Spectrum. I was very happy with it. All the commands were already programmed in and all you had to do was to press a key.

When Paul saw the computer, he said "That's not a real computer, that's a game computer!" We kept this one for a few years and then dad and I went out and bought another one – an Amstrad 286. Now, I could see what Paul was getting at.

About 5 years later, Paul suggested that I buy a new computer again. He suggested that I write to his manager at Dixons, where he worked at the time, telling him how much I needed a computer. I paid half the price. It was an Amstrad 9512.

I sold my computer, and got my money back. So you could say I didn't pay a penny!

During 1980, I asked Paul about upgrading my computer. He said he would buy all the items for me, and I gave him the money. He brought it round and set it all up for me. I really did love that computer. I had this computer until I moved house in 2001.

Eventually, Paul and Pauline moved into their new house. I was relieved to get back to normal. Life at home went back to our old routine and I got the big bedroom back again.

## Chapter Twenty Nine
# Becoming Independent

When I was about fifteen I can remember when mum or dad took me to Lewisham Hospital for my usual check up. I can remember Dr. Gann telling mum that she had taught me everything and it was up to me whether I wanted to do things myself or for mum to do everything for me. At the time it didn't really bother me whether I did things myself, as I was quite happy the way things were. It wasn't until I did the course on 'The Handicapped Person in the Community' that I realised that Pauline was right when she used to say "do it yourself."

To start with I was very keen on the idea of being independent, but it was very hard work. Pauline was all in favour of it. Mum was all for it too, but because I was slow at doing certain things she would automatically take over and I would just let her do it instead of saying, "No, let me do it!"

All she was thinking about was the time! Sometimes Pauline would have a go at mum for giving in to me.

Pauline also used to say, "What is going to happen when Julia gets older?"

I don't think mum or dad could answer this question. I couldn't answer that question at the time as I wasn't clear of the answer myself. It was all up to me to make my mind up what I was going to do when I got older but it wasn't until I was 28 that I made up my mind what I wanted to do with myself, but it had to be in my own time.

Sometimes Pauline used to get me very annoyed, especially when I could do something one day and I couldn't do it the next day. She would say, "If you could do it yesterday then why can't you do it today?"

I replied, "I don't know why!" All I knew was that I had good days and bad days.

Sometimes we used to argue over this. I felt that it was not my fault if I couldn't do something – it's just the way it goes. When we argued about other things mum would say, "For God's stake stop arguing you two. You are getting on my nerves!"

We either stopped or we carried on until one of us gave in!

The next part is very important. My parents took the view that they wanted me to become gradually more independent and help out more around the house. I don't think my parents realised what impact their views had on me, but Paul and Pauline did. My main worry at the time was about how to do things around the kitchen. I would need a lot of gadgets and aids to help me in the kitchen, and we did not have the space for these things.

One of my dreams was to spend a whole year with Paul and Pauline to kick-start my independence. However, deep down inside me I knew I wouldn't do this as I was still quite apprehensive of my sister and my brother-in-law because of the way they made me feel.

If this had happened, I believed I would have been able to cope with cooking and everything to do with the kitchen as Pauline would have pushed me to do things for myself.

I knew that my parents wouldn't always be with me and there was nothing I could do about it. One day I had a fantastic idea, but thought that my parents might think that it would be too big a risk and that it would be too much trouble for them. The idea was to get mum and dad to go on holiday for a week and leave me behind. This way I could find out what I couldn't do and see if I could find other ways of doing these things. The more I thought about it the more I wanted to have a go. I knew a week wouldn't be long enough to try everything but it would be a start.

I knew just the right person who would agree and support me during that week. This was my friend Katie. I decided that the next time I visited Katie I would mention it. Katie was all for it! I had to get my nerve up to tell mum and Dad. At first they didn't really like it but, after an argument, we all agreed that it was a good idea. I had to agree that Mr. Baldwin, a neighbour down the road, and Katie would be the ones that kept their eyes on me. If I ran into difficulty I would go to them. I didn't like Mr. Baldwin very much and I knew that I would call on Katie more than him. Katie was like a second mum to me.

As time draw nearer and nearer I was really excited and looking forward to my experience. At last, the day came when I said goodbye to my parents and then I began my adventure!

I reported every day to Katie what I had done and what I had had to eat. There were two things that I can remember doing very clearly. On Saturday, I did a lot of cooking because at that time I was going regularly to Allerford Chapel. On Sunday evenings after the service, a group of young people would spend a couple of hours' fellowship in somebody's house. As my parents were away, I thought it would be nice to meet in my house. I made some cakes and other things. The evening went off very well and we all enjoyed ourselves. Secondly, the night before my parents came home I made another cake and made something with real strawberries and cream mixed together with a bit of ice-cream. While I was pouring it into glasses to put into the fridge I broke one of the glasses but managed to clear it up without cutting my hand. I did some chicken drum sticks for them in case they were hungry when they got home from their holiday. There was one thing I forgot to get that day which was to buy some extra pints of milk.

The whole week worked out very well and I didn't face any real problems. It was just a case of working it all out beforehand so I knew exactly what I had to do, and spending time on how I was going to achieve what I wanted to do.

The only big problem I had was carrying 'used' hot water in a saucepan from the cooker to the sink. I could only find two ways of dealing with this problem – either to wait for the water to get cooler and then carry it over to the sink, or to put the dish cloth in the saucepan to soak the water up and then carry the saucepan from A to B. This method would depend on how much water was left in the saucepan. This saved water spilling onto the floor and onto me (which I did a couple of times!) If, after boiling, the saucepan was only a quarter full, I could carry that without any problem. If the saucepan was full up though, I would have to put one arm around it and hold the handle with the other hand, which felt a lot safer.

Mr Baldwin used pop in every day and I believe he also popped in during the evenings. I must admit that I did get a bit frightened in the evening and some strange noises would make me jump here and there. I believe that Mr. Baldwin reported to dad how well it went and how well I behaved that week. Thank God that he didn't know everything I got up too because I didn't tell him. My parents were pleased to hear that everything went smoothly and that there were no serious problems that I couldn't handle. Having Katie in the background worked out really well, and I knew that I could call her at any time. My parents said we could do it again but we never did.

Until Pauline started to bring it up, I never thought of leaving home. During my late 20s I began to wonder what I was going to do if anything happened to my parents. Deep down inside me I knew that I could cope in a flat of my own if I had everything arranged to my liking. I wasn't sure whether this could be done as it would cost money, and where would the flat be? Apart from this, I would be faced with a lot of new problems, like changing a light bulb, changing the bed, fitting a plug, the hoovering and many other things. There were a lot of things that I never did at home, not because I didn't want to, but because I didn't need to because dad was there. These factors didn't put me off but the biggest problem was finding out how to go about it.

As far as I can remember in 1984 I told one of the staff at The Ladywell Day Centre that I was thinking about wanting to leave home. We decided to contact Ms. Veronica Watts, who was in the housing department, and specialised in people with disabilities. The funny thing was that she helped my mum when she came home from hospital, so I knew Veronica quite well. We met up and discussed this before I told my parents. Veronica agreed with everything I told her and we both knew that I could cope on my own.

She told me about the Independent Living Scheme (ILS) which the Borough of Lewisham had started. The idea was to get four or five physically disabled people to live together in a house. Each would have their own room but would share the sitting room, bathroom and kitchen. There was a home-help and nurses visiting daily for those who needed it. I was over the moon about this idea and Veronica said that I could go on and be completely independent in the future. I had to have an interview with the other flat mates to say whether they would like me to join them and they said they would. The next step was how I was going to tell my parents.

I spent quite a long time thinking about how my parents were going to react. I honestly thought that dad was going to be the most difficult one to tell as I was his little girl. I told mum first as I thought she would be easy, but I was wrong! When I told her she went off the deep end and threw questions at me that I couldn't answer at that moment.

The sort of questions she was asking me were – "How are going to do your buttons and shoes up? How are you going to carry hot water from A to B when cooking? What are you going to do when the light bulb goes out? What about the house-work etc.?"

I knew mum was right about these things and I knew that I could find another way of doing them, but at that time I just had to say, "I don't know!"

Mum must have thought that I was mad especially when I couldn't answer her questions.

I thought "Oh God, how is dad going to take it? Will he be worse than mum?"

What will I do if he says no. If that was the case I would just keep trying to convince them that I could cope in the end. Anyway, I left it for a couple of weeks and when dad took me to the Ladywell Centre, I told him on the way about me leaving home and he replied, "If you have made up your mind, you will do it, won't you?" I just couldn't believe my ears! No doubt, mum and dad had had many discussions about it.

My first house was 11, Bargery Road and dad and I arranged to meet Veronica there to have a look round. The workmen were still working on it at the time, putting in all the adaptations that were needed. Dad asked Veronica some questions and in the end he was pleased and satisfied with the whole idea. It took them over five years to complete. When they first started planning the house there were five disabled people who were going to live there: Terry, John, Joe, Elaine and Viv. Terry and Elaine had other issues going on at the time, and could not wait for the house to be finished so they found another place to live. Viv became ill for little while and then the council found another flat for her. On the ground floor as you walked in there was John's room – No. 1. On the left, ahead of you was another which led to the stairs, and as you walked past the stairs there was the shower room on the left with a sliding door. The shower was specially made for people in wheelchairs. The floor was made in a certain way so the water would go down the drain in the middle of the floor. On the right was a high toilet and a wash basin. Then there was the laundry room, the kitchen and the lounge, which did look nice. It had an old fashion fireplace, a coffee table, a settee and a dining area with a table and four chairs. We had French windows leading out into a big garden. At the back was a small car park where Joe could park his car. Straight through the kitchen was Joe's room – No. 2. Very tiny, and he could hardly move around when he had the bed down. It was good job that he had a bed settee. I certainly wouldn't want to be the one who got it down and put back in the mornings! The kitchen was well planned and everything was the same level so I could slide the saucepans along from A to B.

I had a slight problem with the cooker as I couldn't turn the knobs. We got the electric people to put a gadget on each knob so that I could hold and turn at the same time. Upstairs on the right was the front room – room no. 3 (the biggest room). Next door to that was another laundry room; after that, there were two cupboards opposite the stairs; next there was room 4; then you turned right and there was a bathroom with a toilet; then there was another toilet room and then room no. 5.

At first I was going to have room 4 but as Viv wasn't ready to move into Bargery Rd. they said that I could have room 3, which was at the front. I was really pleased about this as I liked to look out of the window to see what is going on. Also I could keep a look out if I was expecting a visitor because I couldn't always hear the door bell. As I wasn't involved in the beginning when the planning started I didn't have any choice about the colours in my room. The walls were painted a light blue and there was a blue carpet and I was happy with this colour. In each room there was a sink and a cupboard.

There was one thing that I had to have and that was a bank account. Up to now dad wouldn't let me have one because of my writing and I agreed with him as I knew I wouldn't be able to write a cheque if bought anything in the shops, especially when you have to sign it on the spot. I couldn't control my writing. Most of the time I got Maureen to write the cheque and I signed it. Now I get my friends to help me. I only had to wait seven months to move in but John and Joe had been waiting five years. I moved in on 16th September, 1985. Unfortunately I had just started a college course – 'Computing for Women', so dad did most of the moving for me. He also put some shelves up for my books. Dad and I went shopping to buy a fridge, a television and a cupboard. To put the cupboard up dad had to ask his next door neighbour to give him a hand. As we only had one room I couldn't get everything in it so I left quite a few things at home. If I wanted something, I could easily go and collect it.

John, Joe and I got on very well together. We had a couple of meetings with Veronica, the home help and two or three other people who were involved. The home help said they would put me on their books because I did need help here and there with hovering and housework. Mondays to Fridays we had Maureen (home care) who was really excellent. She would do almost anything. At the weekends we had Sylvia and she was just as good as Maureen. At first John used to have the night nurses to put him to bed but after a while he did without them as they used to arrive so early that he didn't want to go to bed. He had a day nurse to come in daily to see him. Some of the nurses got to know me, as I would see them on my way out. Maureen or Sylvia would do my shoes or buttons up. They would hoover my room and help me to tidy my room from time to time. This is helped me to manage with some things which I found very difficult when Maureen or Sylvia were available. Housework, especially hoovering, used to take a lot of energy out of me.

I could never push the brush lightly across the carpet. It took anything up to half-an hour or three-quarters-of-an-hour just to do my room and it really did make me all hot and bothered. Nine out of ten times, I would get someone to do it for me if they didn't mind. The other thing was putting the duvet on my bed. This is how I coped with this problem: In the morning, I would take the cover off the duvet and the sheet off the bed, which I could do very well without help. However, trying to put the clean cover on would take me hours! I would lay the duvet on the floor, turn the cover inside out and match the corners up to the corners of the cover and slowly pull it down. If there was an opening in the duvet cover right across the bottom it was quite easy, but sometimes the cover would only have a small opening, and then it would be jolly difficult.

On the door of each room there was a spring that made the door heavy and if you didn't come out quickly enough you would get a bump on your bum. I asked dad if he could take the spring off. We didn't bother to tell the council and dad took four off and we put them in the cupboard. We agreed that if an inspector came round dad would put them back on the doors but this never happened and dad never had to.

I never used the shower in the bath in my bathroom because I didn't feel safe and I was frightened that I might fall over. Instead, I would get up early and have a shower and wash my hair in the downstairs bathroom, which was a lot better and also I didn't bang my arms against the walls. Sometimes I used to wash Joe's back and he would wash mine. After a while, when I felt it was becoming a regular habit I wouldn't do it any more. Joe was very good at massaging when I used to get a pain in my neck and shoulder. I would get Joe to rub the cream on it for me. We had only been living there a few months when we received our first bill. The bill was much too high and we knew we hadn't used over 9,300 units of electricity. I believe the council paid most of it in the end.

When I first moved in, one of the biggest problems I had was cooking a meal and carrying it upstairs to my room. There was no way round it.

Sometimes I would eat in the dining room, but this made me feel that I had to be very careful in case I made a mess. Nine out of ten times, I didn't really bother to eat properly. I would go out and eat at Pizza Hut, Pizza Land or the Wimpy bar, or go home and have dinner with mum and Dad, and twice a week with my friend Roland.

The next problem was dressing. I couldn't do buttons up or tie my shoe laces up. As we had a home-help in the house, first thing in the morning, I would call her up to my room and ask her to do me up – in a polite way of course! Over the past five years, I managed to find a way round this. To do my blouse up, I did the sleeves and three or four last buttons down the front with a button hook, but left two or three buttons at the top so that I could put the blouse on like a jumper. Then I had a problem doing the top buttons up. I couldn't do them with the button hook as it wouldn't work so I had to wear something underneath until I got somebody to do them up for me. If I wore a jumper on the top of the blouse it didn't matter whether the buttons were done up or not. To do the buttons up myself, I used to put my finger in the button hole, then put my finger on the edge of the button the other side and push it through the button hole. I would then press the button down and pull it through the other side. My mum and I found another way of doing my buttons up. We got some Velcro, which you could buy in a long strip, cut it into squares, cut the button off the blouse, did up the button hole, sewed the button on top of the button hole and then sewed on the Velcro underneath. All I then had to do was to press the two sides of the blouse together. We had the same idea with wrap-round skirts and kilts. We would replace the inside button on the skirt with Velcro and then cut the buckle off the kilt, and replace that with Velcro. Mum used to hate this bit because the material was a lot thicker near the buckle and getting the needle through was hard work – but she did it. I could then manage to press the two sides together on my own.

A few years later, the Velcro company brought out button-shaped Velcro. I can remember one day, I was on the bus and a lady sat next to me and sat on a bit of my skirt. I went to get up to get off at my usual bus stop. I had my bag in one hand and only had one hand free. I knew the lady was sitting on my skirt and I tried to get her to move a bit but she didn't until I tried to get up. However, this was too late! I put the bag on my arm so that I could hold the hand rail with one hand and my skirt up with the other. When I got off the bus, I quickly walked towards the wall, made sure there was nobody looking, put my bag down between my legs, quickly undid my skirt and did it up again! I t was most embarrassing!

To do the buttons up on my shirt sleeves, I always used to use a button hook and did the button up before I put my arm through. Sometimes it took me a while to get my hands through, but I did it.

For eighteen months John, Joe and I were very happy with the way things were going. The only thing that did get me mad was the price of the gas and the electricity bill. The agreement was that we would divide it into three. I thought, and I think Joe did too, that this was very unfair because we were out all day and John was in most of the time. He should have paid more than us, but we just couldn't work it out that way – so we just paid whatever it was.

After about eighteen months, we all started moaning and complaining because Social Services told us that there should be five people living in our house, not three! We began to wonder what sort of people we were going to get to join us. Nearly everybody thought that we were so used to being our own little group that we didn't want anybody else. This was true in one way – having another person or two would mean that we might have to change our time table. For instance – use of the kitchen – could it be used by five people? Not without working out who was going to use it first and a system of turn-taking. We had a meeting and Veronica told us about Janet, the new girl, who was going join us. I was looking forward to having someone upstairs with me to be company, as I was the only girl there.

We accepted Janet and she moved in. When I met her I thought she was very pretty and attractive. I also thought we were going to be good friends and maybe go out together. As time went by, I found that this wasn't possible so we went our separate ways and didn't get on very well. I became quite frightened and nervous of her. I didn't know what to do or how to handle the way I felt. Anyway, we did have some laughs. One particular day, Janet was doing some toast quite early in the morning when the fire alarm went off. John couldn't do anything as he wasn't up yet and I knew that he had difficulty reaching it. I didn't know where Joe was either. Anyway, it made me jump and it was loud. We had to press one button to turn the alarm off then press another button and hold it until it had reset itself. Nine out of ten times, we took our finger off too soon and the alarm would go off again!

I really tried hard to get on with Janet, but it just didn't work. Once, when she was having a bad day, she knocked me down the stairs! This really did shake me up. I just didn't know what to do or who to tell. I should have told dad but I didn't as I was a bit worried about what his reaction would be. So I told Roland and he went behind my back and phoned my dad. Dad rang me up to see if I was all right and he reported it to Veronica. I had a bruise on my leg. Veronica and the team began to realise that she wasn't suitable for our group, and they agreed to find Janet another place.

Over the next few months before Janet left, I became very nervous and jumpy. I was really scared in case it happened again. I'm glad to say that it didn't. Because of this, I spent a lot of time with my friend Roland. Anyway, eventually Janet left Bargery Road. We were back to three of us again!

The next person Social Services put in with us was Susan. Susan was a deaf girl and was about 25 years old. I liked her and again I thought we might get on together, but communication was difficult. I let her use my computer to see if it would make our conversation any easier, but in fact it was even more confusing because whatever she was trying to say it didn't always make sense. Eventually, we went our separate ways. I didn't really want this to happen as I did want company.

I had difficulty understanding Susan's speech as she was profoundly deaf and we would just say "Hello" and "Good-bye". Then, one day at about two or three in the morning, my door bell rang. I answered it by the phone system, and it was the police asking me if I would come down to identify my flat mate? I must have kept them waiting for about ten minutes. The police told me they had picked her up somewhere in London (or she might have gone to them). They thought that she was underage (she was in her 20s) and vulnerable. I didn't think much of it at the time and I just wanted to get back to bed! I told Susan's social worker when he came down, and thought that was the end of the matter. One day when Susan came into my room, I asked her about that night, and she wrote on my computer that she had a pain in her head that day and needed to get out. So I kept this on my disc and when I saw her social worker again I showed it to her. Susan disappeared a second time and the Police called and woke me up again, in the early hours. I began to get cross because this was my home and I was NOT a carer! The experience of being woken abruptly, awareness of my vulnerability as a physically disabled person to intruders, and the possibility of bad news was disturbing.

After my experiences with Janet and now Susan I felt Social Services were using us as unofficial social workers for people who needed support. Bargery Road was intended to be for housing, not a Social Services unit. However, to social workers it was seen as a substitute for hostel accommodation (where support workers or a warden would be on site). Because I noticed Susan was going out very late at night I decided to watch her next time. It was quite puzzling. When she left the house she hid her purse or handbag in the front garden between the wall and the bushes and walked off, presumably without her keys or I.D. I mentioned this strange behaviour to the home help for Bargery Road and left it at that. It turned out that she was getting on the bus and going to London or wherever she wanted to go, getting picked up by the police and being brought home to our flat. Because she was not breaking the law in any way, they could not keep her in custody and would bring her home. When I told the police that she was 25 years old I am not sure that they believed me.

There was something else that annoyed me about Susan. Sometimes when my meal was cooking, if I wasn't in the kitchen at the time, she would just move my saucepans off the cooker and start cooking her own food. I wouldn't mind if she came to tell me or if she was in a hurry! It was very hard to work out who used the kitchen first. Most of the time I would let her go first because sometimes I was quite wary of her. In the end, Social Services agreed to put a Baby Belling cooker, a microwave and work surfaces upstairs in our laundry room. This meant that we were not so overcrowded as we had two places in which to prepare and cook our food.

One of my friends called Jack, who used to use me from time to time, came to visit quite a lot in Bargery Road. We got friendly again, like we did a few years ago. I had to be very careful and alert when I was with him. Over the years he was a friend in many ways. Anyway, one weekend I was supposed to go camping with the disabled guides. Before I left to go to camp, the home help told me that Jack was seeing Susan. I was upset about this and it also made me feel embarrassed in front of the other people in the house. I decided not to go camping for the weekend and stayed in my room. Jack later came to see Susan. When he came up the stairs, I was ready for him and asked him what he thought he was playing at! He gave me some lame excuses, but after that, I never really trusted him again. However, I still kept on good terms with him as I felt I might need him at some time in the future.

One day, we had a meeting to discuss a fifth person coming to join us. I did not like this because it would only make the problem with the cooking and laundry worse. Really, we had no choice in the matter. The person's name was Lucy. Lucy had been ill before she moved in, and it was soon clear that she had not fully recovered. This was made obvious when, one morning, I got up to go to the bathroom and found the bathroom was in such a terrible state that I screamed! Maureen, the home help, came running up and when she saw the bathroom she made Lucy clean it up (with her help). It took me a long time to use the bathroom again.

Lucy's behaviour also drove me up the wall. Lucy craved company and would not leave me alone for a minute, literally. She would run the washing machine, which was next to my room, late at night or early in the morning (Susan sometimes did this as well). If I shut the door, the noise was bearable, but the vibrations still drove me crazy. She also walked around completely naked and it took a few weeks of nagging by Maureen and myself before she stopped doing it.

Another shock I had in Bargery Road was, one morning, I went into the bathroom and saw a huge spider in the bath. I screamed my head off and Maureen came running up asking me what the matter was. When I told her, she just laughed and got rid of it saying "Honestly, Julia!" I believe she saw the funny side though.

When I was living with my mum and dad, I used to wash my hair in the bath. Later, when dad put a shower in, I was able to lean over the bath and wash my hair using the shower attachment. Because I am left handed and the taps were on the left hand side, it was quite easy to do.

When I wanted a bath, my mum or dad used to turn the water on and fill up the bath for me (if the taps were too tight to turn). To get in and out of the bath, I would put a chair next to the bath, put a towel across the chair and over the side of the bath, and then sit on a chair and swing my legs over the bath. I could then slide into the bath.

To get out of the bath, I would get hold of the door handle which I could reach from the bath, stand up and transfer over to a chair.

When my mum became disabled, Social Services gave my mum a seat to go inside the bath, which was handy for me too. They also put in a handrail, which helped us both in and out of the bath.

Social Services eventually found Lucy lodgings with somebody who was paid extra to care fore her. However, this was unsuccessful and she moved into a home, I believe. After a few more months, they managed to find Susan a flat. I was amazed when Susan gave me a lovely frying pan as a farewell present, which I still have. She had often been so inconsiderate in her behaviour that the gift seemed to be out of character.

In 1989, I applied for a transfer. Janet knocking me over started me thinking about it. I heard, unofficially, that the council were intending to convert the upstairs of Bargery Road into a 2-bedroom flat. If this were to happen, they would want me out, so I put in the transfer request. I was offered a ground floor flat in Blackheath, next to the railway line. It was far from my friends and Ladywell, and to get to it you would have to walk across a large car park next to the station, or down a side street with few houses, which meant that it would not have been very safe in the dark. The entrance of the flat had a heavy door, which lead into a dark hallway, which put me off as well. When I opened the door, I was not impressed. It was dirty and in poor decorative order. There was a large hole in the wall where something had been removed and the rooms seemed small. I turned it down.

I was later offered a ground floor flat in a converted terraced house in Catford, which was only three doors away from Kitty, who had been a friend since school days. I looked round the flat – first with a friend, Irene N, who I knew from the WRVS shop at Ladywell, and later in the day with Roland. Both said I would be a fool if I let this one go. I agreed at the time and accepted the offer and moved out of Bargery Road. Joe got married and moved out of Bargery Road. This meant John (and his carer) was left the entire ground floor, including a big garden – so he got what he wanted too.

Me in a school photo at Plassey Road Primary.

Washing-up duty at Guide Camp.

My dad at his retirement party at Twinlock.

Me and mum at a party at Ladywell Day Centre.

A stroppy teenager – me!

Me visiting a Romanian Orphanage.

Roland and me on holiday in Ireland.

Keiran and me at The Titanic restaurant, Cobh, Ireland – 2002.

Jo, my P.A. – behind bars in Ireland!

Edina and me in the grounds of Blarney Castle in Ireland.

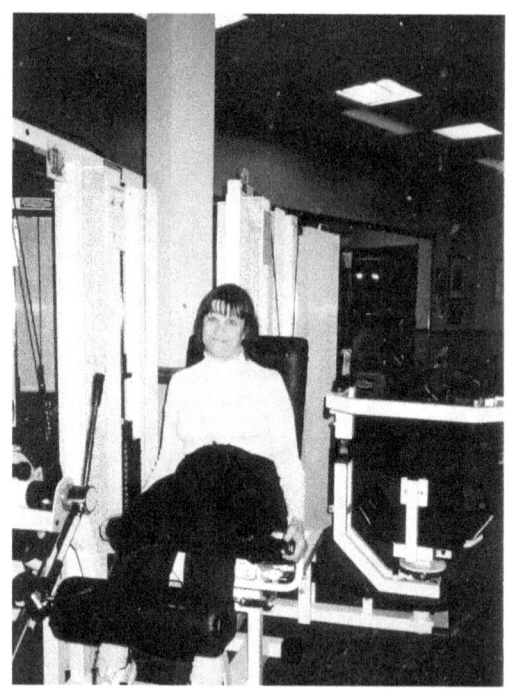

Working out at Eltham Fitness Centre, November 2002.

Me being accepted into the WRVS. The two Renes are on the far left.

With Georgie and John in Lake Garda, Italy in 2006.

Rosie and me – Christmas 2006.

In Portugal, stroking the dolphins at Zoomarine, with Georgie and a keeper.

## *Chapter Thirty*
# Teddy Bears

When I was living in Bargery Road, I was a bit lonely and felt fed up from time to time. One day while out shopping in Eltham, I went into Boots and I saw these lovely teddy bears. I pick one up to have a closer look at it. As it was done up in a bag, I couldn't see much but it was gorgeous and very soft so I bought him. On the way home in the bus I decided to undo it and have a look. I was really pleased with it and the lady who sat next to me in the bus also liked it. She told me to call it Bengie, as I didn't have a name for it – so I named it Bengie.

As I liked Bengie so much I decided to buy another one exactly the same because I knew his fur would go funny after a lot of cuddles. I named him Jason and when I put the two bears together I could see two different expressions on their faces. Bengie was wilder looking while Jason looked friendly, happy and alive. This was the time where I learnt that you can get more out of a bear when you give it time. Somehow, Jason became real and has his own personality. I took him to Ladywell Centre and everybody liked him. Irene N really did adore him. Roland could make him express different emotions by the way he held him.

I started buying bears, but only the ones I liked. When I realised I had over fifty teddy bears in my flat I decided to stop but people started buying me bears as presents. The bear family started growing even faster and was getting out of hand but I still kept them all. A couple of years ago I bought a teddy bear from an Eltham toy shop. The label says "Toyland, made in Israel". I can't find very much out about this bear. He is golden brown with felt paws and is 18 inches (45 cm) tall. I named him Rollo and didn't take much notice of him as he looked miserable, so I left him at Roland's flat. Over a period of time I started to talk to him and make a fuss of him. Then Rollo began to change his expression and now is alive and happy.

Collecting bears, I began to think about the ones I had when I was younger. Ever since I was little there was a teddy bear in our house. I always thought it belonged to Pauline. I asked mum if it was a present when Pauline or I were born, or was it just given to us. Mum told me how Teddy came to join us. When Pauline was five and I was three, one of the neighbours gave one of us a bear and the other a doll. I never really took much notice of the doll, and I don't know whether we had a name for her, but she had a beautiful dress, which was all handmade, and a china face. Pauline certainly did play with the bear a lot and you can tell it had been loved by both of us by the state of its fur. We used to put a little dress on him. He must be at least 38 years old now. When the bear 'retired', he sat on the bed in mum and dad's bedroom upstairs. Many years later, I think Pauline may have taken it with her when she moved house, as well as the china doll.

In my teens, I asked mum to buy me a teddy bear of my own. She bought a lovely yellow one with black ears about ten inches tall (25 cm). I kept him for a long time but he disappeared while I still lived at home and I never found him.

I often wondered if there was a teddy bear collectors' club. Then I bought my first teddy bear book, "The Ultimate Teddy Bears Book" by Pauline Cockrill. Inside there were addresses to get information and magazines but I never got round to writing to them.

On November 29th 1992 at Greenwich Town Hall there was the first South East London Teddy Bear Fair. I'm really glad that Roland told me about it because he wasn't going to. I arrived in the afternoon about one. I'd never seen so many bears! Hundreds of them and not two looked the same. Most of them were very expensive and people were going round with their cheque books. I had never seen so many people, and at some stalls it was difficult to get a close-up look at these bears – never mind those people who were in wheelchairs! It was fantastic and I treated myself by buying a Paddington Bear and a teddy bear magazine, which I used to get regularly. Now I have a few limited edition ones and a good number of books on teddy bears. Roland says I am an arctophile. After I hit him for being rude he explained it meant someone who loved and collected teddy bears.

I still collect teddy bears, and now, in 2007, I have over 103 bears in my collection. I tend to just go for the 1/10 edition bears which are more rare.

## Chapter Thirty One
# Counselling and Teaching

This chapter is about two particular courses that I went on where, really and truly, you had to be in employment. However, because I did voluntary work, I was able to get in that way.

I became really interested in counselling when we went to Avon Tyrrell Branagore for a weekend introduction course. This was run by a lady I used to know, called Gill (my old guide leader), who thought I might like to come along.

I was told to catch a train from Waterloo to Brockenhurst. On Friday 19th April 1985, dad agreed to take me to Waterloo Station and put me on the right train. We said goodbye to each other. While I was on the train, I had a funny feeling being in the middle of nowhere, but I knew where to get off. It was a lovely view looking out of the window. When I finally arrived at Brockenhurst I asked one of the railwaymen to direct me to Avon Tyrrell. He told me to catch the next train and get off at Christchurch. I wasn't very pleased about this but I thought I had better check this with the police as I didn't have much time on my hands.

The policeman said it was right, so I had to make my way back to the train station. I paid another £1.50, which I didn't mind, but I didn't like the thought of going up the stairs to catch the train with my suitcase! Anyway, I managed very well as there was hardly anyone about. There was someone waiting for me at Christchurch Station. I felt very pleased with myself. I don't know why but I had a feeling that I was going to enjoy this course.

The food was delicious and, apart from the work, it was like living in a hotel. I met some very nice people. I enjoyed the course and I did get a lot from it. Mind you, I did get a bit embarrassed during the sexuality session because we had to think of all different names that a man would call his penis. Believe me, there were some names that I've never heard of! As I liked the course so much, from then on I knew that counselling was exactly what I wanted to do. I was so sorry that the course was over that, for the first time, I cried in public.

One of the leaders, Gill, came across and put her arms around me to comfort me and she didn't mind at all. There could be two reasons why

I cried – one is that I enjoyed the course so much and the other is that I could not or do not like saying goodbye to people.

I returned to London with two people who had been on the course, so I had company and pleasant conversation. We arrived at Waterloo Station and said goodbye to each other. I went to phone dad and he came to collect me with the car. While I was waiting, I went to have a drink.

In September of the same year, I applied to do an RSA counselling course. The main problem was that it was in South West London and difficult to get to. Dad agreed to take me over the first week, so we knew where it was and where to get the buses. I asked him to come in with me so he could fill in the enrolment forms, but unfortunately he couldn't do it because he didn't have his reading glasses with him. One of the staff filled the form in for me.

Everything went well until home time, when I was supposed to be going straight back to my flat in Bargery Road and to my parents' house. I might have got away with it. The reason why I was going back to my parents was to show how quick the journey could be. Well, Joanna, one of the students, offered me a lift to Brixton as it was on her way home, and she thought it might cut my travel time. I accepted her offer, knowing that I could get a P4 from Brixton to Lewisham and a number 36 home, cutting out a bus. At 10pm I was still waiting for a P4 to come along, so I went into the railway station and the person working there told me that P4 buses did not run after 9.30pm in the evening. I thought 'HELP!' How do I get from here to Lewisham? The railwayman told me to walk to the end of the road, get a number 37 to Peckham and a number 36 to Catford. I decided to do what she said, but walking down Brixton High Street really did scare me. On the way to the bus stop, I saw a man with rainbow-coloured hair. I had to keep crossing the road to get out of people's way.

What a relief it was just to get to the 37 bus stop! I couldn't see a phone box to give dad a call and I certainly wasn't going to go out of my way to find one! Even when I was in Peckham there wasn't a phone box in sight. In my mind, all I could think of was dad waiting for me. He was going to be furious with me. When I finally turned into Fordel Road, I could see dad in the distance. He certainly did have a go at me. When I told dad what happened, he understood and no more was said about it. It was gone midnight before I got to bed that night. It was the most terrifying evening I had experienced. Never again!

About halfway through the course, a male student said that I should not be on the course. Terri, the tutor, looked at me and said "Well, Julia, are you going to sit there, or are you going to have a go at him?" For a minute, I was shocked and had a lump in my throat. Eventually I took a deep breath and threw questions at him – "Why shouldn't I be on this course? What right do you have to say that because I am disabled I can't do counselling? You are the one who shouldn't be on this course because you are not seeing me as a person!"

Even Terri said that he should not be on the course! I said that my disability was my problem, not his, and that as I couldn't hear everything that was being said, I was the one losing out, so what was his problem?

This man was shocked by my response. In my mind, I was wondering what the other students might be thinking or whether they might join in. At the end of the evening, most of the other students said "well done". It certainly did me good to have the argument in a class. My self confidence was boosted. I had been belittled by an able-bodied student because of my disability in front of others and I had stood up for myself without getting emotionally upset. That student came up to me afterwards to apologise and asked me to forgive him. Would I forgive him? What do you think? I did – a couple of weeks later.

I ended up enjoying the course and was pleased to be accepted by the majority of the students as an equal, especially as most were teachers or social workers. It is a course that I would recommend to anyone who wants to learn about themselves. As well as teaching me counselling skills, it helped me to grow up and gave me confidence in myself and when I am with people. Three books 'Freedom to Learn', 'On Becoming a Person' by Carl Rogers and 'A Woman in your own Right' by Anne Dicken, which I read as part of the course, changed the way I thought a lot. Carl Rogers' statement that "We all have a right to be what we want to be," encouraged me to be more assertive and not to defer to others just because I was disabled. In the past, I had often kept my real views or feelings to myself, not contradicting people even if I felt strongly about it.

There were two types of counselling skills I experienced during the course which I did not like. One was where the client is counselled by different counsellors, one after another. During this exercise I sat on the floor, because it was more comfortable for me. I noticed that only one counsellor sat on the floor with me. I thought that was good because she came down to my level and this made me feel a lot better. The others sat on the chair, which made me feel as if the counsellors were looking down at me. The other type of counselling was where you counsel each other for about 15 minutes – this was called co-counselling.

For my extended work piece, I went to Woodlark Camping Site as a helper with Charlton Park School, looking after disabled teenagers. I had two girls; one could manage fairly well on her own but needed some help, and the other girl was similar, but was very slow at doing things. This girl really tested my patience because she would not accept any help when it was clear she needed it. Usually, she ended up having to accept help, having wasted time and having created more work. Then when she was late, I would get the blame. If you tried to hurry her, she could get a bit stroppy with you so it was better to let her get on with it.

At mealtimes, we took it in turns to feed the ones who could not feed themselves. I had three teenagers to look after – two of them could feed themselves, but just needed me to put an apron on and paper napkins around their necks. I just had to keep my eyes on them and help them when needed. The other one had to be fed. At first, because he had difficulty with swallowing, he spat some of it out and dribbled. The first time I fed him, I couldn't eat my meal at the same time. It made me feel sick and turned my stomach over. By the end of the week I could feed him and eat my meal at the same time. I never thought I would be able to overcome my initial reactions as I did.

One of the girls dropped her glasses down the toilet and I could not face putting my hand in the loo, even with rubber gloves. I went and persuaded another helper to fish the glasses out!

In each tent there was a whistle to be blown if one of the teenagers wanted something or needed help. Late one evening, we were relaxing and drinking coffee and all the teenagers were in bed. We heard a whistle and the duty helper checked all the tents, but found no one to be awake. Just after she returned, the whistle started again and someone else volunteered to recheck the tents. It was then I realised it was my hearing aid whistling! Luckily, they saw the funny side of it!

These things I will always remember from the camp, when I look back.

Between 1993 and 1994, I decided to take up teaching, by doing the City & Guilds 7306 examination, which is the equivalent of the NVQ Level 3. I had to go for an interview. They were quite happy with the way I answered some of the questions, but when I came out, she looked at me and said "What are you going to do about your teaching practice on the course?" This teaching practice was something we all had to cover on the course, and involved standing up in front of everyone on the course and teaching for 10 minutes – a microteach – on any topic. I said, "Don't worry about that. I've got it all worked out." I knew I was going to do a session on Disability Awareness. It worked really well, and I think the tutor was amazed. I got very positive comments afterwards, and was told that this helped fellow students with their approach to disabled people, and also regarding helping members of their own family. I involved all the students in role play for this. One activity was learning how to lift a person correctly and transfer them from chair-to-chair. One student was particularly thankful for this as she had to lift up her mother on a regular basis.

The only problem I had on the course was the 30 hour teaching practice in an outside classroom. Being a member of the Ladywell Day Centre, I took two or three people for a computer lesson to teach them the basics, and then took another person to help them with spellings. This was quite good, but it was not enough hours. The college agreed to help me out by letting me teach in one of their classes for people with learning difficulties. I taught them self-defence. I had been on a self-defence course specifically for disabled people, which was really effective and enjoyable. I could then pass this on to others. I was observed teaching this class, and it worked out quite well.

There was another problem, which Roland helped me with. This was to relate all the work I had done to the specific papers I was given to answer. This involved lots of cross-referencing and took ages. I was glad to see the back of it! As a result of doing this cross referencing, I was able to help another student in the class with their cross referencing.

I was really pleased that I did this course, and completed it.

I would love to have done the next stages in teaching and counselling, but could not. No matter how hard I tried, I would never be able to get the 100 hours teaching practice needed for each exam.

The good thing about this course was that I won an award for being the best student of the year (the Grinling Gibbons Award for Education for outstanding achievement in teacher training) and a book voucher.

By this time my dad was no longer alive, but I would have loved my mum and dad to have come and seen me get the award. Unfortunately, this was not possible as the awards were given upstairs and therefore my mum was unable to get up the stairs to see it. However the college did put it on a video for her, although I don't know if she ever saw it.

*Chapter Thirty Two*

# Work

Over the past six years my self confidence got better as I gained more independence and experience by mixing with all types of people. I realised the centre no longer fulfilled all my needs and that the next step was to gain work experience or employment.

When Roland became a clerk in the office and the other clerk was on sick leave I asked him if I could give him a helping hand there. The reason was that I had in mind to gain work experience. As Roland knew me very well, he knew that I wouldn't do any jobs that were too hard for me. I did have some problems answering the phone because of my deafness and slowness in writing. If they were short messages I could memorise them. When the other clerk returned I only helped when I was asked. I did learn how to use the photocopier and I enjoyed the work. But after a while I became bored as I was not allowed to learn new skills and the other office staff were not interested in allowing or encouraging me to see if I could do other office tasks.

I realised that most of the staff didn't like members helping out and it made me angry. The management said they wanted to encourage members to get involved in running the centre but when it came down to it they were no different from the staff. After a while I realised they were very keen for you to help when they were short of staff but when the staff returned you were shown that you were not wanted. Another lesson I learnt was that people meeting me for the first time didn't take me seriously; I believe this is because I looked so young and maybe the way I talked. Most assumed that I had learning difficulties.

In September 1990, I applied for a job as a liaison officer at the Lewisham Association for People with Disabilities ("LAPD"). I was confident that I could do the job, though I appreciated that there would be problems because of my disability. A week before my interview, Katie, who was on the interview panel, told me I would not get it because of my lack of work experience. As she had encouraged me to apply, it completely destroyed any hopes I had. Until then, although I realised my lack of work experience and disabilities counted against me, I at least thought I had a fighting chance. This was because I was on the LAPD Executive Committee, and also was part of the Education Committee.

My friend, Morris, and I did try to role-play the interview, but this didn't do me any good because, after what Katie had told me, I felt completely deflated and did not think I had any chance of being successful at the interview.

At the interview, the first one I ever had, I did not perform well. I could not relax and was too nervous. Also with cerebral palsy the more nervous or tense you are the less control you have over your body movements and speech. Not surprisingly I did not get the job though Katie told me the interview was good experience. The experience upset and depressed me for months afterwards. If a disabled organisation would not take my application seriously, what chance did I have in finding a job? How could you gain work experience if no one would give you a chance? My partial deafness and inability to write quickly caused problems it was true – but they could have been overcome if the goodwill had been there.

Several months later, I was introduced by my friend, Kitty, to her course organiser. Kitty was unemployed and on a general training course run by the Elfrida Rathbone Society. The course organiser asked me if I would organise a course on disability for their trainers on one day a week, for four weeks. After the LAPD affair, it revived my hopes and I felt that it would be good experience. I worked hard drawing up a programme covering the nature and problems caused by different disabilities; sessions involving finding out what it is like to be disabled (e.g. wearing a blindfold); and inviting various professionals to give brief talks.

When I presented my ideas to the course organiser, she told me that she just wanted me to talk about my experiences for about an hour and a half over two days. As the course was meant to help the trainees consider care work, I felt that my planned programme would have been more helpful. I did what she asked, but although the trainees seemed to find it interesting, I felt that I had wasted my time.

A lesson I did learn was to get promises of payment in writing before doing any work. They originally said they would pay me £20 but in the end they only paid £10 – and that was reluctantly. I hoped to get a reference from them for my profile but decided it wasn't worth the trouble and told Kitty I wanted nothing to do with them again.

In September 1992 under an agency called Lewisham Employment Initiative (LEI), the centre employed a new tea bar lady who had learning difficulties. LEI aimed to find employment for people with learning difficulties. People with learning difficulties who were interested in getting work were interviewed to find out what they would like to do and what abilities they had. After realistic goals were agreed, they tried to find a suitable vacancy from contracts with employers which they had built up. They helped with practice at being interviewed and if the person got the job they worked alongside them until they were settled in the job.

Dawn introduced Heather of LEI to see if she could help me. However we found out LEI was only funded to help people with learning difficulties. I thought the way the scheme worked would be ideal for people with physical disabilities, especially those like myself who had been disabled since birth. The difference is that disabled people often have the brains but not the physical ability and do not need someone to work with them all the time or for so long a period. Heather agreed with me and we decided to see if we could get a similar scheme set up for physically disabled people. We started with a meeting attended by myself, Heather representing LEI; representatives from LAPD; Ladywell Centre management and Lewisham Council's Equality Officer. More and more meetings followed with more organisations involved but we never seemed to get anywhere, they just ended up inviting even more organisations to attend the next meeting. I began to feel that it was all talk and the original aim had been forgotten, and that the meetings were a waste of time and energy.

In September 1992 Heather with the agreement of LEI started to work with one or two physically disabled people including myself, as an extension to the service. If successful it was hoped that LEI funding would be extended to cover physically disabled people. Of course, high levels of unemployment and increasing job losses made it even harder for the disabled to find work.

One of the jobs that Heather and I did together, with another member called Barbara, through the LEI, was putting on a disability awareness course at Marks and Spencer in Bromley. However, unfortunately this did not work out as well as we had expected it to. Heather invited a man, David, from another organisation and we had a big argument about the content of the training day. He wanted the first half of the day to be devoted to a great deal of detail about disability – transitional models, medical models, etc. However, we thought that, for staff in M&S, it would be more practical and to the point for them to learn about how to go about approaching the disabled person; the best way to help up a disabled person if they fell over while in the store; or they might just need help on how to communicate with, for instance, a blind person to help them find the things they want, etc.

In the end, we did what David suggested in the morning, but we were not at all impressed with the outcome – in fact we thought it was a load of rubbish! In the afternoon we had a session on role play. This worked well as we showed the staff the type of problems that disabled people face all the time in shops. One of these was at the till point: If a person is disabled, the shelf where you are expected to sign a cheque is much too high for a person in a wheelchair to reach. Another problem was that a lot of the stock is often very high up and difficult to reach. Also, If you have problems with sight or have a hearing impairment, what do you do about contacting staff to come and help you? This made the M&S staff more aware of the difficulties disabled people face.

At the end of the training day, Barbara, Heather and I agreed that the afternoon session was a lot better – and the staff at M&S also agreed.

After a while, Heather came back to me and apologised for getting David involved and having so much time spent on the theory of disability. She realised that Barbara and I could do a better job of organising an event for disability awareness and training on a more practical level. However, this was after the event and because it did not go as well as we had hoped, I felt that another door had been closed to me.

I have thought quite a lot about jobs I could do and would want to do. At first I thought I would like computer work but soon realised it was unrealistic because my disability means I will never be able to touch type and I tire easily. I would prefer to work in a library or in an advice or information centre. I have also thought of working with a Christian organisation as I can do some routine office tasks. A way forward for disabled people like myself is if an employer would be willing to reorganise the work that has to be carried out so as to create a job which we could do. The job would involve work that has to be done but work that we could realistically do independently.

## Chapter Thirty Three
# Dad Passing Away

It was on Christmas Eve morning of 1989, just like any other Christmas. Dad was going to get up early to go down to Tesco's to buy the turkey. Mum got up first and went to the bathroom to get washed and dressed. When mum went back in the bedroom she found dad was on the floor in pain. Mum managed to get down stairs and into her wheelchair. She phoned Mike, who lived a few doors away and worked in the Ambulance Service, for help. Mike looked at dad and called an ambulance straight away. Dad managed to walk down the stairs and into the ambulance.

Mum phoned Pauline and me to tell us what had happened and I decided to ring mum from Ladywell when I arrived to find out the latest. Ladywell was only 10 minutes from the hospital. Over the past year, I had been worrying about dad's health and had always thought that if he ever went into hospital he would never come out. I am a bit confused about what happened to dad after he first arrived in the hospital. I remember waiting by the centre for Irene N and bursting into tears as I told her the news. She comforted me and I went into the WRVS shop with her as normal, though I was still worried.

At about midday, Maurice told me that my dad was very ill and that Pauline was coming to the centre to come with me to the hospital. I started crying again because I realised how serious it was. Maurice arranged for my mum to be taken to the hospital by a social services coach. The drivers volunteered straight away when they heard about the problem. I think Pauline and Maurice must have agreed that the hospital needed to be told that mum had to stay in a ward there. I could not look after mum, and Pauline lived two hours away by car. On Christmas Eve it was too late to arrange alternative care at such short notice.

The ward staff were extremely good. They agreed to keep mum in until her future arrangements could be sorted out.

When I saw dad lying there on the bed he looked so peaceful apart from the tubes and wires that connected to the different machines. I just didn't know what to say to dad, and realise now that I was in shock. People assured me that he was going to be all right but I knew he wasn't. All I did was to say a few words and tried to kiss him and then I went outside to pray and ask God to do what was best for dad. I cannot remember how I got home. I believe Paul, my brother in law, took me home. I do remember I couldn't eat anything.

On Christmas morning I walked round to mum's house and met Pauline. She told me that dad had past away. I just burst into tears and had a good cry. During the night mum and Pauline decided to turn off the life support machine because they had been told that even if dad had survived, after so many hours the likelihood was that he would have been severely disabled. I felt they made the decision my dad would have wanted them to make.

I cannot remember much of the day but remember visiting mum in hospital and having a Christmas dinner with her. Mum was put in a lovely ward which didn't look like a ward. Each patient had a nurse to look after them. I could have gone back with Pauline but I said no as I wanted to be alone.

I went back to my place and in the late afternoon phoned Roland, who was staying at his parents', to tell him my dad had died and my mum was staying in hospital. Roland phoned me back soon after on behalf of his mum and dad to invite me to stay the night. Jack, who was an old friend, gave me a lift to Thamesmead before he started his work mini-cabbing.

Roland's parents gave me a lovely Christmas dinner. Roland was surprised to see that I ate it all. As his parents lived in sheltered accommodation there was a guest room for me to stay in. Boxing Day went by quietly and during the afternoon we went to his sister's and I spent the time with Roland's nephews and nieces playing chess and draughts. Roland's brother-in-law, Steve, took us back to Roland's flat. I stayed there until after my dad's funeral in the New Year. Dad was cremated at Lewisham Crematorium. I can't remember very much about it or how mum got there and back to the hospital. My mind was still blank and I don't remember very much of that day as I couldn't believe it was my dad.

Pauline had sorted out all dad's clothes and personal papers, giving me the papers that involved me. She was concerned about how I would cope and it became clear that she thought dad had done a lot more for me than he actually did. This upset me a lot. Dad did do a lot for me when I first moved into Bargery Road, but after that he was only involved if it was a D.I.Y. job or if asked him for advice.

She seemed to think he gave me a lift to and from Ladywell every day and said I should take a cab. In fact he only usually gave me a lift in very bad weather or if I had something heavy to get at the shops (e.g. my bean bag). Most of the time, I got about by public transport.

I feel that Pauline had left home so long ago that she just did not realise how much I had progressed in becoming independent since I was a teenager. I never went to Pauline with any problems I had because I felt that living so far away and having a family it would only worry her. Although she is my sister, I could not relax or confide in her, although I wanted her approval.

Dad owned a Montego car at the time he died. Sometime during the year before he died, I went to make some enquiries about the possibility of me driving the car, as a disabled person. My friend, Denise, took me. The number of tests they gave me was unbelievable. At the driving centre, I drove an adapted car around the grounds. They told me that I would need a few extra mirrors and an additional strap to hold me in my seat more securely. They also said that I had a 50:50 per cent chance of being able to learn to drive. They said that the best way to do it would be for me to buy a car, have it adapted to my specifications, and then get someone privately to teach me to drive. Because of my disability, they estimated that it would take me about twice as long to learn to drive as it would otherwise.

Maurice at the Ladywell Day Centre had a Mini Metro (I think). He let me sit in the car, and I quite liked the feel of it. Before my dad died, he was thinking about changing his car to an automatic, so that I would be able to drive it. Unfortunately, he died before he was able to do this.

At the Ladywell Centre, there was a girl called Sylvia. She was unable to talk. She used to lift her right and left leg up to indicate 'yes' and 'no'. Although she was unable to talk, when my dad died, she was a great comfort to me as she could look at me in a way that conveyed that she knew what I was going through. We sat down together and cried together. It was an amazing experience and one which I had not experienced before or after. I think that she later went into a home that used to be called The Royal Hospital for the Incurable. I hoped that I would be able to go and see her one day.

As I began to recover from the initial shock of my dad's death, I realised that I had to think about mum, who was still in hospital. I remember telling Maurice that I would not let mum go into a residential home as I felt it would kill her. I wanted mum to go home after various alterations had been done to her house, and have a go at living on her own, with help from the Social Services. If it was found that she could not cope, then fair enough. I would accept that the only alternative would be to try and find a decent residential home.

When I went to mum's house to collect things for her I often bumped into neighbours who assumed that mum would be going into a residential home. They were shocked when I told them we were hoping she could live at home again.

Over the next couple of months, I visited mum nearly every day and became quite friendly with the nurses and patients. The physiotherapists and occupational therapists worked with mum to find out what aids and alterations had to be done and tried them out before doing some home visits. Once again, Veronica, the Housing Officer for disabled people, was involved.

A couple of years earlier, she had also put a handrail up the stairs and raised the fridge up to make it higher so that it opened above the level of the ramp put in by the kitchen door. The kitchen wasn't much of a problem. They lowered the sink and put blocks under the fridge to make it higher so mum could get to them easily.

The next thing was to make the living room into a bedroom as well. We took the settee and armchairs out and put them upstairs in one of the bedrooms to make more room. We cleared out shelves so that mum could put her clothes and personal things in them. Paul brought mum a TV with a remote control for her to watch in bed.

Mum and the physiotherapist asked me if I would look around for a hard bed about 18 inches (48 cm) in height. Honestly, you ought to have seen the expressions some people gave me when I visited shops and started measuring the beds – I felt a fool! Mum had told me that the height that the bed should be was just above my knee. I was looking at all the beds, measuring the bed heights against my knee.

The shop assistant came up to me and said, "What do you think you are doing?"

I explained to her that I was looking for a certain bed at a certain height for my mother. Unfortunately, she wasn't very helpful so I just walked out. I then went to another shop in Catford. The assistant was so polite, came round with me and could not do enough for me. In the end, we found a bed that mum would like – hard and the right height – and a headboard to go with it. The men who brought the bed round were excellent. They made it up, fitted the headboard on and put the bed where I wanted it. They even put the rubbish in the bin for me. When I went to tip them they wouldn't take it.

The British Legion paid for a "Life line" style service as my dad had served in the R.A.F. during the war. My mum had a button on a cord which, if pressed, alerted a 24hr control centre which called neighbours, family or the emergency services. The phone in the hallway enabled the control centre to speak and hear mum if they wished to, or if mum pressed a button on it. Mum came home and she had the hospital discharge officer visiting twice daily to start with and getting her shopping. They came for about eight weeks and then she had the home helps take over.

At first they visited twice a week but this was increased to three times. Eventually, it went back to twice a week. The organiser made sure mum had a home help that she could rely on and trust. Meals on Wheels were provided daily but mum was not keen on them. After a short period she cancelled them when she was confident she could cope with cooking.

One time, I remember, not long after mum came home when we had a hot spell with the weather my phone rang and it was Maurice from Ladywell saying he would collect me with Pat (bathing nurse) and go to see mum. Well, I didn't know what to think. I kept calm. The Social Service drivers had gone to pick mum up but had no reply and saw her on the floor. They had contacted the Centre through their radio. I can't remember how I saw mum that morning as Pat and Maurice took care of everything. Pat was convinced that mum had had a blackout and so hadn't gone to bed. Mum was all right but we did get the doctor in.

Roland came over while we waited for the doctor. The doctor didn't do anything but said mum was O.K. Roland insisted that the doctor call the District Nursing Service to arrange some help for mum in getting up and going to bed for a while.

Another experience in Bargery Road that will stay with me for long time was this. At about four o'clock in the morning, my phone rang. It was the Lifeline telling me that mum had pressed her button and they could not get an answer. I got up and dressed hurriedly, grabbed my keys and went. I was quite frightened, having to walk the streets in the early hours and worrying what had happened. As I tried to open the door with my keys, mum opened it for me, I don't know who was more shocked. It turned out mum had got up early and had pressed the button without realising it and had not heard the phone speaker. She was wondering why I was visiting her so early in the morning! We both had a good laugh, and I ended up sleeping on her settee.

When mum came home from hospital she had an ulcer on one of her feet. I don't know how it developed or whether it started while she was in hospital. I believe it was the shock of dad dying that brought it on. She had a nurse coming in to dress it but it got pretty bad and painful. The nurses tried all different types of creams and none of them seem to work. Mum got quite cross on occasions when a cream she thought was working was dropped to try another one or when they bandaged her too tight.

After her eight months at home, mum had to go back into hospital to have an operation to improve the blood supply to her leg. It was successful but didn't help heal the ulcer, as was hoped. The doctors tried everything they could think of to heal mum's ulcer without amputating her leg. The different treatments often had some initial success but in the end they failed. They then began to consider amputating both mum's legs but eventually decided to amputate just the one with the ulcer. I asked Shirley Chaplin, a centre member who mum knew, to visit mum and talk about her experiences as she had had both legs amputated but had felt a lot better.

In August 1990, after a lot of discussions with doctors, physiotherapists and other professionals, mum agreed to have the leg amputated. A physiotherapist worked with mum to get her ready for the operation.

After the operation, the physiotherapist and occupational therapist worked with mum to strengthen her use of one leg and look into ways of coping with general living. Mum did look and feel much better after the operation which showed how much the ulcer was making her ill.

One doctor upset mum by telling her she would be able to have an artificial leg and he was told off by the staff nurse. He hadn't read her notes and did not realise she had M.S.

After ten months she came home and again surprised everybody by how well she adapted to living on her own with support from the home help and the nurses who put her to bed. Unfortunately while mum was in hospital she got an ulcer on the other foot and she had the district nurse in to treat it for her.

There was a problem mum had when she returned to the centre, which was getting off the toilet. She had to ring the buzzer and wait for an attendant to come. Sometimes mum had to wait ages. Mum used to hate asking for help, which I don't blame her for, because it is not the same as going on your own.

Anyway, in late 1992 we had a new aid in one of the toilets for mum to try – this was another seat which was put on the loo at a level to suit my mum. Mum liked it and found she could use it, provided it was securely fixed. The centre manager had it fitted permanently and afterwards, mum could manage by herself.

Mum coped very well with her independence, and went to the centre twice a week having her hair done and seeing the chiropodist there on a regular basis. She went back to attending the monthly evening socials run by the M.S. Society. All I used to do was just make sure she was all right. I used to get her personal shopping and pay some of her bills for her.

Towards the end of 1993 I wanted to do something special for mum. Mum had gone through a lot over the years but had always been there for me. I wrote to Ann and Nick on the BBC programme "Good Morning". They were asking people to write in with nominations for "Christmas surprises". However, I got no reply so had to think of something else.

In March, I saw Torvill and Dean on T.V. talking about their new Ice Show and realised mum would enjoy it. Seeing an advert, I got Roland to find out about the dates, prices and wheelchair access. Roland booked 4 tickets for the first night of the show (the Saturday afternoon performances were booked up). As mum needed a helper, I asked Christine and Hilary, who worked at the Centre, if they would like to come. They agreed and Hilary volunteered to take us in her car. Mum really enjoyed the evening and the Ice Show was excellent. Mum and I were able to relax because Christine and Hilary were very good at their job and easy to get on with. They even stayed to help mum into bed so she did not have to rely on the night nurses. Quite a few years later, Hilary passed away.

Thinking back, there was something that dad could have done to make it easier for mum, although I can understand why he did not choose to do it. I felt he could have considered putting a lift in to take mum upstairs. I don't think he would have considered this, as he would have been worried about it bringing down the value of the house.

The other idea that my mum had was to sell the house to the council, and do a swap for a house that had wheelchair access. When they looked into it, dad said no because when the house was sold, the owner got half, the council got half, but you still had to pay rent (I don't know how true this was).

Another thing was when Social Services first put the handrail up, they did not put a piece of wood between the rail and the wall, and mum pulled the rail away from the wall and could have had a nasty accident. Social Services had to come back and re-do it.

The first time that Social Services got involved with mum, dad asked them if they could raise the floor up in the conservatory to the same level as the kitchen floor so that mum could get out into the conservatory more easily. Unfortunately, they said that it could not be done. My dad certainly proved them wrong. He did the job himself. To get out from the conservatory into the garden, he changed the one big step into three little steps, so that mum could get out into the garden in her wheelchair more easily. He even installed a toilet in the conservatory in the space where the larder used to be.

## Chapter Thirty Four
# Holiday

My first real holiday away from home was not too successful as I went with a friend and not my parents. I cried quite a lot of the time.

I did enjoy going to camp with the guides. With the guides I went to Cudham, the New Forest, Blackland, Foxley and Paxmeads, R.A.V.E. horse riding and Switzerland. Over the years I can remember some of the things that happened at camp.

Kizzy was one of my closest friends. When we are at camp we always wanted to be together. Eventually Kizzy and I were given a nickname – the terrible twins – because of the things we did. The leaders always wanted to separate us but didn't succeed because we wouldn't take any notice. We wanted to be together, and together we were!

At one camp, Kizzy and I went into the woods to get some wood for the camp fire. In the wood there was a great big hole in the ground. Kizzy bent over to look down the hole and she saw some wood so she looked at me and said, "Well?"

I replied, "Oh No! Don't look at me, I'm not going down there. What do you think I am?"

Anyway, Kizzy went down, saying that it was muddy. As she picked some wood up she fell over while she was throwing the wood at me to catch! I started to laugh and said, "It serves you right! You shouldn't have gone down there in the first place!"

When she got up she was covered with mud and started to panic as she cried out, "Oh Julia, how am I going to get out?"

I wasn't much help because I was laughing and replied, "The same way you got in."

Eventually Kizzy managed to climb out and because we laughed so much I lost my balance and fell backwards. When I got up, I had a patch of mud around my bottom! When we arrived back at camp they starting laughing at us. Kizzy told me to turn round and they laughed even more. Then the guider came over to us to find out what was going on. She asked, "Where have you been? I told you to get some wood not to get muddy!"

Kizzy and I replied, "We got the wood!"

The guider said, "If you found that wood in the mud, we can't burn it because it will be wet!"

We just looked at each other and then she started laughing and said, "I can't ask you two to do anything without something happening!"

Then she told us to go and change our clothes.

Another time when we went wooding, we found a whole pile of wood. We decided to carry as much as we could back to site and when the guider saw us she said, "Good, go and get some more."

When we returned with the second load she was puzzled and asked us how we came by it. So we pointed to where we collected from and she said, "Oh no! You two just don't bother to think or ask before you take it!"

Kizzy and I replied, "Well, you did tell us to use our own initiative."

The guider just looked at us and gave up on us and told us to take it back as the wood belonged to someone else.

One year I went on holiday with my friend Roseanna to Seasalter. We went with a group and we all met at the Station. We arrived early and then I burst out crying because I thought I didn't want to go.

mum just said, "Shut up!" But I didn't stop crying until it was nearly time for Roseanna and me to get into the train. Then we said, "Good-bye" waved to the mothers and off we went.

Roseanna and I slept in the same room with eight others, and we sat together at meal times. We went out together but we could not play together because of my disability. Roseanna could run around but I couldn't.

I can remember two things about that holiday. Firstly, there was a little girl who could only walk on crutches, so when we went out to play she would be in her wheel-chair and her crutches would be lying around somewhere and whenever I saw them I would walk with them and pretend that they belonged to me. The number of times I used to get away with it, but one day I didn't bother about the crutches and one of the helpers said to me, "Here – Julia, what about your crutches?"

I said, "Oh! they don't belong to me, they belong to that girl over there!"

Another time on that holiday I can remember something else that happened. I was crying bitterly because one of my teeth had fallen out! When the helper found out what I was crying for she said, "Oh! I'll tell you what we will do! Tonight we'll put this tooth under your pillow."

We did just that.

The next morning when the helper was getting me dressed, after I washed, she told me to look under the pillow. When I lifted my pillow, I found a sixpence lying there. So I gave it to the helper to look after for me. The tooth had gone.

There was one year at camp which I will never forget. Kizzy and I were in our tent talking before going to bed. Kizzy really did frighten the life out of me. She rubbed her eyes to make them red (while I wasn't looking) then she rested the torch on her chin and switched it on. I looked round and screamed! For that second I thought I saw a vampire as her two eye teeth made her look like Dracula!

One year I went camping at Elm Farm Riding School. I had a great time and Kizzy was with me. The funniest event that I can recall was while Kizzy and I were riding. One of the girls in front fell off her horse and landed in some horse manure. Kizzy and I got told off for laughing, which we couldn't understand because we thought it was funny.

During the last evening we were given a certificate to say what we had achieved with our horse riding. I could mount and dismount a horse with assistance and could stay on my horse while it walked, without help. I could ride it at a trot if someone led it by its rein etc., but there was one test I just couldn't do which was to gallop. This was because of my balance and keeping my head steady – the hat was also too big for my head and I couldn't see where I was going.

I could go on writing a lot more about camping with Kizzy as we went on so many camps with the guides. And Kizzy would love me to do just that! There was one holiday when the guides went to Switzerland on 13th – 28th August 1970 to celebrate the Diamond Jubilee. I will always remember because one of my other friends had an operation to have her bunions out before she came away with us and her feet were in plaster. We had to laugh at her because of the size of the boots she was wearing.

We all met at Victoria Station at 3 o'clock, said good-bye to our parents. At 4 o'clock we left for Folkstone Harbour. At 7 o'clock we got aboard the boat to Bouloigne, and then onto our sleeping train (I didn't get any sleep!), We had to change at Barie Station. We arrived in Interlaken at 10.30am then took a coach to Wilderswil. At 11 o'clock we arrived at the Victoria Hotel.

The weather was mostly warm, but we had a few rainy days. We visited places to have a look at around Wilderswil and Interlaken. We took a boat trip to Thun-Thuneersee and had a packed lunch at Brienz. We went to church in Interlaken and visited the mountain Murren by train. We also had a coach ride to Grusse aus Luzern for the day. We visited a place called Grindelwald by chair lift and had look round the village. The most beautiful place, to me, was when we went to Schynige Platte by a special train – the view was fantastic.

We then visited the Guides' Chalet at Adelboden. We were split into groups to have a look round and I had never seen anything like it. The views were really fantastic you could see mountains and trees.

Our journey home started at 6.30pm when the coach took us to Interlaken from Wilderswil. Then by train to Basel at 7.45pm. Then we had a night train to Bouloigne at 11.45pm. I have told you about most of the places we visited from my log book.

Jimmy Saville was the patron of the Across Trust, which was (and still is) an organization that took disabled people on holidays, but with a difference. They had coaches which were called Jumbulances. They looked like a normal coach from the outside but inside they had six beds down one side and ordinary seats down the other side. There was a small kitchen at the back where they kept the food. There was also a loo. One of my friends had been on one of these holidays and said they were very good.

In 1977, I decided to go Germany in a Jumbulance. It was very expensive but dad said I could go as I was paying for it. I had to get a passport, and decided to get a ten year one, so we sent it off, hoping that I would get it back at least a month before I went so I could get the German money. Dad had to phone the passport offfice when my passport was late in arriving as we were starting to panic. In the end the passport arrived two days before I went and I asked my adopted granddad if he could help me to change my money, as he could get it more quickly then I could – this all went well.

Dad had to take me to Westminster for the picking up point and then I said good-bye to dad and off I went. On the way to the ferry we gave the leader our passports and we stopped at a convent to collect our lunches and put them in the heater and we had our lunch on the boat.

In Germany we had a fantastic time. We visited different places – we went on a boat trip on the river Rhine and we went passed an old castle and a lot of people told me that Dracula lived there. This frightened me a bit but I decided not to believe them.

We had some lovely beer garden parties. I had a lovely helper as she was young and good fun to be with. On the last night, I shall never forget, my helper's boyfriend, who was in the army and called Richard, turned up. My helper said to me, "My boyfriend wants you to go over there."

So I went over then he asked me to put my hands out and shut my eyes. He gave me such a big cuddly bear. I was over the moon and I didn't know what to say to him. I thanked him very much and took him back to my table. The bear was so big that I had to think how I was going to carry it.

When I went to bed that night everybody wanted to see my bear, so I took it to bed with me. Because it was too big it had to lay on top of my bed. The next morning at the breakfast table before we started our journey home, that bear went round from table to table as everybody wanted to hold 'Richard' (named after who gave it to me). We said good-bye to the people who had looked after us and then we were on our way home again.

The bear went from person to person on the Jumbulance. On top of the Jumulance were two emergency sirens in case of emergencies (there was always a doctor or nurse on board with us). When everyone wanted to hold Richard, I thought to myself 'poor thing', but I didn't mind because I knew once I got it home, Richard would be with me forever!

I brought some cigarettes and a bottle of Whiskey (for my dad – although I did try it once!). Dad collected me from Westminster and before I got out of the Jumbulance, I found a way of holding my bear. To be honest I didn't really know what animal it was. I put his two front paws around my neck and the two back paws around my waist. If you took a quick look at me you would think I had a real animal with me. Dad couldn't believe his eyes when he saw it. I don't think he thought much of it but mum did.

During the holiday, one of the helpers gave me a copy of a poem from a card, but she didn't know who wrote it or what sort of card it was written for. I really do like the words and it means a lot to me. It goes like this:-

### FRIENDS

If nobody gave us a helping hand,
And nobody seemed to care,
If all the prizes of life, went to the strong.
And nobody gave us a share,
If nobody had the time to give,
A thought, to you or me,
And we had to struggle, as best we could,
What a hopeless world it would be.
Lending a hand to help the weak,
I am lightening another's load,
Doing our best with a willing heart,
Can brighten a lonely road,
Tis on something to live for,
Someone to love, that the purpose of life depends,
But there's nothing to equal the gladness, and joy,
Of making and keeping **FRIENDS!**

In 1979 I decided to go to Rome with the same organization. This time I didn't have any problem with my passport. Again dad took me to Westminster to pick up the Jumbulance. We did the same as we did when we went to Germany. I met my helper on the coach and she was a lot older than the one I had last time. She was very friendly but because I was quite able in some ways, she had difficulties knowing when I needed help and when I didn't.

On the journey I wanted to go to the loo and my helper said she would come with me. That I didn't mind, but when she came right into the room with me, I just couldn't or wouldn't go. This happened a few times and then she said she would wait outside. This was a bit better but I still couldn't go! In the end I decided to hold my water until we came to our stop.

We arrived at our first destination which was a place in Austria and on the way home we stopped in Switzerland. I ran away from my helper straight into the building and found the ladies'. By this time I was bursting to go! It was a lovely relief after holding it for so many hours. We had four days in Rome and we visited some lovely places and there was one which displayed all pictures from the time Jesus was born until the time he died on the cross.

Now I have done an art course I probably would have appreciated this more than I did then. One of the nuns said that she would take me and my helper around the convent, but I believe I went to the loo and when I came back they had gone. Now I wish I had looked around the convent as over the past few years I have often wondered what it was like inside because some can be really beautiful.

I didn't get a chance to lay down on one of the beds in the jumbulance to find out what it felt like. I can understand when people say that some journeys are too long because I don't think I could lay in one place for a long time especially if you are severely disabled, but I must say the staff really did go out of their way to look after their passengers.

When Roland was at Ladywell, I was on a course for a year, studying Government and Politics, just to get the basic background. I was invited to go to Strasbourg and Brussels to see how the European Parliament and European Commission worked. We were allowed to ask questions and meet some of the members there. I asked Roland if he would like to come with me, and he said that he would. I was amazed that he wanted to come.

While we were there we also visited the First World War Museum, which was very interesting. We stayed in several hotels, some of which were really posh. In one hotel, there was a mini-bar fridge, and I told Roland not to drink anything from it because it was very dear.

During one mealtime, I asked for a chocolate mousse for my desert. When it arrived, it was the size of a basin! Everybody at my table had a piece of it and said how lovely it was. I still couldn't finish it, and asked Roland if I could take it up to my room. He said, "No way!". Luckily for me, one of the other members of the group took it up for me anyway! Even then I could not manage to eat it all.

Another time when we went out one evening, it was raining and we got really wet but we didn't get cold because the temperature was still warm.

During the year 2000, Roland and I decided that we would like to go to Bethlehem with the Jumbulance. We paid all our money but then a couple of weeks later they went bankrupt. However, we were lucky enough to get our money back (after threatening them with court action).

The Jumbulance service was bought up by a company in Scotland, who still organize holidays for the disabled (but now only to Lourdes).

During the 1980s, I believe, I went to Brittany in France with another day centre called Arthur Morris. I shared a room with another girl from the day centre. Also on holiday with us was a man from the Ladywell Day Centre, called Alfie, who I got on well with. Everybody thought we were going out together, but we weren't really.

A lot of people were moaning about the holiday because they felt that there wasn't much to do there, but I said that a holiday is what you make it. I did have quite a good time on this holiday.

When we came back home, Alfie didn't come to the centre for a couple of weeks and some of the members were getting a bit concerned about him. They knew that I knew where Alfie lived, and that he was a good friend of mine. I said that I would go round and see how he was. Unfortunately, when I got there I had the shock of my life. Alfie let me in and we had a short chat and then he asked me if I would like a drink and something to eat. His flat was quite bare and I said that I would ask a lady called Katie, from Social Services Committee, if she could get him some decent second hand items for the flat like a cooker, table and chairs and some furniture.

The kitchen was quite nearby, and before I realised it, he had picked up a knife and was pointing it towards me. The only thing I could think of was to get out quick. I managed to leave quickly and went for a bus ride to calm me down.

After a couple of weeks, I found out what was behind his behaviour. It turned out that because he had a drawer that was stuck, he used to always use a knife to open it, and that was all he was preparing to do!

I said, "why didn't you bloody well tell me that in the first place?" He could really see the funny side of it, and so could I.

I went to Jersey with my parents. We flew over and dad hired a car for the week. We stayed at St. Hellen's and the hotel was very good, including the staff. At meal times we had a very friendly waiter and he was very good to mum, and remembered her because he was on duty every time my parents went. They managed to get the same room as well.

Every day we visited a different part of the Island and we found one place that we really liked for afternoon tea, and I believe it was convenient for mum and her wheelchair. Opposite our hotel there was a castle out in the sea. When the tide was out you could walk to the castle and take a boat when the tide was in. I asked if we could go out there. Dad agreed and we left mum on the promenade while we walked out to the castle and had a look round and then we came back.

As the weather was very hot, while mum was waiting for us she caught the sun. Her nose really did get burnt and dad and I took the mickey out of her. It was very painful and she had a blister which made it worse. I just couldn't stop laughing!

In our room there were three beds. We pushed two together and left one on its own. Mum's bed was near the bathroom to make it easier for her wheelchair, and my bed was near dad. As dad had a habit of snoring, one night when he stopped breathing it really did frighten me. I decided to wake him up to see if he was all right and he was. Anyway, for rest of the holiday I couldn't really sleep. Mum told me that he did it a lot at home. This did worry me for a long tiime afterwards and then I found out that it doesn't hurt the person.

There were a couple of places that I would have liked to have seen but we didn't know where or how to get there. One was the German Hospital which was built during the war and the other was the glass church. As my parents had been out there a few times they brought me back a book and post cards of these places. I'm glad I didn't go to the German Hospital because dad said it was very, very cold and frightening, but it gave you a good impression of what it was like during the war days.

In November 1991 after I finished my O.U. exams, I booked a holiday in Majorca with Christian Holidays who used Thomson's. Roy and Olive drove me to Gatwick Airport along with Roland to see me off. We set off at about five in the morning. It was dark and pouring with rain. Luckily Roy is an experienced driver who knew the route and we arrived in good time. We had a drink and they saw me off. An Airport employee took me in a small electric car to the plane and helped me belt up.

Though both Christian Holidays and Thomson's were told that I needed help with my luggage at the airport, nothing was done. Later we were told it was because we had not told Christian Holidays what specific help I needed and because we had phoned Thomson's and not put it in writing. Roland had to ask the Thomson agent at the airport to make sure I was helped. Unlike Heathrow you walk straight into the plane from the gangway. There were no steps to climb which explained perhaps why they looked so blank when Roland insisted I needed help getting into the plane.

The contrast with Aer Lingus, who had been so efficient and caring on my trip to Ireland, could not have been greater. The staff at Majorca airport were good with helping me off the plane and luckily a young female tourist, who I asked to help me, took my case from the Customs to the coach for me, even though she was on a different tour.

When we arrived at the hotel, a fellow tourist carried my suitcase to my room. I found that I was the only person in my room (a double) – which was really great. This meant that I could do things the way I did them at home without being embarrassed by another person in the room.

The first problem I faced was at the evening meal because we had to line up to get the starter. I just asked Lorna who was on my table if she could give me a hand. Lorna was only too happy to help. I didn't want Lorna to have to be my helper at every meal time so I sat at her table for breakfast, another person's table for lunch and another person's table for supper. This way I got to know a lot of people and I felt that I wasn't relying on one person.

I sat with Leo and her friend. It was really great to see that the Lord had heard my prayer as I was asking God who could help me to have a bath and wash my hair. After a while, Leo asked me if there was anything that I really wanted to do but couldn't do. I admitted I needed help getting into and out of the bath and washing my hair. Leo agreed to help saying that her experience as district nurse meant she was used to it.

Leo was great fun to be with and we certainly had some good laughs. One laugh was when she tried to get me out of the bath. I was trying to climb out her way and we both slipped and we just burst out laughing.

On Wednesday, Leo asked me to join her table for the rest of the holiday. I didn't know what to say as I didn't want to hurt the ones I had been with and also we would have to tell the waiter. Nobody minded and there was no bad feeling, which I was grateful for. Leo and I had become friends. I also made friends with about ten of the other tourists.

During the early mornings and evenings we had a time of prayer and bible reading, which you didn't have to go to but I went to most of them and found them quite a blessing. The outings were organised by Thomson and they had to be booked and paid for on the first evening of our stay. One of the outings was to a cave, which was very beautiful. I had to have quite a lot of help walking down the steps as there were so many. Once down there you could sit on a seat. The lights went out then a boat went by playing music, different shades of light around the cave made it very fascinating. It was worth all the effort of getting down there. Coming back, I didn't want to walk up all those steps so I went on a boat. I put my hand in the water and it was lovely and cold.

Another outing was to a jewellery factory and it was fascinating to watch. They must have very steady hands. I bought a pair of earrings, which I gave to Margaret as she did a lot for me.

On another outing we went up the mountain by coach, which was very beautiful. It was frightening when you looked out of the window because we felt we were right on the edge of the road.

I became friendly with Elizabeth and her friends. One evening I was invited to have coffee with them in their room. As Elizabeth works in London, when we got back, I met her in her dinner hour and we had lunch together and exchanged each other's news.

Most evenings at about 9pm, I would go for a long walk along the beach with Eric, Stuart, Lorna and Brian. We would chat, laugh, look at the stars in the sky and sing praises to God. On the last night we agreed to go to the beach to see the sun rising the next day. Lorna asked me to wake her at four in the morning, which I did. At 5am, we were all ready and went to the beach and watched the sun rising. It was really beautiful.

Leo and her friend said that I could stay with them on the journey home. I was very pleased about this because it meant I would have nothing to worry about. I said good-bye to all the friends I met, and thanked the ones who helped me. We were over an hour late getting back to London. David and Roland were waiting for me. Leo and I said good-bye at the airport but have kept in touch.

The following year, I went to Ireland on a coach tour with Pat P. and we had a good time and got on really well. She took some photographs and wrote on the back where they were all taken.

I went to Ireland again, later, with Roland – another coach tour. This time we went to a different part, where Bally Kissangel was filmed and it was exactly the same! It was great. We also went to visit the Blarney Stone (but didn't kiss it!) This was the best trip of the holiday.

Roland took a picture of me outside a pub near the door, and I think I must have looked drunk. Unfortunately, none of the pictures came out and we were disappointed.

We went back to Ireland again with Edina, who is a friend of Roland and mine. We visited Kieran and his family and went to eat at a posh restaurant called the Titanic. It was out of this world.

The next year, I went again with Jo, but because I was not well, we could not meet up with Kieran. We went to a zoo with Jo and we were allowed to pick up some of the animals. I had a rabbit on my lap. When Jo went to pick it up, it weed all up her sleeve. When she put the rabbit back John shut the gate and took a picture of her while she was trying to get out.

One day we were driving down a country lane and John said "Here comes the cow". Jo thought he was talking about her. When we got a bit further she realised John had seen a herd of cows!

In 2003, I went on holiday with Through the Roof to Cyprus. I had a lovely carer, called Georgie. We both wondered how we were going to hit it off, but there were no problems and we got on really well. Her boyfriend, John, came with us and was looking after another man (who was a bit of a so-and-so).

We hired a car for a couple of days, which was very helpful, and we went on a couple of trips around the island.

Ever since that holiday, I have kept in touch with Georgie and John and we ring each other every other week.

Georgie, John and I went back to Cyprus the year after, but not with Through the Roof. We were not expecting to meet up with them on that holiday but we did. One morning at breakfast, Jenny came over to me and said, "Was it you who spoke about having difficulties going to church on the Don McClean show on Sunday morning?" I said that it was me. Jenny told me that Don had got through to her as I did not get back to Don. Don asked for my details and sent me an autographed picture of himself and a pen for Roland.

Jenny Edwards is the lady in charge of the disabled Christian holidays. She also works alongside with Master Sun, who are a Christian holiday company. After my last two experiences of being on holidays organised by Jenny, I feel that any problems relating to our care, falls to Master Sun and not to Jenny. Any carers that come with us on holiday must be Christian. They must fill out a form detailing their religious practices. If the carers do not comply with the Christian standards set out by Master Sun, then they are not allowed to accompany the disabled person on holiday. The task of having to tell the disabled person that they cannot take their own carer, because of religious reasons, falls to Jenny.

The reason why Master Sun insist that all carers must be Christians is that during the holidays, there are several worship meetings that we are encouraged to attend. In my opinion, the main qualification that carers should have when accompanying a disabled person is that they provide good care for the person they are working with. Whether they are Christians or not should be a secondary issue, and should not stop them from accompanying the disabled person on holiday. I therefore feel sorry for Jenny sometimes, as she has to go by Master Sun's rules and has the job of telling some disabled Christians that they cannot bring their own choice of carer or personal assistant, who they feel comfortable with.

On a different note, Jenny sends out the 'Come Fishing' tape, which is sent out every month. On one side are some hymns and songs and an update on the activities of Through the Roof, and on the other side is a bible sermon given by Jenny. Jenny makes a really good job of these and sometimes I feel that these tapes are a blessing to me.

In May 2005, Georgie, John and I decided to go to Portugal. The holiday offered swimming with dolphins and this was my main reason for choosing this holiday.

We had thought about going to America, but because my eyesight was so poor we thought that it may have been a waste of money until we knew what the outcome was after my operation. It was much easier to swim with the dolphins in Portugal.

Georgie e-mailed the people at the dolphin swimming centre and it took quite a while for them to e-mail her back. In the end, we asked Roland to contact them directly. They told Roland that they would make an appointment for me to see the supervisor at 1 o'clock on $3^{rd}$ May, and she would say a final 'yes' or 'no' as to whether I could go in to swim with the dolphins. If I could not, they would say that I could sit on the edge of the pool and they would come up to me. This was ok, as I knew that I would have contact with the dolphins one way or the other. Roland made a point of saying to me not to get too disappointed if I was not allowed to get right in with them.

We went to meet the supervisor with an open mind, but they decided that it would be too dangerous for me to swim right in with the dolphins. However, they said that if I went back at about 3.45pm that day, they would allow me to play with one of the dolphins accompanied by one of the staff. This is what I did. I was able to get out of the wheelchair and sit on the ground sideways. It was still quite difficult for me to be able to stroke the dolphins in this position and I couldn't really see them very well. Having said this, I was satisfied at being this close to a dolphin and being able to touch one.

Later that evening when we got back, Georgie said that she would love to go in the water with them. This would give me a second chance to stroke the dolphins again, but this time to be more prepared, e.g. to have my swimming costume on and take my trousers and shoes off, and put my feet in the water and be able to get more close to them. This time it went really well. I got loads of kisses, I rubbed their bellies with my feet and I saw a little baby dolphin of eight months old. They both talked to me! Then they waved goodbye to me with their fins. The adult dolphin's name was Toby and the one I saw before was Lula. This was very worthwhile.

When you go for the day to the dolphin centre, you automatically get a video of your day to bring back with you. Georgie is going to give me a copy of this. We could understand why it would be so difficult for somebody like me, who is not a strong swimmer, to go in with the dolphins, and why they made this decision.

After we had done this, Georgie read out the e-mail that she had received from them, stating that they were not trained to take disabled people into the water with the dolphins. It was good that Roland had rung them up directly and sorted this out for me.

In the evening and during the daytime, Georgie and John read a lot to me. John would bring his own book – 'Running with the Moon', by Johnny Bealby, and I took my own book for them to read to me, which was the autobiography of Max Bygraves.

We did a lot of talking over the holidays about all sorts of things. We went to the beach a lot and eat out on a couple of nights. I enjoyed the Chinese meal the best, and also Pizza Hut. The English restaurant was not so good as the food was too salty.

We had a very good cab driver – we could not have asked for better. He was so friendly and helpful, and we managed to get him both times we went out.

This is the first holiday I had ever been on where it had been really hot for the whole two weeks. We came back really brown and Edina was very jealous of me!

When Georgie, John and I got back home, Roland was here and we all got on well. Rosie started to play with John's bag strap, which was so funny to watch because she was so excited.

During Easter week in 2007, I went to Lourdes. This was one place I had always wanted to go to. It was a very interesting holiday as I learnt so much about Sister Benedict's life and times. I went on my own, with a carer who was organised for me by the Across team. We travelled to Lourdes by Jumbulance.

Tim and Lesley took me to the pick-up point at Maidstone and I said my goodbyes to them.

I had a really good time. We had three helpers/carers for the duration of our trip, who were all sisters. Two of them could play the flute, and the other one was an excellent singer. She could sing in Latin and it sounded amazing.

On the way there, we had an old Jumbulance, but on the way home we had one of the new ones. You could really see how they had been improved. There was more space for your legs and there was a footrest that you could put your feet on. There was more choice of meals on the journey, probably because of a better kitchen. You could eat and drink at any time you wanted.

A couple of days after I got home from the holiday, I opened my handbag to take out the remainder of the money that I had taken with me on holiday. I had about 300 Euros left, and Roland and I panicked because we could not find it. Roland kept looking but with no success. In the end, we had to email the Across and let them know. We thought that it may have fallen out onto the floor of the Jumbulance. I knew that my helper was going away on holiday and we had to wait for her to come back. When she came back from her holiday, she got in touch and told Roland exactly where to find it. She had zipped it into a side compartment of my handbag. This was a new handbag and the zip was right at the top – in a different place to where it was in my old handbag, and not easy to find.

It was such a relief to find the money.

Roland and I decided to ask Helen, Tim and Lesley to see if they could find the place in my handbag where we had found the money. Not one of them found it! Lesley even had the same handbag and she still didn't know it was there.

I am hoping that the helper I had will come and visit me, as she said she would.

*Chapter Thirty Five*

# Verdant Lane

I decided to take a flat in Verdant Lane and signed the Agreement on 6th October, 1990 and moved in on 16th October, 1990. Kitty and her mum lived just down the road and helped me to wash all the paintwork. As some of the floorboards were wet, I had to call the council in and they replaced the pipe under the bath, which was broken. The plumber refused to put back the hardboard around the bath saying it was the carpenter's job! I didn't bother because I didn't know how long I would have to wait and managed to put the hardboard in place myself, but was unable to do the screws.

As my father was no longer with us I had to arrange moving myself. At that time I used to belong to a Christian fellowship which met in Deptford Town Hall and the pastor said they would help me when I moved, but they never did. It was David, Alan and Roland who helped me move. Alan had a small van which meant it took four to six journeys to move all my stuff. David also fitted new curtain rails and hung my old curtains. For my birthday and Christmas present, Pat B. bought and made up the curtains for the kitchen and bathroom and hung them up. It was a nice present.

Kitty came with me when I selected the carpet and the shop came and measured my flat and estimated the cost. I accepted their quote, and they fitted the carpet and I was very pleased with the result. As there was no heating in the flat, I bought a gas fire for my living room. Roland took the measurements and went with me to the Gas show room when I bought it. In December, Pat B. told me about Creda electric heating which used "Economy 7" electricity. I thought this might be a good idea and decided to have a heater in the living room, the hall and the bedroom. The Electricity Board gave me a gadget to help me turn the switches, which worked well. I had the heater in the living room so I could be sure of heating in case the heater or gas fire failed. The problem with the Creda heating was that it didn't really warm the flat up. It just took the chill off which wasn't much good if you wanted to relax.

The next job was the kitchen. It was very difficult and I just did not know where to start. I had to ask the lady from upstairs to light the pilot light for the hot water when it went out on me. There was a tall cupboard in one corner which I had removed, and Albert, a friend, covered up the old fashioned ventilation duct which made the kitchen very cold. Albert and his son-in-law wallpapered for me. It took them ages! Stripping the old wallpaper off, they found five layers on top of one another and had to borrow a steam stripper from a friend of theirs.

I decided to buy an electric cooker rather than a gas cooker because I thought it would be safer. There was no pilot light that might need relighting and no risk of gas escaping if I had trouble turning it off or lighting it. It had two ovens, a large oven at the bottom which I could use if I had guests (who could remove the hot meal from it for me), and a small oven which I usually used because it had a pull down door on which I could rest my meal until it was cool enough for me to lift safely. It also had a glass top, which I thought would be easier to clean.

Dawn G., who was in charge of the office at Ladywell and is a friend of mine, showed me her washing machine because she thought it would be the ideal model for me. I liked it because the push buttons made it easy for me to operate with my disability. The tumble dryer was also useful because I tend to wear a lot of jumpers and trousers. My mum paid for it and Dawn went with me to the shop to order it. I arranged for a plumber to plumb it in. One of my friends told me about Robin, who was a carpenter, and had fitted their kitchen for them. I wanted a worktop, the level of the cooker, right round to the sink so that I could slide things across without lifting – for example, saucepans with hot water in them. He put cupboards under the worktops with a space for the washing machine to go in. Robin finished most of the job and was supposed to come back and finish the edges of the worktops but he never did.

It didn't work out as I hoped. The washing machine stopped me from using the corner cupboard and the washing machine was longer than the worktop and got in my way when I used the microwave oven.

Veronica, the Council Housing Officer who assisted disabled people needing aids or building alterations, come round and gave me a few ideas as to where to put the washing machine but there wasn't a satisfactory solution. I couldn't move the microwave to the other side as there were no electric points. The microwave oven also prevented me from sliding the saucepans across the work surface to the sink.

The next problem I had was the wall under the sink – which was wet and had black patches here and there. When the council came to investigate they said it was coming from the washing machine. I didn't believe them because the washing machine hadn't been there long. The council plumber came to fix it and I think he cured it – but I couldn't be sure because the wall still looked black and damp. Then I had water coming in through the kitchen roof and once again the council dealt with that.

I had never liked the bathroom but I cannot put my finger on the reasons why. It had a funny smell which I thought came from the old pipes underneath the bath. The bath was old fashioned with high sides and very difficult (if not risky) for me to get into without help. I preferred washing in the kitchen and having a bath at a friend's than using my bathroom.

After living there for two years, the council agreed to replace the bath with a shower and also fitted a hand rail from my front door to the front gate. In winter the path was often slippery. The shower was fitted but when I used it the water went straight through the 'water proof' curtain making the floor wet and slippery and there was a long delay fitting the shower seat. Veronica arranged for a new curtain to be fitted but it took over eight months for them to fit the shower seat. As I needed the shower seat to hold on to in the shower, I was unable to use it until the seat was fitted, and had to bath at a friend's house. The controls for the shower were too difficult for me to handle, so I used to leave the shower running and switch it off and on by pulling a cord which controlled the mains.

The handrail in the front garden came away from the wall because the section nearest the wall was moveable to allow dustmen to remove my wheelie dustbin. This had to be re-fixed more securely.

I have often had problems when contacting my local Housing Officer. Some of the staff there often seem to lack any patience or understanding when dealing with people with speech or hearing problems. One Housing Officer thought I owned and drove a car, which was in fact my upstairs neighbour's, and seemed unable to accept that I had any disability. When I asked Roland to contact them on my behalf he encountered similar rudeness and an unhelpful manner. For example, informing them that a cheque had not been credited to my rent account despite the bank confirming the Council had cashed it was met by them asking if he lived with me – despite him having explaining why he was phoning on my behalf!

When I was living at Bargery Road, as I have said, I had Maureen or Sylvia to fall back on when I wanted my room tidied or hovered. I was promised that I would get a home help when I moved into the flat. Unfortunately, I didn't inform or remind them. As it got put back further and further, my friends reminded me that I had left it a bit late and felt that I would not be able to get one. I thought they could be right. I only wanted one once a fortnight – I felt that the home help may not be a regular one and I might have different one each time. Because of this, I did not bother to chase it up.

When I first moved in, Kitty's mum gave me a hoover but I found it too heavy for me to use. I couldn't push the brush along the carpet. Pat B. and I went to Alders in Bromley to buy some items and their staff were excellent when we told them what I wanted. They got down three or four different types of hovers for me to try out. After I tried them all I particularly like the 'Electrolux Lite 1000' (they also helped with the iron and ironing board.) The hoover was easy to use, moved around on wheels, and changing the bag wasn't too difficult – and Roland used to do that for me. When I did the hoovering I couldn't push the broom backwards and forwards as I pressed too hard and it got stuck in the carpet. The only way I could use the hoover was by using the narrow tube bit without the brush and go from side to side. This worked very well but it took a long time. I used to wash the kitchen floor by hand. Sometimes I think it is better by hand.

Cooking could be a problem because I had to be careful and work out what I could cook or make before hand. There are things I would love to eat, for example, pancakes. I could make the mixture with the hand mixer but frying and turning them over is too difficult to attempt. Another example, is separating the egg white from the yoke. To do this I used a Betterware dish. I used to crack the egg in – any stray shell would stay at the bottom – and move the dish from side to side to separate the white from the yolk. This worked very well.

I liked the traditional glass milk bottle because of the neck. I could lift the bottle by the neck using one hand and pour milk from it by resting the bottle in my arm and lifting the bottom with my other hand. The modern glass squat milk bottles have no neck which means I cannot use them as I can only lift them using both hands. I do use this method for most bottles like salad cream etc. Another technique I've discovered is sticking blue tack round the top of a bottle to get a better grip if it is hard to unscrew. A T.V. show had suggested putting a rubber band round the top. One night I could not unscrew a top but realised I would not be able to put a rubber band round the top with my disability. I thought blue tack could do the same job and it worked.

I now have cartons and have to use a plastic gadget with which I pierce the carton and pour milk through. I prefered Marks and Spencer's cartons which had arched rather than the usual flat tops because the latter would tend to spill over when you pierced them. I am really pleased to see that Marks and Spencer have improved their carton of milk by having a pull on top. I'm sure lots of people find their milk a lot easier to open. I used to use my finger to push the top bit backwards, then I had to hold those two bits back, then I used to get the fork and stick it where the join was at the middle, and pull it towards me. This used to open the lid of the carton and then you could just pour it out. The other way I used to do it was to turn it round to the side, get a knife, put the knife in, in the shape of a 'v', push that bit down – which made a pourer, and then just pour it out.

When I used to buy yoghurt or a similar product with a sealed foil top, 9 out of 10 times when I tried to pull it open, it would tear or break off and I would have nothing to get hold of to pull back. The first time I tried to open it a different way, I tried to put a spoon through the foil. I had to press hard and it ended up splashing out everywhere.

The other method I tried was to cut around the edges with my sharp-bladed vegetable knife, which was small and more easy to control. That did the job just right! I had to be very careful how I held the knife though!

Because I could not use a tin opener, Social Services gave me one that you put on the wall with a little tray under it. It had a magnet on the tin opener so that when the lid had been taken off, the tin would stay up there. I would then pull the lever to let go of the tin, and the tin would fall into the tray. Then I used to get a tea towel, fold it in half, and then half again, put it against my chest and then pull the tin towards me, so that if I spilled anything it would go onto my tea towel and not into me. I would then carry it to the saucepan and pour the contents in.

I had to have Ribena in glass bottles because when I poured from the bottle I held it in my arm when I lifted it by hand. The plastic bottles, unless half full, would often spill over as my arm squeezed the bottle because I jerked or lacked control over my muscles. I can't peel grapefruits or oranges because of my hand control, and sometimes they can be too big for me to hold. I have even tried cutting them in half and then cutting round the edges but this is too mucky. I can peel tangerines and satsumas if they are soft, so I do not eat them that often! I did used to eat grapefruits and oranges at the Ladywell Centre with Irene and Irene in the W.R.V.S shop. They would peel them and cut them up for me. Mind you they had to be sweet otherwise I would put some sugar on them or I wouldn't eat them!

For peeling potatoes, I used to get a tea towel, put it over my lap by sitting on the floor, put the potato in between my legs, get the peeler and peel it with my left hand and turn the potato round as I went along. That used to work very well. The peel used to go all over the place and I had to pick it all up but it did do the trick. I used to have a gadget that could slice and cut the potatoes into chip shapes, which made life easier for me. The only trouble was that sometimes I used to cut my hands because it was so sharp, but I soon leant my lesson.

I found the microwave very useful for cooking, the only trouble I had was with ready made meals that had a film across them. I found it very hard to peel them off, even more so if you had to leave it on until after the meal is cooked. They rarely seem to leave a corner bit to help you peel it off and it seldom comes off in one go! I usually cut around a corner with a knife before I put it in to give me a start when I take it out. When I made hot chocolate in the microwave I only filled the mug three-quarters full at the most, in case I jerked when I took it out and spilt it over my hands. When I got it out I wrapped a towel around my hands and the mug before lifting it. I tried with a tea towel but it was too thin and not big enough. I would top up the hot milk with cold milk. I would then get a straw, stir it up, and drink it.

Because I could not carry too much, I had to shop in small amounts, often buying my meals daily. Roland often bought the heavier stuff for me, like Ribena, washing powder, bleach etc.

When I lived completely on my own I had to find a way of doing my top buttons up. If I put a jumper or T-shirt over a blouse with a collar on it, it used to take a lot of fiddling for me to get the collar straight. I overcame this problem by holding the first jumper's collar with my teeth while putting the second one on so that the collars were even. I learnt to do my shoe laces up over a period of time, but could not do a double knot.

I preferred to have my shoe laces tied up in a double knot because it was very difficult for me to tie them up if they came loose while I was out. When I first started doing my shoes up I could only do one bow, which wasn't always tight enough, and I would tuck the end in my shoes so people wouldn't see it. I could later do two bows and eight out of ten times it was enough. I still got people to do them up for me occasionally.

One occasion I won't forget, was when I was walking down Lewisham High Street and my shoelace came undone. Seeing a copper walking toward me, I stopped and asked him if he would do my shoe up. He gave such a look and asked me if I could not do it myself. He reluctantly did do it for me. I wonder if he was thinking that if he bent down I might hit him on the head!

Up until 1992 people always had to do my coats up with a zip for me. One day when I bought myself a new jacket, I got it home and realised it did up on the boy's side. As I am left handed it was ideal because it meant that I could do it up myself. After a little practise I found a way to do it, by holding the right side of the zip still by bringing my right arm across if there was nothing to hold it with, and pulling the end of zip in with my left hand. This worked very well but it was easier to sit down doing it as I had more control and was more stable. Sometimes it could take ages, especially when my hand could not get hold of the zip properly, when I was in a hurry or when there were people around me.

Early one winter morning, I got up and went into the living room, shutting the door because it was cold. When I tried to leave the room I just could not open the door! I knew that Kitty, who had my spare keys, could not open my front door as I had the chain on. I rang Roland up for suggestions. He said if I could unlock the window lock and open the window a bit, he could open the window and climb through. The only alternative was to smash the glass panel on the front door so the chain could be undone. It took me over half an hour to open the window. In the meantime I had phoned Kitty who knocked on my neighbour's door and he managed to climb in through the window and open the living room door by tightening the screws on the door handle. Because I was cold, Kitty lent me her jumper. She really wanted me to ring up the Fire

Brigade, but I said no way! Roland arrived while this was going on, having come straight over by bus. He was not amused when Kitty and I explained that we thought he might not be able to climb through the window. The neighbour who had done so was a senior citizen in his 70s. After this experience, I never again put the chain on my door.

Just as I moved to Verdant Lane, they brought out a new bus route with a stop a few steps from my front door. Kitty was quite annoyed because they had been living there for years and wanted a stop to be put there. The 284 bus would stop there and went to all the places I went to – Catford, Ladywell (near the Centre) and Lewisham.

Another experience I went through when I moved to Verdant Lane was a delay in my income support payments. Shortly after I moved my old payment book ran out but no replacement arrived. I had informed the DHSS when I moved and it turned out that they wanted me to put in a new claim, but no one told me. In the meantime, I received no money. I did not experience the same hassle when I moved to Bargery Road.

## *Chapter Thirty Six*
# Forest Hill

During the 1990s, I was getting really fed up with living in Verdant Lane. The more I stayed there, the more problems I was facing. To begin with, I didn't like the bathroom – it was really creepy. Some people will know what I mean – there was a really weird atmosphere. I would have a quick wash, but then would come out again as soon as possible. The council replaced the old bath with a shower, but it still didn't make much difference to the atmosphere. The whole flat was not designed for anybody with a disability. In the end, I decided to get hold of Veronica, the housing officer for disabled people who dealt with my mum and was now assigned to me, and who knew me quite well. She also helped me to get in to Bargery Road.

When Veronica came round to visit me, she was very shocked to see the accommodation that I had been given. She agreed to take me on again and wrote a stiff letter to the housing officer who gave me the flat. When Roland and I first looked round this flat, we were impressed by the size and the space. However it was only after I moved in that I realised how cold the flat was. There was no central heating and I had to buy a gas fire out of my own money. I also had to buy an Economy 7 heater to help heat the flat. I managed to work out how this worked eventually, but it still seemed like a big waste of money. The kitchen was less than ideal and the bathroom was not equipped for anyone with a disability.

In the end, through Veronica's help, I got offered a nice modern maisonette, which was partly central heated in Normanton Street in Forest Hill. I decided to take everything I had with me to Normanton Street from Verdant Lane. The only problem I had was that I had to dump the gas fire.

Normanton Street had a large living room, quite a big kitchen, a bathroom and one bedroom. Again, I managed to get all my things in. I had to have it decorated by a friend. I was quite happy there. There were lots of shops just round the corner, where I made some friends, and a bus stop nearby. I got friendly with the neighbour who lived up the road, who was a Christian. The lady above me was very helpful and used to keep an eye on my place. However, as time went by, a couple of things began to happen to frighten me.

Roland and a few of my friends thought that I would benefit from having a home help. My friend, Pat B., managed to find me a home help, who was a friend of her mum's. The home help was called Marina. I used to pay her £15 every 3 weeks and she would clean my flat thoroughly. She was a good worker and I got to know her quite well and was very grateful to her. I will tell you one thing that she used to do. She would take all my teddy bears down off the shelves, wipe the shelves, and put them all back up again.

I have now lost touch with Marina. I heard that she later was doing a part time course at college, and I hope she achieved what she wanted.

One day I had a frightening experience. Outside my front door, there was a path and one day when I came home from Ladywell I got inside, went to take my jacket off and went back to the front door to pick up my letters. As I looked at the front door I saw a man standing there, which panicked me. The door was still shut but I could see him through the glass. I rang up Roland, and he phoned the police. The police came round quickly but he was gone.

Another thing that frightened me was as there was no gate to the front garden, if anyone wanted to get the attention of the lady above me in the maisonette, they would stand in front of my window, and this happened on several occasions.

Another frightening time was when the police came banging on my door. When I answered it, they said they were looking for somebody upstairs. I said that the only person I knew upstairs was a lady. This made me a bit wary.

I used to spend a lot of time at Roland's place, and come home now and again. One particular day I came home and found the bottom pane of glass on my front door had been boarded up with wood. Had I had a break-in? I thought I would go in and be prepared for the worst. I had a quick look round and thought it was odd because nothing was missing. I went back to the front door and found a little booklet from the police, saying that they had broken-in. I rang up Roland and explained to him what I had found. He rang up the police station and they told him what had happened.

Because no one had seen me for a while, the neighbours thought that I might have had an accident, and called the police. The police had to break in to check the flat and then boarded up the glass again.

I had a garden when I was living at Forest Hill and Verdant Lane. Because they both needed a lot of work doing to them, I did not take a lot of interest in them and was not prepared to spend money on them. Therefore, they just got left.

When I moved to Woolwich in the year 2000, I had an area in the back and the front of the house where I could grow roses and other plants. It was only when I moved here, to my bungalow in Woolwich, that I started to have an interest in the garden, because I felt that this was the place where I wanted to stay for a long time.

## *Chapter Thirty Seven*
# Friends

This chapter is going to be about my relationship with Carl and male friends.

I started going out with Carl because he was a member of the Penny Farthing Club. At the time I wanted to find out where one of my male friends, Jack, lived. Carl and I went out to different places without success.

Carl and I decided to go out on a weekly basis to the pub. Sometimes we went on a day's outing to either Margate or Ramsgate. Most of the time I paid my share. Carl and I went out on and off for about ten years or more. I liked him, but didn't love him. I suppose you could say I just wanted to go out with someone. During the ten years nothing changed, we were happy to be friends. I could not have a serious relationship because I felt I would not have been able to have spend the rest of my life with him. We never talked about marriage.

I wrote a poem about our relationship at the time, it went like this:-

> Do I really want to marry?
> This man I'm supposed to love?
> Do I really love him?
> Does he really love me?
> And yet he never shows his love,
> I know he isn't a Christian,
> There's so much to think about,
> All the fors and againsts,
> Money isn't the problem,
> Housing isn't neither,
> All the things I ask myself,
> Could I bear to live with him?
> Have I enough patience for him?
> Would I really let myself go?
> To be what he wants me to be,
> Its not only the give and take,
> Yet I know all the answers,
> But how do I tell him?
> As he is so good to me,
> When I just take him for a friend.

One evening we went out for a drink, and he told me that he did not want to see me anymore, because he had a new girlfriend. I was shocked to find he had a girlfriend as I had no idea he was seeing anyone else. Deep down inside me, I was glad that he had found someone else, but on the other hand, I was sad because we had been friends for such a long time, and I wanted our friendship to continue, but I knew this was the end.

Pamela, Carl's new girlfriend, was a very nice person, in her own way. She was inclined to be bossy and wanted to have her own way in everything. I met her after Carl asked me to join them for a drink (I wish I hadn't bothered). We went into a pub and while Carl was buying the drinks, Pamela asked me all sorts of questions, about my relationship with Carl. At that time I felt it had nothing to do with her, but she kept on about it. "If I had known him for ten years, why hadn't I married him?" I didn't know what to say to her because we never really thought about it, and I told her that I didn't love him.

I hoped this was the end of the matter, but I was wrong. She was very persistent so in the end I got up and walked out. Then no more was said until a couple of months later, when Pamela bumped into me at Lewisham. We went into Littlewoods to have a drink and she told me she was engaged to Carl but there was something wrong. I was pleased to hear the news, but rather surprised. We said good-bye, but another couple of months later, we met up again. Pamela had changed and I couldn't put my finger on it. She had mixed feelings about Carl, and started agreeing with me about the way I felt towards Carl. After all this talk about Carl I was pleased to hear that Pamela had finally realised the way I felt about him.

There was one occasion that really did shock me. Pamela asked me to pop in for a drink; when I arrived Carl answered the door in such a bad mannered way that I thought why on earth did I bother – so I just turned round and walked off. Eventually Pamela went back to her previous boyfriend. Pamela used to invite me down to Ashford where they lived for the weekend. I put it off as long as I could, and then finally managed to find enough courage to go and visit. We used to meet at Bromley South Station and catch a train to Ashford, then take a cab to her house. It was a lovely area with only a few houses here and there. Her house was surrounded by fields. Over the weekend her boyfriend Tom took us out and it was very enjoyable. Sometimes I used to take my homework, otherwise I would become bored. Most of the time when I was with Pamela, she tried to mother me which irritated me. But I still liked to be friends with them.

There were three occasions which were quite frightening at the time, but now I can see the funny side. One day when I was due to go home, Tom was at work and Pamela had agreed to walk with me to the bus stop which was about half a mile away. But when it was time, she said she was unwell – having asked me to stay another day, which I had said no to. Having thanked her for having me, I began to walk down this long country road, which was nerve-wracking. What if I had a fall, was abducted or got lost? How relieved I was to arrive at the bus stop and it was lovely to see other people waiting there. I gave Pamela a ring when I arrived home.

The second occasion was after another stay when we all went to Maidstone to go round the shops and have a drink in a pub before I caught the bus home. My bus was due to go at 4pm (the last one). Pamela liked shopping and window-shopping, and time went by. As it got nearer and nearer to 4pm. I started to panic about missing the bus, but Pamela took no notice. I did not know where the stop was but luckily Tom, her boyfriend, kept reminding her about the time. We just made it at last minute, literally. Pamela's behaviour made me think twice about going down to stay that often. Another time, I did actually miss the bus and had to get a train from Maidstone to Bromley South. This was really nerve-racking as I did not like to get on a train on my own. What a relief to get home! After this our friendship slowly began to end.

There was another man who I used to go out with who I shall call Roger. He was friendly and helpful, but I felt I was unable to have a relationship with him, because he seemed to think more of his family – I don't have that kind of closeness in my family. It must be lovely to be like that (my parents always kissed me good-bye before going out and good night before going to bed as you never know what might happen). We used to go out on a regular basis to a pub in his car. We used to have a good laugh, though sometimes it was boring. I liked it better when he bought his friend with him.

There are two experiences which I remember quite well. The first one was one Christmas when Roger and his friend and I went up to London to see the lights. Roger parked his car at Forest Hill so that we could catch a train to London. We walked down Oxford St. and Regents St. and went into a pub on the way home, where I was glad to sit down for a while. When we finally got back to Forest Hill, Roger suggested that I could get a bus home even though it was nearly 11pm. I was furious and in the end Roger agreed to take me home.

One of Roger's closest friends was in hospital. Roger used to take me to see him. On one occasion his friend had a break-in, but what Roger didn't tell me was that his friend's wife had told the doctor who advised her not to tell her husband. Unaware of this, I thought it was best for him to know while he was in hospital, because if he got upset he would have the medical attention he might have needed. I noticed that Roger's friend was very calm and in a way he was glad I told him, but his wife was furious with me, which I could understand and didn't blame her for.

A good few years ago when my real grandmother was alive and I was at 'Trinity' I had a letter from a young man who wanted to meet me. I invited him to tea. When he came, I was very wary of him and wanted to get rid of him. All he seemed to want to do was to kiss and cuddle and put his hands everywhere. There was granny sitting in the armchair saying that he was a nice man. Mum and I thought that he was a bit of a lad and was glad when he went. I have no idea where he got my name and address from or who told him about me.

As you will notice Roland is mentioned quite a few times towards the end of my book. He started working at Ladywell Day Centre in 1983 as an attendant and a handy man becoming the office clerk in 1988. At first I didn't take much notice of him, but as time went by we started talking and slowly we got to know each other very well and we have become the best of friends.

Roland really got involved with me when I was living in Bargery Road, because I became frightened and scared. He was always there to help me through it and I could phone him up anytime I needed to talk – day or night. From that time on, I realised that I could rely on him and then he started doing jobs for me which I was unable to do for myself.

In 1989 Roland decided to go to college and get a degree. At first this worried me, because I didn't know if I would still be able to see him but he reassured me. During the second year of his course he was thinking about giving it up because of personal reasons. I was only glad to be able to help him and he was able to continue his studies. Over the years I have known him we certainly have had some good laughs and I will mention a few of them.

One occasion I will never forget, we were in the kitchen. Roland was washing up and I dared him that he would not splash the water over me. He proved me wrong, as he threw about half a saucepan of water over me. I just stood there with my mouth open and completely speechless. Ever since that time I have never dared him again!

Another time which comes to mind was when I did a collection for Roland's leaving present at the Centre. I certainly made sure that I went round to everyone, though I wasn't worried if some of the members were unable to contribute, at least they were asked. I asked one of the staff who was going to the office for money and I didn't realise that Roland was behind me. He was very cross with me because he thought I was asking for money directly. What Roland didn't know was that I had asked the staff member beforehand.

Another time was when Roland was getting ready for an interview. He went to polish his shoes using a liquid polish. When he went to apply it, the sponge top fell off and liquid polish shot everywhere. He had to scrub his hands and legs where it had splashed, dry out his shoes and soak it up from the carpet. Roland was not amused.

Sometimes I wonder if Roland is more disabled than me because of his accidents and mishaps over the past years. Like the time he opened his washing-machine forgetting he had not drained the water out before switching it off earlier. His kitchen was flooded. Since I have known him he has gone through several pots and poached egg pans through forgetting he has them on the stove. He has locked himself out twice emptying rubbish – his front door slamming on him. Roland says I have less accidents than him because I am disabled! He says my disability means that I have to concentrate more on what to do than he does.

## *Chapter Thirty Eight*
# Romania

In this chapter I am going to write about my trip to Romania and the two friends I went with. I will tell you how I got to know them. I will not write anything personal about them. It will be based on my feeling and friendship towards them as a brother and sister in Christ.

When I left King's Church I didn't know where to go to worship. James worked at Bondwell, which was a day centre for the mentally ill, and often popped into Ladywell Day Centre to buy goods from the W.R.V.S shop. He told me that he held a prayer meeting on a Friday night in the "Cabin" just outside Ladywell Day Centre and invited me to join in. The Cabin was similar to a portacabin and was run by a charity group as a cafe for users and residents of the two council homes and the day centres in the Ladywell complex. Since the closure of the homes, the Cabin has been pulled down. After some thought I decided to go along and found I enjoyed it. The group was small and most of the members had learning difficulties. We used to have a time of sharing each other's news then a time of worship and Bible study.

James and his wife, Tracey, had been going to the Ukraine during their summer holidays to help people. Because they had done this several times, they had made some good friends. In June and July 1991, I helped James and Tracey to type out the Bible messages and where to find them in other countries' Bibles. I really enjoyed doing this work and then I brought some goods for the children, like plasticine and moulds.

While they were on the journey, Ron and Olive came and took over the meetings until they returned home. Ron and Olive certainly made a good job of it. The only thing that was missing was that we had to play music tapes instead of having James and Tracey playing their instruments during worship.

Ron and Olive became friends of mine and they helped me for a time when I was doing a correspondence bible course. As they became more involved in their mission work, I began to feel a bit low in myself and I didn't carry on with my Bible studies. I hoped to return to them in the near future. Whether Olive would still be able to carry on being my Guider or whether I would have to find someone else to take her place on my return to my Bible studies, I was not sure of.

I would have liked to have gone on that trip with James and Tracey but somehow I didn't think it was the right time. But I knew that The Lord would allow me to go one year.

In July 1992 after we did a lot of praying, I finally had my wish to go to Romania. I will not be able to tell you all the names of the towns we visited, but will tell you the countries we went through and I will not mention anyone's name – they will just be called friends.

On the first weekend of August, Roland came over to help me pack my bags and I gave him my house keys to look after. I gave him another job to do, which was to keep his eye on mum and do her little bits of shopping. Another job I asked Roland to do was to make me four music tapes to take away with me. He made a very good job of it, as he knew the right songs and hymns to pick. James came to pick me up about midday and I asked him to check my bags. I had to take out two or three items. I didn't take my camera as James said he would take any pictures I would like. I said good-bye to Roland.

We went back to James and Tracey's place to do the last minute bits and pieces and had something to eat then off we went. We spent a night with Tracey's family who lived in Folkestone. During the evening we all went for a ride and took the dog for a very long walk. Tracey's brother made it interesting because he told a bit about the history of the place. It was great fun. We got up very early the next morning at about 4am. We had our breakfast and caught the 5am boat to France.

We drove from there to Belgium. We spent the whole day in Belgium and went round one of the markets. We bought some toys for the children, had a good meal then travelled on to East Germany and spent a week with friends. I really did enjoy being with this family. I enjoyed looking through their religious books, it was fantastic. Again, we had some prayer time and I was looking forward to seeing them again on our way home. We travelled to meet another friend but unfortunately he wasn't at home. We went back on the road, and while James was driving, a van overtook us with a religious sticker on the window so we decided to follow him until we caught up. We then managed to stop the van and introduced ourselves to him. As we had nowhere to stay that night, he invited us to stay with his family – so we followed him to his house which was in the mountains. I was amazed to see how big the family was. I was surprised to see so many children! I can remember at least eight. The lady's husband left us there while he went to work. We had something to eat with the wife and children and had a good time while we were there. During prayer and worship time we tried to exchange songs. I was quite surprised that when a song is sang in a foreign language, the tune remains the same.

We then moved to another part of Germany to see another friend. He made us a lovely cherry drink and it was delicious. We went for a walk and ended up having a paddle in the water. I was amazed to see how different parts of Germany are from each other. We visited a religious shop to collect some items. I saw some pictures which I wish I had bought. One was a picture of The Bible family tree and it was so colourful.

After leaving Germany, we went back on the road again, but this time it was going to be a lot tougher. We took as much drinking water from our previous stop as we could carry. Because it was a long bottle, James had to make me a special straw. He did this by making a tiny Split in one end of the straw and pushed a second straw into it. This straw really did work and I was surprised how long it lasted.

While we were driving through what was then Czechoslovakia, we stayed at a hostel for a night. We were able to pay the bill with our German marks. During the next day everything was going fine until the van suddenly decided to break down. The Lord was good to us because He allowed us to stop right in front of an emergency telephone. Tracey did the talking on the telephone as she was able to speak German. While we waited for the police to come, somehow The Lord told me what was going to happen. He told me we were going to be towed back to a Hotel to stay and that we will have to leave a lot of our luggage behind.

The police came while we were eating and did all the necessary arrangements. We were taken back a few miles to a hotel. As it was a Saturday nothing could be done to the van until Monday as most people didn't work at weekends. It was a lovely area with quite a few animals. While we were staying there, the weather was very hot. We didn't have any Czechoslovakian money so it was difficult to get anything. Tracey had to go backwards and forwards to the telephone to sort out what could be done about the van. We slept in the van and had our food. We were allowed to use the hotel showers, which we did to cool ourselves down. We ate quite a lot of their ice cream, which was delicious.

Early Monday morning, Tracey was told that we were going to be towed back to Vienna. This journey was long and tiring. As we had to get into a small space, I had to curl my legs up under me. We stopped at a car-hire company. We had to wait quite a while to sort out what car we could have and eventually we found a company that would allow us to go to Romania. They agreed to let us park the van in the car-park and agreed to take the van back to England, after we returned with the car.

Then we had to sort out what we could take with us as we now had a car instead of a van. We put all the Bibles in the car first. Then we added the toys for the children, and items of clothing for the babies. Then lastly we added our personal belongings and leaflets with Bible messages on them which we had been folding along our way. I had to leave my bible behind, which didn't really please me, but I could understand. When I wanted to read the Bible, Tracey let me borrow her one.

Because it was getting late, we stayed in a hotel, which was fantastic. We drunk some of the soft drinks in our hotel rooms thinking they were inclusive. They were not! We had quite a bill to pay the next day. The only problem I had with these hotels was I couldn't unlock or open the doors.

When we stayed in Vienna I put my personal belongings in with Tracey and James and left my room unlocked. After breakfast we made our way to Hungary. We slept in the car. I really don't know how we managed it, but we did. In Hungary we stayed with two of their friends. They knew that I was interested in conductive education, which is specially designed for children with cerebral palsy and uses exercises and physiotherapy to help children learn. We asked their friend if it was possible to visit a school, and it was.

The place we visited was fantastic – I had never seen anything like it. As we arrived there late in the afternoon, we went round the residential part. It wasn't like a residential school; the staff and the students all worked together and on the same level. I had a go on some exercise machines. Then we went to have a chat and coffee with some of the head staff. The helpers didn't want me to leave. They would have been quite happy for me to stay with them for a while as I would like to have done, but I couldn't. They had a few animals there and I saw one of the girls giving a kitten a bath. We had a look round their rooms and they were fantastic as the students could have what they liked in their room. In one room there was an enormous picture of a view. We took some pictures of the children. We thanked them and said good-bye. I would very much like to visit the place again.

As we were staying with two friends in Hungary, it was easier to get to Romania for a day, which is what we did. We visited a children's orphanage and had a good time with the children there, showing them the toys we had brought them. From there we went round to the babies' unit. We had to show the staff what we bought them before we were allowed in. Some of the babies were really gorgeous and it made you feel as though you wanted to pick them up. Some of the babies grabbed hold of my dress and I had to pull myself away. There were a couple of babies all tied-up, to stop them from harming themselves. When I first saw them, I thought they were born with no arms because they were all wrapped up. On the way out there was a little boy standing there, so I knelt down and put my arms around him and gave him a cuddle. Before we said good-bye, we had to wash our hands. Then we made our way back to Hungary.

The two people we were staying with in Hungary looked after us very well. Their son was on holiday and he took us out to different local places. One place I shall never forget was a swimming pool, which was fantastic. It looked like a normal building from the outside and inside you had a pay-office, canteen and changing rooms. We went through the showers and then walked through a cave, with our feet in the water. Then here and there we would come to a waterfall. When we came to the end, it opened out into the swimming pool. It was really lovely. I have never seen anything like it. The next day we moved on to the Ukraine.

We stayed with another family in the Ukraine and I really enjoyed my time there. When we first arrived at the house, Ruth the youngest daughter was the only one in, so she made us welcome and gave us something to eat and drink. After this Ruth grabbed hold of my hand and took me inside the house. She took my shoes off and glasses and I had to lie down on the settee for a while. I wondered where I was going and felt a little frightened at first. A few minutes later, Tracey came to find me, and I stayed there for about half-an-hour before getting up again. I must assume I looked tired but why she did it is still a mystery. However I found her very helpful and we became quite friendly despite the language barrier. We certainly did have some laughs. One morning she tried to help me get dressed – she put my dress on back to front and did it up. I had to get Tracey to help me get undressed and put it on again. We all laughed.

The only problem I had was going to the loo. The toilet was in an outhouse and had a wooden seat and was dark. There was no sewer to take it away and no water to flush it away. The height and angle of the seat made it difficult to sit on. Tracey and the girls came up with an idea, and I was quite happy with it. This gave me another alternative to overcome using the toilet. The idea was that I used a bowl whenever I needed the loo, which could be put somewhere private, and which could then be emptied.

We had quite a lot to eat there. To my surprise we seemed to have tomatoes at most meals. I really did enjoy their doughnuts. They were delicious, softer and sweeter than the ones in England.

We went round visiting some of the hospitals, which were terrible. I'd never seen anything like these. The smell was awful and turned my stomach over but I soon got used to it. The loos were even worse. It certainly made me grateful for the clean hospitals we have at home in England. We took some bibles with us to give out to the patients and staff.

We did some preaching outside the hospitals, which was really great because we gave them leaflets with messages taken from the Bible on them. Most people read them, which surprised me. Back home in England people often just throw them away. The other thing I noticed was that when we gave them a Bible they would hide it and come back for another one. I was amazed and decided to tell James. From then on we were careful to whom we gave the books. Some of the people wanted to give us money for the Bibles, but we refused to take any.

Before leaving, we wrote some post-cards and sent them off to our families and friends. Just before we said our thank-yous and good-byes they wanted to give us a present. I didn't think it was right to tell them what I would like. They gave us a Russian doll and a money box and I was very pleased with them.

From there we went back to Hungary for a couple of days. We stayed in a friend's flat. His mother, who lived with him, certainly made sure we had plenty to eat. We were outside the block of flats when we saw a young girl with some puppies. I went over to her and stroked one of the puppies. After a little while a young man came to join us (her brother I think) and he could speak English. He tried to persuade me to take the puppy home and I said that I would like to, but unfortunately was not able to.

Paul, our friend who we were staying with, wanted to come back to England with us - a youngster on the streets could translate what Paul wanted to say. Tracey and James agreed to let Paul come back with us. I thought this was God's way of getting us to understand what Paul wanted. If it wasn't for the puppies we probably wouldn't have bumped into these youngsters.

We started our journey back to Vienna, but instead of having three passengers we had four in a small car. Can you imagine all four of us sleeping in a car? I was all right because I am small and can curl up my legs. Tracey sat in the front, Paul slept in the driver's seat and James, with difficulty because he is tall, sat at the back.

Eventually we arrived in Vienna late in the evening and we wanted to book into a hotel again. However, we didn't arrive till 2am so we slept in the car again. We got up early the next morning to take the car back and to put our belongings in the van so that we didn't have to carry our heavy stuff with us. To our surprise the van had already been taken back to England. So we had to carry our belongings with us. Tracey had to do all the booking for our journey home by train. We were hoping to get off the train in Germany to visit their friends, but the train didn't stop there. We were unable to get a nightsleeper, so we had to get an ordinary train. We had a couple of hours to spare so we went for a walk. When we finally got on the train, we had a terrible time trying to sleep, but we did doze off here and there.

When we finally arrived in Paris, we had a whole day and night there. We went for a trip on the canal and it was really lovely. We met two nice people and we had a chat with them. That night in our hotel, we were going to have tea in our room and I just went to sleep.

When I woke up, Tracey told me that while I was asleep a fire engine passed by, and without waking up I had sat up and then laid down again. I noticed in our room that we had an extra toilet, which I thought was for washing your feet. It was only when I got home someone told me what it was for!

We finally caught our train from Paris to Calais and a boat to Dover. Here we had to get another car, which wasn't really necessary because we were going to ask Tracey's brother to collect us. We spent the weekend with Tracey's family.

The different church services in the countries we visited were very interesting. If I could go again I would take the chance. I would certainly take more than one dress because I wore mine for two weeks and it only had one wash in all that time.

I really enjoyed this trip with James and Tracey. I learned a lot and it also made me think how lucky we are to live in England.

## Chapter Thirty Nine
# Open University

Earlier in my book, I wrote about how I began school and which schools I attended until I left Charlton Park school at Easter 1969 when I was seventeen years of age. I attended a typing course at Downham College and then I attended Trinity Centre in Faversham Road. I did some English and maths work with staff at the Centre. I attended the Bromley Workshop for nine months and then I went back to Trinity Centre. Later I went to the Portland Training College, which is in Mansfield, for further education. I was sent home after three months because they felt I did not need their specialist help as I could cope with an ordinary F.E. College having reached the required educational standard.

I came back to Trinity Centre, but I was very restless and didn't know what I wanted or what I could be capable of doing with my life. I was very depressed and even tried to take my own life, by taking first mum's tablets which made me drowsy and I was kept in hospital for observation for one night; then I took some of dad's tablets which first made me ill for about a week. I even tried to cut my wrist, but a little cut was quite enough for me!

I wanted to be different from my fellow members and I was sure I could achieve more than what I was doing – just sitting around all day. I felt I was not learning anything at Trinity. I was bored and began to look around to see what I could do. My sister had had a good education and had a good job and I am sure I was envious of her.

I heard of the Open University first from the T.V.. I think during 1978 I made up my mind to take an O.U. course as I felt I wanted to follow in the wake of a friend who worked in several ways for the welfare of people in the community around her. I also wanted to go further in my education than the Ladywell Day Centre was prepared to offer me.

I started by doing the course on "The Handicapped Person in the Community". I particularly enjoyed this course because I learnt about different disabilities and how disabled people coped with life and this helped me personally.

I passed this examination and received a certificate. I went on to take other courses. I studied Social Work in the Community and a Foundation Course – Making Sense of the Society. The Tutor gave me extra tutoring if I arrived early for the class. I think the obligatory week of Summer School at Keele University gave me confidence and having Katie to do the writing for me was a great help. I'm sure it was the impetus enabling me to be successful in the examination. My dad told me that the tutor said she didn't think I would pass the examination. When I did get my certificate she wrote to congratulate me and to apologise for her remarks.

Katie sometimes also made me feel incapable and would put restrictions on what I wanted to do outside study time during summer school. For example she would not come with me to trampolining or come out for a drink.

I also studied 0' level Sociology at Downham College in a mainstream class but I did not have anyone to take my notes for me. I had to use another student's notes and I feel my written exam was not very good. The way I used to get the other student's notes was to get a carbon copy of what she had written. I passed the 0' level English examination in 1980 with a C grade, but I found it quite hard because of my difficulty in writing. I had to dictate my answers to questions to a scribe, who would then write the answers for me.

I then went on to do a Computer Course for Women. The reason why I went on this course was because I did not know anything about computers. This course was aimed at women, but was a mainstream course – not just for disabled people.

The course consisted of several subjects: English, Arithmetic, Computer Programming and Electronics, and took about nine months to complete. The subject which I enjoyed most was the computer work and the least enjoyable was the electronics work. The electronics consisted of wiring connections and finding out the mechanics of the computer. Lectures involved a lot of writing and all this was "fiddly" and difficult for me to handle because of my disability. The rest of the class, too, became less and less interested until finally there were only about four students attending the lecture. One tutor knew that I wore a hearing-aid but unfortunately the other tutors were unaware of my inability to hear easily. Sometimes I didn't answer a tutor when I was called and they thought I must be concentrating on my work; and when sometimes my hearing-aid "whistled" they thought it was the computer! During the last week of the course we did not use computers and when my hearing-aid "whistled" the tutor was quite surprised and shocked to learn that I was deaf and that she had not been informed. Although the course director knew she had not passed on this knowledge to the others tutors! The tutors who took us for our computer lessons knew the difference between my hearing-aid and the computer whistles.

There were only two problems I had on this course – these were writing and getting my dinner. On the first week, we had our English lesson and we did some writing. I told the teacher that I could do my writing by kneeling on the floor. The teacher said, "O.K." I did some writing for about half an hour and then I stopped as my arm and legs were aching. The teacher came over to me and gave me a hand, I told her what to write down. I felt quite worried about what would happen when it came for me to write an essay. Anyway, on the next English lesson there was no problem. The tutor arranged for me to have a computer. This was great because I used it for most of my writing and I also did Maths as well which made it a lot quicker all round. The only lesson I couldn't have the computer for was Electronics, and yet they did a lot of writing in that class.

The College had three separate buildings. We were mainly using Wickham and Breakspears buildings. For the first few days I went to the Wickham canteen. I didn't really like their meals and they were not very helpful with carrying the tray for me. The following week I decided to try the Breakspears canteen. It was a lot bigger and to be honest I didn't know where to start. I saw a lady in a white coat so I went up to her and asked if she could help me to carry my tray. She replied, "Yes sure!" She was great, just the right person I'd been looking for. My problem was solved. Melita would come round with me and let me tell her what I wanted, help me to get my money out, and cut the food up and open my drink. When Melita knew that she wasn't coming in she would even arrange for somebody else to take over. Believe me, I don't think I had ever come across such a caring person in a college canteen. When I left the college I still saw Melita in Lewisham from time to time and we would have a chat.

During my time doing Computing for Women, the local paper, "The Mercury", took a picture of me to advertise the course – I have still got it to this day.

The course finished in March and the examinations were in June. There were not enough students for us to take the computer exams and I already had 0' level English so I was very surprised to get a phone call one Friday in June asking me to go into the college on Monday to sit for the Maths examination. You see, I had not contacted the tutor since the end of the course and had not attended the discussion meeting about the exam. I did not expect to be sitting it because I had not done any work since the end of the course. However, the maths tutor said that I was quite capable of taking the exam. My father phoned the college and said that I was very concerned about the writing as I could not write except by sitting on the floor and I could not use a pencil (this was obligatory apparently). Would I be allowed to use a computer? The answer was *NO*, but I could take someone with me.

It was too late on Friday afternoon to ask the manager at Ladywell. When I asked her on Monday morning if there was anyone available to go with me to the college by 1.30p.m, she replied that she could not spare anyone at such short notice! Time was getting on and I told Peter I couldn't do it. He said, "Don't give up Julia, just go!" I left the centre at 1 o'clock and arrived at college by a miracle at 1.30pm. I was shown to my desk, on which were my paper and pencils, although I had said pencils were of no use because, as I had to press hard, I continually broke them. I told the tutor that I must move the desk forward so that I could sit on the floor with the paper on the chair. The secretary and the tutor expressed concern and asked if I could manage and I answered, "I've no choice, have I?" Then the exam started and after about a quarter-of-an-hour the tutor came to me and said that I was to go with her to a separate room and someone would come to write for me. This took about another half-an-hour. The length of the exam was two hours and I did not get any extra time but I did not need it. I finished the paper within an hour and a half!

I came out of the college on the day of the exam at 4.15p.m and had just fifteen minutes to get to MacDonalds at Catford to meet my friend, Pat. I just arrived on time! All I wanted was a very large coke. I was so thirsty as I had had no lunch or any drink. Pat said I must have drunk more than a pint of coke and this made both of us laugh! The end of it all was that two months later I received my certificate – I had a distinction!

Towards the end of that course, Computing for Women, I went to see the College Careers Officer to discuss what I wanted to do next. I told the Officer that I would like to go on another course within the college – and that was word-processing. The careers officer and the tutor of my class agreed that I could do it. So one afternoon, I went across to the other building to get the application form and when the receptionist saw me, she said, "Oh no! you won't be able to do it so why don't you join a typing class?"

I replied, "No, I don't want a typing class, I want to join a word-processing class!"

Then she asked me, "How many fingers do you use?"

I answered, "One finger!" She said that the course wouldn't be suitable for me. I just walked off and went to see my tutor and told her what had happened. She said that she would look into it for me. I realised that if I got on this course I would have to miss a few of the Thursday afternoon sessions. A couple of weeks later, I was told that the teacher was going to let me have a go for a month to see how I could cope! I was so pleased and I thought, Yes! – I will prove it to you that I am just as good as any of the others, despite my disability!

On Thursday 9th January 1986, at 2.0'clock I started the word-processing class. I felt very nervous and I was worried about the tutor's attitude. After the first lesson I felt I had coped very well. I felt that the tutor (Alan) was quite scared or not sure how take and treat me. During the second week it was the same feeling. I had to ask Alan to fill in the work sheet as I couldn't write that small. He was very nice about it and he agreed that he would do the work sheet for me. Everything went well. Watching the other students – they had one rule and that was that when you typed 118 into the printer, you had to use both hands to feed the paper into the printer.

When it was time for Alan to show me how to use the printer, I said "I can only use one hand." He said, "That's all right, I'm going to allow you to do it", and said, "Do you want me to show you how to do it, or do you want me to leave you to it?"

I replied, "I would like you to go away and I will call you back when I have finished."

About quarter of an hour later I called Alan over. I believe he was surprised at the results. I thought to myself, yes! – one up for me! Anyway, just before I put my coat on he came over to say that I was doing very well and I could carry on coming to class. He admitted that I was just as good as the others. One thing I was pleased about was that I could go at my own speed – all the worksheets were laid out on the table at the side of the room, and you could work through them at a pace that suited you. The computer we used was called a WANG. When the course finished, I felt pleased with myself as I managed very well. I left the course a little bit early, and the reason for this was because the weather was snowing and icy, and I was worried about using public transport in such conditions and worried about possibly falling over and hurting myself. I was sorry to miss the last week. One thing I wish I did was to find out what Alan thought of me!

Early in 1985 a friend at Ladywell Day Centre told me about a short weekend course for people wanting to know about counselling skills and how to help people to deal with their problems. I thought it over and decided that I would go to find out what it was all about, especially as it offered places for disabled people. This weekend counselling course introduced me to the topic of counselling. I found that counselling was important to me and it gave me confidence and also change my life, as I have written about later.

In September 1988, at Ladywell Day Centre, Roy started as a part-time computer tutor. He was employed by R.A.D.A.R., which is a charity which helps disabled people in many ways including education.

Roy had to interview interested members and then choose one to teach for twenty-five weeks. When he interviewed me, I was interested in learning Bliss which is a communication system for children without speech. I told him what I had done on computers at college and apart from this I didn't really know what I could learn from Roy and I thought there would be a waiting list so I didn't put my hopes up too high.

Maurice, a member of staff at Ladywell centre, told me that Roy was going to start taking me on, on Monday-week. I felt pleased about this as I had a feeling that I might gain something from the course. For the first couple of weeks, we talked and worked on the BBC computer, which I didn't like because it was too slow. I had had enough of them at college! Working with Roy there was nothing I could do about it. Robert (Manager of the

Centre) had been thinking about getting the PC 1640 with the money raised from the WRVS shop. Roy started teaching the database and I liked that very much.

Within four weeks he asked me if I would like to take the exam. At first I didn't know what to say as I didn't think I was ready for it. Roy had more confidence in me then I did! Anyway, I did it and passed. The next subject Roy taught me was the spreadsheet. I enjoyed this one too and it was just a little harder as there was more to learn. After five weeks on the spreadsheet, again Roy asked me if I would like to take the exam. With the spreadsheet I made sure that I had a lot of practice during the week. I was a bit worried in case I couldn't remember all the commands. Again, Roy was more sure than I was. I got through it! I had one more to do which was word-processing so I didn't have to decide – I just went for it. With the word-processing programme (Mini Office) I didn't really like it as I had to learn most of the commands before the computer did anything. I also knew I had to be more careful when I took the exam as I'm not very good at spelling and have to watch and read every word in case I misspelt them! I made sure I had a lot of practice as I had a feeling that I might forget something. Anyway, during the exam, everything went well until I had to change the right-hand side margin. My mind just went blank. Roy said I could have a look at my notes, which I did. Yet even now I believe I made one mistake. We still had some weeks to go so we decided to do some work on the basics. This was good because it refreshed what I did at college, on the Computing for Women course.

Roy and I had some good laughs. After I finished my course with Roy, we did get the PC 1640 computer but it was too late for Roy to give me any lessons on it. From 1996 – 1998 I went on to do levels 1, 2 and 3 in Wordprocessing, and levels 1 and 2 in spreadsheets and database. I then did Health and Safety level 2. All these were done at Lewisham College.

I have found that it is very important that tutors understand, or are willing to try and understand, the difficulties that my disability can cause me on a course. I can write only with difficulty, which means I need either a word-processor or someone to write from my dictation. If I have someone to write it down for me I need to be confident that they understand the way I think and appreciate my hearing and speech problems, especially as they are not obvious to the casual observer. If they are taking notes on my dictation it is important they take them down as I want them, not as they think they should be. I feel that it is important to take courses that end with a certificate in order to prove what you are capable of, especially as people tend to disbelieve you if you are disabled.

Most of the courses I have done have been in mainstream classes and have given me confidence, not only in my ability as a student, but confidence to stand up for myself. It has also taught me not to be afraid of asking for help, though I try to do as much as I can independently.

In 1990, I decided to do another Open University course. I chose the A102 Art Foundation Course, as I had already passed the D101 (Making Sense of Society) foundation course. At that time, you had to pass two foundation courses if you wanted to get an O.U. degree, but the following year they reduced the requirement to one.

The course literature said you did not need to have any background knowledge, but I think you do. I thought the course would be difficult but it was much harder than I had anticipated. To understand the meaning of the arts you need to have a knowledge of history, which I lacked. The evening classes were held at Avery Hill College but I gave up going after a few weeks because I could not hear the tutor properly and he spoke very fast. I tried taking a tape recorder to record the lecture but it didn't work because of the background noise, and the tutor's voice didn't stand out. A letter to the tutor explaining my problems got no response so I stopped going to the evening class and carried on with the help of Ronald and others.

Will, an Assistant Manager at Ladywell, helped me with literature as "Hard Times" was one of the set books and Will's hobby was Charles Dickens and his works. For music, the set piece was "The Messiah" by Handel. I liked it very much but Roland was not amused because every time I saw him I played it repeatedly. It drove him mad! I struggled because you had to discuss the harmony (tune), texture (loud or soft), rhythm (the beat) etc. The music tutor who came to Ladywell went through the music with me but because of the limited time, I didn't find it that helpful. However, Irene (a friend of mine through the WRVS) put me touch with a fellow churchgoer of hers, Elizabeth, who was a music teacher. She spent a morning going through my notes with me, patiently explaining the terms I didn't understand, and how you used them to discuss piece of music. Philosophy was beyond my understanding but Roland explained it to me as we went through the unit and helped me to do the essay.

In Art History I thought I would get a very good mark because we had to pick six pictures from the illustrated book to go into a big Victorian house and say why I picked them. It turned out I really didn't understand what they required in the essay. I selected paintings that I liked but you were expected to select paintings that fitted the house and created an appropriate image. History I found interesting because it made you think about how history was written and the sources they used.

I chose the summer school placement in London because I was concerned over mum, who had been in hospital for several months with an ulcer on her heels and doctors were talking about amputating one leg. My friend, Margaret, was in the same hospital with a similar problem.

The day before I started summer school, mum had to have her leg amputated. I went to see her from Ladywell but she wasn't back yet from the theatre so I went and saw Margaret, who stopped me from worrying about mum too much. I phoned Roland and asked him to meet me at the hospital because I was getting frightened. When mum came back to the ward in the early evening she looked terrible and was very weak. I didn't like the look of all the equipment around the bed – mum was all wired up and there were bottles and monitors everywhere. I was very worried about whether to go to the summer school or not. However, Roland promised to visit her and keep me informed on how she was.

When I set off for the summer school I had a lot on my mind. I was also worried about what my helper would be like. Usually I had brought my own helper, but that year the people I would have asked were unable to come. A good helper makes all the difference as to whether or not you enjoy and benefit from a summer school. They need patience and understanding of how a disability affects you, and they need to have a friendly personality. It is important that they realise that disability affects every person differently, both physically and mentally, even if the type of disability was the same. Roland came with me to carry my luggage and to give me moral support when I met my helper, Pat 'P', who was a special needs teacher. We all had a drink and by the time Roland left, I felt as if I'd known Pat a long time. Pat and I got on really well together and we became really good friends. It turned out that Pat was just as worried as me; she was worrying that she might have to help someone who she couldn't get on with.

I couldn't cope with the door of the room I was given, so Pat and I shared a room. By the evening I was sure that we were going to get on well together. I phoned Roland to find out how mum was and could not believe it when he told me that mum was up sitting in a chair and looking well, if still weak. It was really good news and put my mind at rest. Roland admitted he was amazed at how fast my mum had recovered from the operation.

The summer school staff lent me a loop system, which was very helpful. Pat carried it from lesson to lesson. The tutors would pin the microphone to their clothing and I would have the loop cord around my neck and my hearing-aid on "T". The only problem was that I couldn't properly hear what the other students were saying in the class. We could also tell that some tutors didn't like wearing the microphone. Pat was fun to be with and most nights we would take drinks back to our room and stay up till one in the morning just chatting about anything under the sun. By the end of the week Pat and I had become really good friends. Pat and I have kept in touch and visit each other still. Pat gave me confidence in myself.

Pat and her husband, Roger, have both now retired and have a lovely bungalow in Northern Ireland.

It was not clear whether mum would be going home to her own house or whether she would go into a home. As I mentioned, some of the neighbours assumed that mum would be going into a home. From what I knew and had heard about residential homes, I saw them as a last resort and wanted mum to be given an opportunity to try living at home again. I felt that, given the right support from Social Services, she would be able to cope. Eventually in October, mum was allowed home and coped very well.

When it came to the exam, I was already convinced I would fail. I took the exam at home, with the O.U. providing someone to write down my answers. Nervous and unsure, I was not helped when the person turned up more than half an hour early. I was hoping to read my notes but was put off. Her manner was condescending and brusque and when she laughed at my answer to a question, my confidence (such as it was) completely vanished and I more or less gave up. I did not attempt to answer part two of the exam. When I phoned Roland later that day and told him what had happened, he knew I'd fail it but said that I could take it again. I wasn't very keen on the idea but Pat convinced me, pointing out I had nothing to lose by trying, so I decided to re-sit the exam the following year. This time I passed, although I only made up my mind to do it at the last moment.

Looking back over the year, I did get something out of the course – it led me to join an Art Appreciation class, which I really enjoyed. I even enjoyed reading "Hard Times" which amazed me.

In Part One of the course, we did History, Art History, Literature, Music, Religion and Philosophy. In part two of the course you used what you had learned to answer historical questions through the use of art, literature and music etc., as sources. This I was not very good at; I lacked historical knowledge which the set text books could not make up for, and even if I had it in my head, putting it on paper was very difficult for me. When I took my English O' Level, we had to read 'Hard Times' and I hated every moment of it. I struggled with the course with Aline (the main English teacher) and Molly (a retired teacher and helper).

In 1991 I took the "Special Needs in Education" course (E241). I enjoyed this course because of my personal experiences, which I gave as first hand knowledge of the problems involved. The big difficulty I had was that E241 needed revising to take account of the recent 1988 Education Reform Act. I did not go to the evening classes because I visited the site with Roland before they started. The site was in Croydon and not that accessible by public transport from Catford. What was worse – to get to it you would have to walk up a dark, lonely and very steep access road or walk across a park in the dark. The tutor came to me once a month, at my flat instead of me going to the classes. The tutor was very good and helpful. As part of the course we had one day in London. My tutor made sure that the classes I selected were allocated to the ground floor. She even gave me a lift to and from the school which was in North London.

In the old Education Act you had different categories of special needs. In the new Act they classify all those needing special help in their education as having special needs, regardless of their very different needs and problems. I disagreed with this because it means the definition becomes meaningless. It grouped together students with their peers, which does not always work because of family problems for example or with a student who is physically disabled. Or for example, it groups together a dyslexic student who is very intelligent with another who has severe learning difficulties. The result is that their different needs and problems are not recognised enough.

Another idea which I agree with, but with reservations, is the policy of trying to teach all students with physical disabilities or learning difficulties in main stream schools rather than special schools. I felt that it depended on the degree of disability and the support needed. With all the cut backs in Education spending, I doubt if the support required would be provided. It would be even worse for those severely disabled children. Not only would they lack the support needed, but they would not have the physiotherapy and speech therapy currently available at special schools. I also could not see main stream teachers being able to reach the same level of expertise as special teachers, considering the daily pressures on them.

The Open University had sent me another complete set of A102 books for me to read in order to re-sit the exam. I was still in two minds about re-sitting it, lacking confidence, and just put them to one side. Two months before the exam I made up my mind to just go for it and try my best. I asked Roland to tell me what to read and learn for my revision. He advised me to concentrate on history and art history in part one and religion, town and country, women, work and moral values and the social order in part two. On the topic of religion, I always got muddled up between the High Church and Low Church.

He pointed out that I had got good marks for my essays and advised I should just concentrate on getting a pass mark rather than worrying about getting a very good mark in the exam. I worked hard in the two months, reading "Hard Times" again, studying the paintings, watching video tapes of the 0. U., T.V. programmes and a Channel 4 programme series on Victorian paintings.

Every week Roland asked me questions and helped me memorise key points in the topics I was covering. I found religion difficult to grasp properly. I was nervous about the exams though I was more confident and determined because of the work I had done. What worried me was my helper after my previous year's experience. The woman who came to do the writing was friendly and understanding. Her manner helped me relax and do my best. When the exam ended, I felt I had done my best and chatted with the tutor who admired my teddy bears.

I had a week to revise for my second exam, the E241. I struggled a bit with part one but my problem in part two was what questions to pick. I felt I could answer most of them equally well and took what seemed a long time deciding what questions to answer. It was nerve racking waiting for the results. When the letter arrived I was very nervous but on opening it, I found I had passed both exams, the news of which I immediately phoned through to Roland and Pat (the summer school helper). Having three credits I was halfway to a 0. U. ordinary degree.

In 1979, I did my first Open University course. If you stopped for more than 2 years, you had to start all over again and the credits you gained on the course were null and void. However, when I went back to the OU in 1990 this all changed, and you were allowed to accumulate your credits until you had enough to get your degree. As well as the 0. U. courses I started the CCPR course for community sports leaders in October 1990. The course was held at Ladywell and lasted about four months. The students on the course were mainly physically disabled but did include some able bodied people. Margaret Badgery who taught sports at the centre had invited me to join. I didn't really want to as it wasn't my cup of tea but in the end I said I would do it, thinking it would be useful when I went back to guiding. The other reason I decided to do the course here was that it was at the Ladywell Centre, and I did not need to go anywhere else to take the course. There was more practical work than written work. Each week there was a lecture for about an hour covering different aspects of sport then about an hour and a half on practical sports games, using different equipment every week.

I faced two problems; I could not really play sports involving the use of my hands because I lacked the control needed because of my cerebral palsy, and I do not have a strong voice to give instructions with. Margaret suggested I practice giving instructions in the sports hall when it was not being used. I only did this once or twice because I knew that I could shout if I had to – for example, if someone was ignoring my instructions.

When we did the First Aid section, Margaret was a bit shocked as I knew quite a bit, having covered First Aid in the Guides and Rangers. The course included running a sport class of your choice for a total of ten hours. I took fitness and relaxation classes at Ladywell, which were usually ran by Valerie Matthews, the centre instructor. The examination involved planning, organising and running a sport activity. Students (able bodied) from other centres were brought in to make the numbers up, and afterwards were questioned verbally on different aspects of the course. Despite my initial reluctance, I enjoyed the course, though I needed constant encouragement, and was pleased when I passed.

After passing the A102 Art Foundation Course and the E241 Special Needs In Education in 1991, I felt really encouraged to go for it, and try to pass my degree.

My counsellor, Sue, advised me that I could put the courses that I had done in the past together, along with ones that I want to do now, and they could all go towards a diploma in Health and Social Welfare. This could then all go towards my degree.

I did the D251 Issues in Deafness in 1996. I enjoyed this course, but I did not get as much out of it as I expected to. There was only one thing that I did not agree with, and this was the suggestion of having ear implants. This would take born-deaf people out of the deaf community at an early age. I think that this decision should be left to the individual to decide in later life.

Most deaf people know the British Sign Language (BSL). Some years ago, I went to a deaf club which was held at Ladywell Day Centre on a Friday evening. I went there for a while and I found it really, really difficult to cope with. Because I have other disabilities, it is very difficult to use my hands for all the signs you need for the BSL, and there was no way I could learn it. The club was very good, and it was fascinating to watch, but I had to give it up because I felt left out. Today, I think they are thinking of making BSL a second language.

I also did the following courses –
'AA313 Religion in Victorian Britain', in 1997
'Diploma in Health and Social Welfare', in 1998

Between 1997 and 1998, I also did a Community Care qualification, but hated every moment of it! The course content was too political. This course did not seem to have too much to do with people, or the disabilities they face, and concentrated more on political correctness.

To get my diploma, I also had to do the K258 Health and Well-Being certificate. To get my degree, I chose to do Religion in Victorian Britain, which I enjoyed very much.

The next one I did was World Religion. Quite often, my friends were worried about me doing this qualification, in case it distracted me from my own religious beliefs, but I believed it would widen my horizons.

During the World Religion course I started to go blind, and all the course books had to be sent to me on tape. This was really hard work, especially as there were all different types of voices on the tapes – some loud and some soft. This meant that I had to keep turning the volume up and down according to who was speaking. The other problem came when every time there was a change of topic, the tape would bleep. This used to drive me up the wall!

Sue was my support worker while I was doing the O.U. course. Sue and I became good friends and she used to visit me at home. She gave me a lot of support and back-up. She also came to see me get my degree. We lost touch for a number of years, but in 2006, I received a Christmas card from Sue, saying that she would be getting in touch soon.

## Chapter Forty
# Religion

When I was eight years old, I started going to Sunday School at St. Andrews (Church of England) in Catford with my sister. I can't remember anything about it but mum told me that the staff took good care of me.

Then when I was 11, mum and I started going to St. Andrews regularly on Sunday mornings and we only stopped when mum was diagnosed as having Multiple Sclerosis when I was 14. I used to like going to church but I did find it rather boring when the vicar gave the sermon as I couldn't hear what he said.

There were other times when I could hear some of the words but not enough to make any sense out of the sermon. This did not make me feel that it was a waste of time as I enjoyed singing the hymns

When I was seventeen, I started going to church again, but on my own. This time I was more committed as I had thought a great deal about my beliefs, and though I still had the same problem of hearing I looked at it in a different light. I felt that God knew I was there in church and it didn't matter to him that I couldn't hear everything.

The vicar was a kind and understanding person. I started to attend confirmation classes, which I enjoyed. We read and discussed the bible and Christian beliefs, but I was very unsure of myself so I went along with other people, instead of saying what I really thought. Finally, I was confirmed by the Bishop of Woolwich at St. Andrew's Church. I attended the services in this church for quite a number of years but gradually my attendance fell off, partly because I began to take up swimming and I joined a club, and also I found that I no longer seemed to get any help from the service.

In 1979 I met Maurice at the Ladywell Day Centre and at once I felt that there was something different about him and I wanted him to talk to me about God and religious beliefs etc.. He was a member of a Free Church and he began to discuss religion with me and I asked him a lot of questions. He either gave, or found, most of the answers in the bible for me. During 1980, he asked me if I wanted to commit myself to the Lord and I replied that I did want to do that. I then repeated a prayer after Maurice. When I had done this, somehow, after a few days I felt different. Everything I looked at, even everyday objects like tables and chairs, I saw in a different light. I can only describe it as a 'sensation' that I felt.

Maurice and his friend John A. (a Christian who worked at Ladywell for a few years) between them bought me a "Good News" bible to show their friendship to me and to help me to develop my relationship with God. Maurice arranged for me to meet Richard, the pastor of a local church who he knew. Richard visited me once a week for about eight weeks and we used to discuss the bible and Christianity. I started attending his church, Allerford Chapel, which was an Evangelistic Free Church. It was also unlike a "normal" church in its layout with no pews but chairs arranged in an informal semi-circular way with a table for communion and a bible reading stand. The service was easy to understand and follow, and the members of the church were helpful and friendly.

When Richard said that I was ready to be baptised, I invited my parents and some of my friends to the ceremony. Dad didn't like the idea of me becoming a church member or my baptism and said he wouldn't go but he relented at the last minute and agreed to attend with mum. The song I chose to be sung after my baptism was "Jesus, take me as I am". This still is one of my favourite songs.

Richard arranged for me to continue my bible study at home with Pat B., another church member, and she and I became good friends. We met every week for about three years for bible study and later when I left the church we met every fortnight in McDonalds in Catford to talk about everyday things as well as the bible. We would work on bible study books, discussing the bible, and then I would type in my answers. Once Pat noticed an error in the book and we wrote about it in our work. When the book came back the work had been marked and there was a note saying I had an excellent tutor as the markers had not noticed the error.

A few months after I had been baptised with water, I asked Richard if I could be baptised in the Holy Spirit. We prayed about this and then Richard came to my house and after we had talked and prayed, I was able to speak in tongues. When I began, the words I spoke didn't make any sense – they were more of a jumble of sounds – and I used this as a way to speak to God. I did not realise that I could speak in tongues before I was prayed for. I gradually became more confident and sure of myself as the weeks went by. I often speak in tongues especially when I don't know how to communicate or what to pray about.

Pat bought a book at the Christian Bookshop, called "Christ's Healing" and she asked me if I was interested in being healed. I said, "Yes" and so we worked through the book. Then we asked the church to begin prayers for my healing, and most of the congregation agreed to do so. During the following years of prayer healing, I was told that I must be set free from any evil spirit that might be in me and those who were praying for me were also told to keep on praying and asking God to heal me.

As time went on I got frustrated and angry because I felt that the church kept on at me to pray for healing but many of these prayers were more about the church becoming famous if I was healed. Nobody had asked me at the time how I felt so I hadn't said anything; it might have made a difference if I had but I felt so frustrated and I knew I just couldn't go on in this way. I believed that too much was being asked of me, so I stopped going to church for five years.

One particular friend from church, who I still see now, has said to me that both she, and other members of the church community at that time, now realise that they did not communicate with me in a very effective way regarding this issue. My friend wanted me to know that, since that time, both she and other church members have learned from their mistakes and had become wiser and more sensitive to disabled people's feelings and their rights to be involved in decision making.

Every year during the time I was a member of Allerford Chapel, I attended a bible week called "The Downs" which was organised at the Plumpton Race Course by New Frontiers International. There we were able to set up tents for services and for sleeping. Some families took their caravans with them. This convention was made up of many churches and there were discussion groups on many different topics. People were free to attend any group which had a topic they wished to discuss and hear about. When I went there in 1982 I felt rather depressed and I began to think about writing a poem to express my feelings and gradually my ideas formed into these words:-

### DOWNS

I spent a week at Downs,
Didn't really want to go,
Afraid of what might come about,
For I felt sure that something would;
But what, I could not say,
Often I had a sensation,
Which I could not understand,
Happy when I was alone with God,
In a crowd I was lost and sad,
Sometimes I would wander off,
To find God and to be alone,
To talk and to sing my songs to Him,
Slowly I grew aware of myself,
Wondering how to over-come,
Though I must have known the answer,
Myself alone must make the move,

> No one else could do it for me,
> But could I just let myself go,
> Then I began to feel a change,
> I could worship God in a crowd,
> I could talk to those whom I feared,
> I found God's Blessing helping me through,
> But I must take my next step alone,
> I still had to ask for deliverance,
> From my fear of living and life!
> How far would I have to go, I thought,
> Perhaps my next step to me would be shown.
>
> 16th August, 1982

There was a girl at Allerford who told me the reason I had Cerebral Palsy was because the umbilical cord got caught round my neck. Even though I know that this is the most common cause of Celebral Palsy I knew that this was completely untrue and she knew nothing about my birth.

Unfortunately in 1988 the leaders of the camp heard from God that they were to stop the gathering at Plumpton.

During 1987, I went through a phase of reading my bible and nearly every time it was the book of Psalms. On this particular day I was looking at Psalms 89: 28, 33, 34.

> "I will always keep my promise to him,
> and my covenant with him will last for ever.
> But I will not stop loving David or fail to keep my promise to him.
> I will not break my covenant with him
> or take back even one promise I made him."

I really felt that these words were for me as it proved that God still loved me. God will keep His promise, which I felt was for my healing, and lastly God won't break His promise. For the following few weeks I kept these words on my mind without telling anybody, even Pat.

I started attending a church in Bromley called The Assembly of God, which I started to enjoy going to. I went there for a few months and then stopped as I didn't want to get too involved. A few weeks after that I was at Lewisham doing my normal shopping when a girl put a leaflet in my hands about the prayer meetings at Goldsmith College which were on Wednesday evenings. I decided to go along and see what they were like. Again, I enjoyed these meetings and started to go regularly. I got to know one particular girl who had a baby and we got on very well together. She came to visit me at my flat, which was fine.

The church had friends in Holland and they had special gatherings twice a year. I decided that I would like to go with them, and I did. To start off with, I paid more than I should and the pastor told me he would give me a refund when we returned. I wasn't too worried about this at first, as they had been very helpful to me. I certainly did get blessed and I felt a lot better in many ways. Then I came home and I went back to my usual routine. I never did get my refund. Perhaps they thought I was giving it as a donation.

One Wednesday, for some reason, I just couldn't attend the meeting at Goldsmiths College. One girl I knew in the congregation got really cross with me and I felt she was saying, "you've got to come ... or else!" This made me feel, "What right has she got over me while I'm not even a member of their church!" I really felt that this was heavy-handed so I refused to go to their services. I had quite a few invitations to attend their meetings but after a while they gave up on me and stopped sending me the letters. From time to time I went back to Bromley 'Assembly of God Church', but I felt there was something missing.

After I left Allerford Chapel, they joined together with Catford Hill Baptist Church and formed King's Church Catford. Allerford had a small building which was too small for its growing congregation, while Catford Hill, though it was also well attended, was a very big church.

In 1988 I went to King's Church again. It was nice to see my old friends again but at that time I just couldn't go back there on a regular basis. I knew I had to get back into going to church but I just didn't feel comfortable so I didn't bother.

On Christmas Eve of the same year my father was taken very ill and I went to see him while he was on the life support machine. I really prayed that God would take his life as I was sure that dad would have a very difficult time if he came round, as he would have been severely disabled and I knew how he would hate it.

I was very upset on Christmas Day when I was told that he had passed away. However, I felt that God had answered my prayer and had given me peace about the situation by stopping my dad from suffering. This made me think, could this be the sign I had been waiting for to go back to church again? I knew what I had to do was to get right with God again, and then get back to church. I kept putting it off, but I visited King's Church. The morning I went, the sermon was hard to understand and it discouraged me. I kept telling myself that I couldn't go back to King's. Then after a few months I knew God wanted me back at King's so slowly I began to attend. This didn't take too long as Pat helped me to feel part of the church again.

The next step I had to do was to make a date with an elder and I picked Ron, who had been my house group leader at Allerford, and his wife, Audrey. I did this one Sunday when Pat was away because I wanted to be sure that I was making the move on my own and not relying on other people. Ron believed that God got me ready for my father's death. When

I was ill I tended to get very fed up and started to talk to God and read my bible here and there. I had a good chat to Pat and she said that if I came back, the house-group I would join would consist of caring people and that I would get all the love and support I needed. In July 1989 I was welcomed back into the fellowship at a family meeting at Allerford Hall, which was still used for the smaller meetings. Pat and I were very pleased because Allerford Chapel was where we had first met and I was baptised.

During 1989, I stopped going to King's. I never started going to a house-group because I didn't think the one they wanted me to join was the right one for me. The reason was, a friend of mum's belonged to that house-group and she said she would visit mum, either when she was in hospital or when she came home, but she never did! I just couldn't be a member of that group, not feeling comfortable with that lady. The other reason I did not want to join a group was because of my hearing impairment, and the difficulties that would bring when being in a large group.

There were times when I felt that God wasn't doing anything for me, like when I was feeling down and depressed. I didn't read my bible or have my prayer time, which made me feel even worse.

Eventually, I got my own prayer book, which was an exercise book where I wrote down things I wanted God to do, and the names of people that needed prayers. Then I turned back to God and realised that He had done a lot for me.

In 1993 I still hadn't found a church to go to, whether it was because of past experiences or looking for something special in a church. For example, being accepted as a person in my own right, and not being seen as a child or someone with learning difficulties. I felt if people accepted me as an adult and not a child, and looked beyond my disabilities to see me as a person, I would be able to take a fuller, more committed part in a church. I liked it at King's but they make me feel small. They did have a loop system which would have made it easier to hear with my hearing aid – it had been stolen – and at that time they had not replaced it.

There was one other experience I went through. For four years, I felt I couldn't communicate with God because I couldn't view my relationship with Him as being like a father and his child. Yet I could talk to my teddy bears like anything. Then one day I turned away from the bears and sort of shouted at God saying "If you are here then answer me?" Within the next few days I knew that God has heard me as He had given me peace and assurance within me. Now I can talk to Him and my bears.

Recently I have read two books, "Unexpected Healing" and "Beyond Healing" by Jennifer Rees Larcombe. The books tell us about an able-bodied girl who lived quite a normal life in the country. She married and had children then became disabled for eight years. She certainly understands the problems caused by disability and how people treat us. The point that I would like to make is that she was so desperate for healing after being able-bodied. It made me think of how I felt when Allerford, and later Kings, prayed for my healing. As I had been disabled from birth I was not so desperate for healing but I did want to be healed.

The church kept on and on telling me to pray and ask God for healing. The more it went on the more frustrated and depressed I became and I felt confused. Several fellow churchgoers said the lack of progress must be because I or my parents were sinful. I began to feel that some people in the church were only interested in using my healing when it came to increase their own fame and reputation and not in me as a human being. My trust and faith in my fellow Christians was undermined considerably and I am now much less trusting. These days I have a much more relaxed attitude to healing. This is partly because I now realise that, having been disabled since birth, it has helped form my personality and beliefs, because it is part of me. If I became able-bodied through healing, it would completely change my life in every way, not just physically. At times the idea scares me. I still believe that God has the power to heal me when he wants to. It is in his hands and therefore it is not my problem.

# Life (1)

The way I see life
Is not the way you see it
The way I see people
Is like being at war
They way I see work
Is just a waste of time
But has to be doe
The way I see music
Is a way to relax
The way I see nature
Is to show
How patient nature can be
The way I see time
It just flies by
The way I see love
Is peaceful and joy
The way I see death
I cannot say
The way I see me
Is what I am
And always shall be
The way I see you
Is just another person!

By Julia Mitchell
September 12 1976

## Life (2)

The way I see life
Is to do God's will
The way I see people
To be like a family
The way I see work
Is to work for God
The way I see music
Is a way to relax
The way I see time
To keep me going
The way I see love
Is to show my care
The way I see death
It will be glorious
The way I see me
Is part of God
And always will be
The way I see you
Is to show that I care

By Julia Mitchell
April 4 1983

This is a revision of the poem I wrote in 1976. After I became a Christian in 1981 I began to see life differently.

## Chapter Forty One

# Mum

Everything was going well for mum except for her foot, which had an ulcer on it. It was during 1994 when mum was beginning to get fed up with her foot as it didn't show any sign of improvement. The nurses and the hospital staff kept trying different treatments and this was getting her down. The nurses, the doctors and mum all agreed that she should have her foot amputated. With this leg, she didn't hesitate, as it was beginning to make her ill. I believe that it was a relief because I think she was in pain with it.

When mum told me, I believe that I was more worried than she was. It was five years since she had the other leg off below the knee. Mum being older added to my worries. I worried whether or not mum could cope with the operation let alone after the operation.

Once again, mum went into hospital and went through the usual procedures with the physiotherapists and occupational therapist. Mum made it clear to the doctors that she wanted it the same length as the other leg. They laughed saying it was not easy to do but they would do their best. Mum was convinced that she was going to be put out with a general anaesthetic but, no, she had an epidural anaesthetic. I don't know how she could go through such an operation without being put out! I was shocked and didn't really know what to think; God knows what mum thought!

When I went to visit her with Roland, she was all wired up to machines and that frightened me. I wanted to know all about the machine. Just by looking and watching I worked out what some of the readings were for. Mum did look terrible but she soon recovered from the operation and the doctor had put her on this painkiller where she had control over the doses. Mum was told by a friend who was in hospital at the same time, to stay on the painkiller as long as she could, but she didn't and after a few days she came off.

Mum and I had a lot of fun. While she was in hospital, her ward had problems with a contagious infection and every time I visited I had to put on an apron and rubber gloves, despite her being in the side ward. On one weekend when most of the patients went home there was only mum and another two patients there. I went to buy some ice cream for us, as it was a warm day. While we were eating we watched the staff clean everything on that ward from top to bottom. They even took down the curtains and put clean ones up. All the beds had to be washed. Mum and I were making the nurses jealous of our ice cream. On many occasions I would take mum to the hospital's W.H. Smith shop and sometimes the drivers from Social Services would come over and talk to us. Sometimes I would take her to the canteen.

While mum was in there, her sister Eva was in the 'E ward' for a few weeks as she had had an accident at home. So I took mum to see Eva. Between you and me I used to find this boring but mum was happy so I didn't mind. Eva gave me a job to do which was to collect her pension, but I didn't really want to do it. I felt awkward about this, as Eva could be difficult at times. I told mum that I had put everything down on paper. This worked really well but I was glad when she went home.

Mum was really pleased with her leg as it was roughly the same length but she discovered the doctor left a few stitches in her and it was a good few months before the district nurse took them out! I was surprised that they could be left in for so long!

Within a couple of months mum went home and soon got back to her usual routine and felt a lot better in herself. She had the support from the hospital home care staff for about a month as well the Social Services. It had been a long time since I had seen mum so cheerful and happy.

After mum had been out of hospital for a while, I went to visit her one Saturday. I arrived to find that the ceiling in the hallway had come down! It was no good picking up the pieces to put them in a bag because they just crumbled in your hand. There was dust everywhere – on the stairs, the banisters, the hallway floor. Mum said that she thought she heard a 'bang', but did not realise what it was. Mum and I did our best to clear up what we could. Then I went and got mum's neighbour, who was on my mum's community alarm list. He came up and cleared it all up for her. Mum then phoned the plumber, and he repaired the piping in the loft that had been leaking. We then had to find a plasterer to repair the ceiling in the hallway before everything could get back to normal.

While mum was in hospital I had a bump come up on my wrist and it wouldn't go so mum told one of the nurses and she put a plaster on it. I didn't think any more of it until about three months later after mum went home. My bump was getting bigger but it wasn't hurting. In the end she, Irene and Roland insisted I went to the hospital. They lanced it and got the infection out. It really hurt and it had to be bandaged every day for two weeks. Mum did it once or twice then Roland took over after that.

For the last few years I had a feeling that one day I would phone mum and she wasn't going to be there.

On 19th March 1996 I phoned mum to tell her that I wouldn't be going to the Centre that day. A man's voice answered and I thought this was odd so I asked if I could speak to mum. It took me a good few minutes to find out what was wrong. The police are not really supposed to tell you over the phone when someone passes away. In the end he had to tell me and he asked me to go to mum's house as soon as possible. When he told me that mum had died I was shocked but didn't waste any time.

I rang Roland to tell him the bad news and asked if he could come right over and he did. I then phoned Pauline and she was just as shocked as I was. Pauline said she would try and get to mum's house about 11 o'clock that morning, which she did.

Roland arrived about 8.45am. I wanted him to look after Marina, my home help, while I dealt with the police. I arrived at mum's house about 9.30am and I was taken into the back room. The police started asking me questions about mum's health and as I didn't see her on the bed I thought she had been taken away by the under-takers. Unfortunately she was still in her wheelchair covered with one of her blankets. The police asked me if we could go in the front room while the under-takers came to take mum. Then we went in the back room again to sort out some of mum's personal items. The police told me how much money mum had in the house. They asked if I would like to check it and her jewels. I just took their word for it and they were amazed, because most people will check it. By 10.15am the police had done all that needed to be done and they asked me if I would like to stay with a neighbour until Pauline arrived. I decided to stay on my own until Pauline came.

This is what I think happened. Mum got up at her usual time and went to the table, either to do her face or to write something. Then she passed away. When the home help came to give mum a wash and help her to get dressed she could not get any answer. The home help and the neighbours went round the back of the house to see if they could see anything. When they got in they found mum had passed away and called the police.

When Pauline arrived we did not greet one another like we did when dad died, we just got down business. Pauline said she would do all the paper work and the house. We had no firm ideas about the funeral as we had never discussed it with mum. After thinking about the funeral and chatting to Pat on the phone, I thought it would be good if Martin (the Pastor at King's) could do the service. Pauline agreed to it. I was going to King's Church at the time. I'd been back at King's for a little while and this was the reason why I wanted Martin, along with the fact that he knew me and had met mum.

Martin and I had a meeting to discuss the service. We decided to get Pat to read Psalm 23 (The Lord Is My Shepherd). Martin had already had a chat to Hilda, as she was a friend of ours and a member of King's. I decided to listen to some hymns, which I taped on the video from 'Songs of Praise'. The hymns I chose were 'What a Friend We Have in Jesus' and 'Be Thou My Vision'. I knew one of mum's favourite songs was

'Memory', sung by Elaine Page. I thought this would be good to play on the way in and out from the service.

On the day everything went well. My two aunts, Trudy and Eva, did not come because of the travelling. Members from the Centre couldn't come because at the time of the service [3pm] the borough transport was tied up taking the school children home. June (a retired attendant) and Rose, an attendant, came on behalf of the Centre. I believe there was a bit of a do as several attendants had wanted to come but could not get time off. Sid and Esther, who I adopted and called Granny and Granddad, were there too.

A few people came back to the house afterwards. There was a little problem – Pauline had to get back because Verity, her daughter, had to do a test for a Girl Guide badge.

The only thing that did disappoint me was I wished the service had been earlier in the day so that I could have arranged for more of mum's friends to come to the funeral. Pauline felt that the service went well.

Most people thought the service went very well and Martin gave a very good speech about mum, her life and interests.

# Hilda

As long as I can remember, Hilda lived in our road
She went to Allerford Chapel
In our house group
"Hello" was all we said
But on Mondays
With her neighbours Charles and Doreen
For a chat and laugh
To have a prayer time

Hilda started visting mum
For a chat
To exchange news
They became good friends
Mum died in "96"
Hilda asked me to visit her
So Saturday afternoon it was
We eat and drink
We chat a laugh
Study the Bible and prayer
Our friendship grew
Went to Stoneleigh* together
Our friendship really took off
I needed her more and more

As weeks went by
My legs and blindness got worse
Hilda became a special friend
Gives me support when I'm dowm
Understands John's feelings
As she does mine
Little jobs that I can't do
There when I need her
She will give me her time no matter what
What more could I ask for?

Looking back over this
I can see how God has worked
And how much we have changed

By Julia Mitchell

Stoneleigh took over the Down Bible Week from 1991 to 2001

## Chapter Forty Two
# Ladywell (Part Two)

During the late 1980s, I began to realise that Ladywell Day Centre was not fulfilling my needs and that the next step was to gain work experience or employment.

I thought that Ladywell wasted a lot of time and energy concentrating on craft work and art. This just seemed to be passing time, rather than using this valuable time to help young people to learn how to look after themselves in the outside world, if they were capable to doing so. If they had spent more time on this, people may have felt more confident to move into a flat with a carer, or perhaps completely independently.

I believe that the Ladywell Centre could also have run meetings with the disabled person and their parents/carers, to encourage carers not to be too over protective and to encourage independence in the disabled person.

I felt that Ladywell just kept people ticking along, but never extended anybody. With all the cut backs, it was even harder to offer any additional services. They no longer had the time to sit down one-to-one, as when staff left they did not always get replaced. Therefore, there was less staff to spend time with the members.

People who became disabled later in life tended to have a better chance of getting involved in work experience than those who were born with a disability.

One of Ladywell Centre's stated aims has been to assist members needing help in managing their disability, living independently or becoming employable – rehabilitation in the words used by Social Services. However, it never had a high priority and was not carried out methodically. The cutbacks at that time meant the effort put into it had steadily declined until 1993 when the Centre more or less dropped it as one of its tasks.

The District Health Authority also considerably reduced its speech therapy and physiotherapy services at the Centre. I feel strongly that there is a need to help those who have been disabled since childhood and are cared for by their parents so that they can live, or at least think, independently. Both parents and the disabled members understandably overlooked the fact that parents aren't always going to be there to look after them. If it is left until the parents die, it is often too late and the disabled person faces a complete upheaval in their way of life, while also having to cope with bereavement. If done while the parents are alive, it can provide advice and support which makes the transition to independent living so much easier (as they do for abled bodied children).

Ladywell Centre changed significantly over the years. Its membership steadily increased while staffing was reduced, as did the hours of tuition provided by the Education Department. The average age of its membership increased considerably. Some 75% were over 65, often over 70. Young disabled people rarely attended day centres, and schools encouraged them to go onto further education or training schemes – regarding day centres as dead ends. The result was that day centres were even less attractive to them because of the dominance of senior citizens.

What concerns me is what happens to young disabled people after they finish further education and training schemes A survey carried out as part of my O.U. studies showed that no one seems to know, although it is known that very few get work. When the Centre Manager and Maurice returned from the two years' C.S.S. course, I really thought that we could change Ladywell for the better. Members were canvassed for ideas on how we could improve and develop the Centre but my hopes were soon dashed. At short notice the Neighbourhood Centre was closed and its membership transferred to Ladywell. It increased our membership by about a third and most were in their 70s or 80s. At the same time, the Centre lost three of its twelve officer posts and the overall number of attendants was only increased by one or two. The Centre Manager's duties were also increased to cover other areas. The result was that the new ideas were never taken up.

I was annoyed by the loss of the hairdresser/instructor and print instructor because the members were given no chance to propose alternatives. The hairdressing service was especially invaluable for those in wheelchairs facing problems of access and transport to normal salons, or those like myself, whose sudden jerks could be off putting to inexperienced hairdressers. As the hairdresser was neither part of the attendant staff nor the centre management, but still an officer, and many members felt they could raise problems or complaints with her informally. The hairdresser prices could have been increased from their very low level and would have paid for the post. Prices would still have been below commercial rates and most members used its services because of its convenience rather than cheapness.

The print room could have financed some of the cost of the print instructor by charging higher rates and perhaps canvassing for more work. The loss of the print instructor's post meant that the print room had to be shut down over a period of time because of low levels of use.

They did have a few members making special birthday, wedding cards etc., for a small price. I felt that if there were more members involved and they charged more, it could be a small business. They could also make new Christmas cards from old cards.

After a while I decided to do something about the decision to delete the hairdresser's post. I asked Roland to help me with the wording and drawing up of a petition to the Council. Redundancy notices had been issued before we heard of the decision so the petition asked for retention of the hairdressing service rather than retaining the post. I decided that it would have more influence if only centre members signed it. Every sheet had the petition on it and I checked signatures, deleting anyone who signed it twice. Another member helped me to collect signatures but I had some trouble explaining to her that it would be no good collecting signatures on a blank sheet, and that members had to sign properly and only once.

We eventually collected over 300 signatures and I handed the petition to the Chairperson of the Social Services Committee, who arranged for it to be formally presented to the Council. The Assistant Director of Social Services was instructed to look into alternatives with the result that it was agreed that Social Services would recruit self-employed hairdressers to provide a service at the centre for three days a week, with the Council letting them use the fully equipped hairdressing salon, free of charge. I was pleased because we at least retained a hairdressing service of sorts which, without the petition, the Council would not have been committed to provide. However, they admitted that the possibility of the post being self-financing had not been considered because of the speed with which the cuts were implemented.

The service provided by the Centre inevitably deteriorated as the pressure on staff increased and they had less time to chat with members and just had to focus on basic tasks. There were two members, who did not agree to sign the petition until the last minute, when they realised that I was getting somewhere with it! – I just couldn't believe it.

I was on the Centre's Representatives Committee for quite a number of years, but found it very frustrating. The Committee had no power and was only advisory. The way I saw it, most of our requests seem to be ignored or not followed through. On the other hand, members often lacked any ideas or failed to argue their points and often just rubber stamped what the Centre Manager had done or proposed to do.

What I would have liked to have seen happening at Ladywell Day Centre covered many areas. I would have liked to have seen the attendants given the chance of getting qualifications so they could move on to better jobs. I believed they should be involved more and taken more seriously. Management only payed lip service to involving them in caring for members, beyond attending to basic physical needs. When it came to the crunch, they were not consulted or involved. Attendants who had a special skill or knowledge should have been allowed to pass it on to interested members if they so wished.

It is important that more attention is paid to the relatively younger members, in view of the overwhelming proportion of elderly people now attending the Centre. Younger disabled people are often deterred from attending day centres because of the pre-eminence of elderly members.

It is important for the younger members at the Centre, who are often severely disabled, to receive one to one care. For example, being read to or assisted with exercises to keep them as mobile as possible – mind you, they did do this with one member. It is important that a speech therapist and a physiotherapist attend the Centre on a regular basis – not only to undertake work with new members, but to undertake reviews of older members like myself who may need refresher courses of treatment as bad habits reassert themselves.

It would also have been helpful if there could have been displays of the various aids and gadgets for physically disabled people, every 6 months or so. A catalogue is not as good as seeing and trying out the real thing. A computer room at the Centre, which members could use for basic training and entertainment, would benefit all members. There, they could learn basic computer skills or play games or use it for education according to their own wishes. Eventually the centre did acquire a computer through the WRVS, which members were able to use.

Computers can be the solution for members who cannot write or communicate verbally. They exercise their fingers and wrists, improve concentration and can keep your mind occupied. The computer gadgets available for severely physically disabled people can open up a new world for them. For those hoping to find work, basic computer training could be the first step on the way to finding employment.

During this time we used to have a teacher from Lewisham College who used to teach computer skills to us at the centre. Then they moved this course to Lewisham College itself. When I left in the year 2000, I do not know whether they carried it on or whether the course was discontinued. I worry that this means that we could end up being more isolated from the community as a whole.

I would like all classes to be open to able-bodied people and the Centre have a pop-in parlour where those independent and mobile could visit to see friends or have a cuppa. The woodwork and crafts classes could be encouraged to produce items for sale to bring some extra money in. Ladywell Centre, while it was purpose-built and had ample parking space, was rather isolated. Ideally, I would like a centre to be near public transport, shops and a library as well.

Looking back over the past years, the Social Services transport has changed tremendously. At Trinity we could get to know the drivers and they would join in our activities, play cards, joke and chat with us. Now the transport comes under the Direct Team, having combined with the school buses and hospital outpatient departments. As schools have priority over day centres this causes problems. The coaches do the school rounds first before the day centre rounds so members can often be late in or late going home. Drivers now have to return to the Depot except for one, which will be left at the centre, so there is less contact. The drivers are often very different in their attitudes: some are really caring and understanding while others are so rude and inconsiderate that you wonder why they do the job.

While I often saw the faults in Ladywell, I must admit that if I had still been at Trinity I would not have progressed as much as I did at Ladywell. Ladywell brought me into contact with many more people of all ages and backgrounds. At Trinity, all the members were like me disabled since birth. Mixing with the members at Ladywell, most of whom had normal working lives before disability affected them, widened my horizons. At Ladywell, I also found that, because of the much larger number of staff and tutors, there was always someone I could go to for advice on practical problems or my educational studies. It gave me the opportunity of doing courses at the centre that I would not have done otherwise.

Over approximately eight years, I became increasingly involved in the WRVS shop in the Ladywell Day Centre. The shop was usually open from about .m to around 2pm, Monday to Friday. It sold confectionery, biscuits, soft drinks, cigarette and toiletries. I used to go to St. Mary's Church in Lewisham for a while and got to know Irene B. who worked in the shop on Mondays and Wednesdays.

One Monday Irene was on her own as her co-worker, Joan, wasn't in and she invited me into the shop and we had a good chat and a laugh. After that I used to join her in the shop every week. I often felt nervous and on edge with Joan, feeling that I had to be careful what I said or did. Yet Joan was a different person on her own, much more relaxed and friendly. In time I became a sort of helper by helping them fill the shelves up. I would serve people who I felt comfortable with, those who had the patience to wait while I worked the change out. Sometimes I could take ages getting the money out of the small cash box compartment. I also helped them in small ways like running errands within the centre etc. Eventually Joan left when she moved to Maidstone. She did teach me that some people are much nicer than you think if you get to know them. By the time she left we were quite friendly. She was replaced by Irene N, one of Irene B's friends who attended the same church. I got on with Irene N straight away and I really enjoyed her company. I looked forward to helping out in the shop on Mondays and Wednesdays because of the laughter and chat.

While working there, I got to know Wendy, Rose, Vickie and Victor, WRVS volunteers who worked in the shop on other days of the week. I helped them in the same way, except for Victor. I often had a chat with Victor when he had his break but only went in the shop to serve people if he left the shop for a few minutes to do something. I didn't really get to know Victor until I asked if I could interview him about his religious beliefs as part of a project for my bible study course. After that, I looked on Victor as a father-like figure. He was very interesting, telling me many stories about his working days as a cook and wartime experiences. Later on I found out he was partially deaf, like myself, and we could talk and joke about the problems this caused us.

We used to call Irene B. and Irene N. 'the two Renes', just like 'The Two Ronnies' on the T.V. Sometimes I used to take in my teddy bear, Jason, to see them, and they used to have a lot of fun with him. Every time I wanted Jason's neck bow done up, I used to get Irene N. to do it because she was so good at it.

When either of the Irenes were on duty, we used to bring in fruit to eat at lunchtime. Because I had a sweet tooth, I would never eat any fruit that was bitter or sharp, and the two Renes used to laugh at me. As time went by, I began to eat more of the citrus fruits, but still not all of them. I used to bring in some unusual fruit, just to try it out, even if we weren't sure what it was – like ugly fruit, passion fruit, and pomegranates. Sometimes, we didn't know what part of the fruit to eat and what part to leave, so we used to experiment.

I used to play jokes on the two Renes. The WRVS had an old fashioned till which used to have a glass 'window' at the top. When they weren't looking, I used to drop some money down the back of the drawer, and when they came to total up all the money I used to say "Are you sure you've got the right amount there?"

Then they would look at me and say, "Why? What have you been up to?" Then they would open up the drawer and find the coins that I had put down the back.

We had a new lady that joined called Mary. She was a laugh too, and I got on really well with her. Every time she was on duty, she used to buy a soft drink for me. It was so nice of her.

Fridays seemed to be a bad day for the WRVS because apart from Irene N they couldn't seem to find a permanent volunteer to assist her since she worked with Florrie. Florrie was such a lovely person, just like the two Irenes – fun to be with. She was found to have cancer and I used to visit her once or twice a week when she was in hospital. I often met her daughters there. Florrie was always cheerful and ready for a joke. In the end she was transferred to St. Christopher's Hospice and though I visited her there soon after the move, I was too late. Alice, who replaced her, was good fun but she had to leave for medical reasons.

It was a great shock when, in October 1993, Irene B. died suddenly. I missed her very much as did Irene N. who was her closest friend. Irene

B. had been at Ladywell for 14 years or so. All three of us used to have a good laugh and I really used to look forward to seeing them at Ladywell.

Those days helping out in the WRVS shop, and the friendship I enjoyed with the volunteers, played a big part in my attending the centre. I also feel that I gained a lot from the discussions we had about life in general.

Irene N. became like a mother to me, just like Sylvia after my mum died. Irene N. unfortunately passed away, having suffered with cancer, on May 24th 2004. Roland and I just managed to visit her in time to say goodbye, and she told me how much I meant to her. The best thing of all was that I was able to put my arm round her and kiss her goodbye, which was something I wasn't able to do with my real mum.

Victor, used to come in once or twice a week. I used to see him as a fatherly figure. Slowly, Victor and I got to know each other and had a good laugh and a good chat. Then one day, he asked me to do a job for him on my computer. This was to type out the whole list of items that we had in the shop, so that he could re-order the things he wanted. We did this once a fortnight.

After a couple of years, he asked me if I could help him with the stocktaking. This had to be done a different way, but I knew I could do it. You had a list of items – with their descriptions. Then you had to write in the prices, how many were left and the price of each item. You then multiplied this number by the price and that would give you the total of the stock you had left in the shop. He was very pleased with the way this went, and we carried on doing stocktaking together.

During the 1990s, Victor became ill, out of the blue. His wife rang up the Ladywell Centre to see if I would go and see him in hospital, which was opposite King's College. I was the only one from the Centre who was allowed to go and see him.

When I got there, he asked me if I would like to take the whole job over, and I replied that I would give it a go. He was quite pleased.

Over a period of time, Irene said she would give me a hand with it, which I was quite happy about. However, we did have one or two problems. I would not order anything until we got down to the last half a dozen. Anything that was slow to go would not be ordered again. This was because sometimes things would go past their sell-by date if they were not selling quickly enough.

Irene and I did the stocktaking together for quite a few years. I used to order different stock now and again, just to give the members a change. This used to go really well. One of the biggest problems that I had while I was doing it was this: if there was something about to go out of date, I would like to knock the price down gradually as it came up for expiry. This way, people got what they paid for. Unfortunately, Irene did not like this idea, and preferred to sell 2 for the price of 1, which did not make much money.

Over the years since it first started, it lost more and more money – this was partly due to dwindling membership as well.

One day, Maurice and I were talking. I brought up the idea of him going on a counselling course because I thought that he would be good at it. It would also give him another qualification. After a little while, he came back to me and said that he was going to take my advice and do a counselling course.

Twice a year we used to hold a sports day. On these days we would sell quite a lot as members from different boroughs would compete in the sports day. In the end they stopped this event.

One of these sports days I will never forget. Katie, a member of the social services committee and the president of LAPD, invited me into the staff room and asked me if I would like a glass of wine. When I accepted, she offered me a sip of her wine – which really made me mad!

Victor told many stories about his job as a cook in Lewisham Hospital. Victor and his wife he were members of Westminster Cathedral, and he was on 'Songs of Praise'. I managed to get them on video, and I've still got it to this day.

When I first started working for the WRVS, I really thought that this would open another door for me, which may lead to me working in the office and using the computer. Unfortunately, it did not work out that way. The person in charge did not really see me as a person with a brain, who could use a computer. He did not give me any encouragement or opportunity. Once again, a door was shut to me.

One of the other jobs I used to do was to buy the diabetic food from Boots and bring it into the Centre. This used to cost about £20 per week. It used to drive me up the wall because I had to explain to the members that eating a lot of diabetic chocolate was just as bad as eating normal chocolate. Eaten in large quantities, it could give you diarrohea and other trouble.

In the year 2000, Boots stopped making diabetic chocolate – and I had to bring in a leaflet to prove this to the members! It was a nightmare.

We had one member who was not allowed to eat any sweets. He used to like buying a certain kind of chocolate and we used to let him buy it. Then, one day, a member of staff came over to us to stop us from selling to him. In the end, we managed to persuade him not to buy any more.

Another thing I had to do was go around chasing members of staff because they had not paid for certain items they had bought. This used to be a lot of fun for me – chasing people for their money, and I believe a lot of the staff knew it!

In 1999, Edith (the WRVS organiser for Lewisham), wanted to change the plan of the stocktaking list. Instead of coming to me, she went to

Irene, and gave the instructions to her. When Irene came back to me, and told me what she wanted, I got cross because Irene could have told Edith to come and discuss this with me, as she knew I kept this on the computer. Instead of this, they presented this to me after they had decided on things. I decided to walk out and let them get on with it, although I still worked in the shop.

I made some really good friends at the shop. We had 2 new female members. One was a bit of a so-and-so, and the other one became a good friend of mine. Her name was Sylvia. Even now, she comes to visit me once a month.

One of the biggest lessons I learnt was this. One day when I was sitting in the dining room talking to two or three friends, one of them said " I don't care what people think about me".

Of course, I believed him. I then told him one or two remarks that I had heard a member of staff say about him. Contrary to what he had just told me, he was very upset and went to find the member of staff concerned and had it out with her.

From this experience, I learned that even when people say that they don't care what anyone else thinks, you know damn well that they do!

This situation was made worse by the fact that the member of staff who was involved did not come back to me directly, but went straight to Roland and told him what had been said. She wrote me a very formal letter, stating that she would speak to me at the Centre, but would have nothing to do with me outside. I said that that was ok by me.

All in all, it took us about two years to become friends again and forgive each other.

## Chapter Forty Three
# Mum's Will

When mum died, I wasn't expecting anything like this to happen. As time went by I began to feel that Pauline wasn't keeping me informed about the will. I visited mum's house one Saturday to check it was OK, only to find Paul and Pauline there. Pauline told me they were waiting for estate agents to come to value the house. I wanted to stay, as much out of interest as to what they did as anything else. Having lived with my parents, and just having been a council tenant, valuations were all new to me. Pauline's attitude gave me the feeling that she did not want me there. Pauline did not tell me what was happening and when I filled in a form to do with benefits, telling them the date of mum's death, she told me off. I was beginning to feel very unhappy about it all.

Katie, who had been a good friend to me ever since I was small, told me that I would need to get a solicitor for my share of my parents' will. I sort of looked at Katie and said, "Why?" She did have her reasons.

We all do silly things when we are young. I knew that Pauline didn't mean them, but Katie had never forgotten them. I was not totally sure, but I needed advice over putting my share into a Trust Fund, so I took her advice.

Katie recommended a solicitor to me, Richard, who was a friend of hers. At our first meeting, I asked Roland to come along in case I had difficulty hearing what was said or had difficulty in explaining things. We discussed my general situation and as a first step Richard filed a caveat on my mum's will. This meant my sister could not get probate on the will without my agreement.

My idea of a Trust Fund soon ran into difficulties. I knew that I did not want Pauline as a trustee, though she could assist as executor, as it meant changing the will. We were not very close and she lived far away. I felt I could not talk to her and also felt very threatened by her. I wanted Richard, Roland and Pat as they lived locally, knew me better and were more aware of the problems that disabled people faced. What ended the idea of a trust fund was a barrister's advice that it would have to be available to others, however restricted its range.

My problem was that, as I would lose my benefits, I would have to live on the money. It would disappear in a few years, leaving nothing to show for what my mum and dad had left me. I decided I would like to buy a two bedroom flat. This would enable me to invite friends to stay and, if my condition worsened as I got older, provide somewhere for a carer to sleep. Pauline had suggested this years ago, but as things turned out I think she forgot.

I asked Richard to another meeting. This time I invited Pat as well as Roland. This was because Pat had been a good friend to me and owned her flat and knew a lot about the problems, as she also was on the lease-holders co-op that owned the freehold. We discussed different ideas: Roland thought I should buy the flat I lived in, as I would get a big discount under Right to Buy. Pat and I were against the idea. It did not help that we were not sure how much I would be getting, only an estimate.

I started visiting different agents, seeing what that had on offer, and discussing ones that seemed promising with Pat. One flat I liked very much. It was in Catford, not far from the shopping area, near the two railway stations and on the 284 bus route, which went to Ladywell and on to Lewisham. Pat arranged for a friend of hers, who was a retired building surveyor, to go with me to view the flat. The flat was in Ravensbourne Park and seemed perfect. The only thing I did not like was that the pathway leading up to the flats looked a bit uneven and could be dodgy in the dark. However I could not meet the price they were asking, though eventually it went for £4,000 less for a quick sale. The owner had already moved to Wales. I felt that if I had pushed harder to get my money, I could have bought it. Pat said it showed that it was not meant to be, but I believe if God gives you the chance, it's up to you.

One flat I looked at was behind Catford library, quite modern with a kitchen/diner. However, this was not suitable as it was an upstairs flat and would possibly be knocked down to widen the road.

Another one I looked at was in Downham, quite a walk from the bus stop. We decided against this as were were told the people nearby were very noisy.

The other flat I liked very much was in Bromley Road. It had a lift and would have been ideal as the buses ran past on the main road. The price, however, was too high.

The price of flats was gradually rising, and towards the end of 1996 it was becoming clear that I would not have enough money. However, my mum's Woolwich account had not been shared out because my sister and I had agreed not to close it until after the share allocation, when The Woolwich became a public company.

I wrote to my sister asking if the money due to be shared out could be changed, so she could have the Woolwich Account while I could receive my share of cash immediately. It would have meant I would have been able to consider flats like the one in Catford. The Woolwich pay out, in six months' time, would be outrun by increasing house prices. My sister would benefit by receiving all the shares.

On Christmas Eve I received a letter from Pauline, completely out of control. I asked Roland to read it but he refused, other than to say that she would not agree. He said he would read it to me after Christmas. He knew that my dad had died on a Christmas Eve. I thought, "Wow, it must be bad." When he did read it, I was really upset. Pauline said she would lose out on interest on the money involved and that the Woolwich's change to a public company was not certain. I felt this was unfair. The shares due to be handed out would be worth far more than any interest that could be earned. She claimed that I had delayed the pay-out of the will and had cost her money because of the caveat.

While there had been a delay, I felt I had the right to seek legal advice. Moreover, it had been more than outweighed when her solicitor had gone on holiday for about three weeks without sending the accounts of the estate to me for my signature. She also went on about the cost of my barrister's advice, when it had been paid for by me, and concerned my personal situation. I felt she was very unfair and any doubts I had in having my own solicitor disappeared. In the end, I left my shares in The Woolwich so I could gain more in the long run. This worked out well, but was still not enough to buy a flat at that time.

That Christmas was the first since mum had died. I had thought my sister would invite me to stay; instead she sent me that letter. I spent Christmas with Roland at his parents'.

On Christmas Day I felt more unwell as the day went on. I felt sick, had a bad headache and my eyes hurt. By the evening I was being sick and I could not see properly. Roland rang his parents' GP's emergency service, who told him that it was a nasty virus which was making a lot of people ill. They advised him that I should be kept warm, given sips of water and paracetamol for the headache. If I was not better in a day or two, he should take me to my GP. I did improve but my sight was still poor.

Roland took me to his GP as I stayed with him after Christmas. The GP understood disability and was very good. He told me I had conjunctivitis and said I would have to have an ointment to put in my lower eyelids four times a day. This caused uproar at Roland's place as he had to do it. Because of my cerebral palsy I could not.

Between us we worked out a method: I laid on the settee and held an upper eyelid open with difficulty. Roland had to hold the lower lid down while he squeezed some ointment in. The more my sight improved the more difficult it was. As my eye instinctively closed as the ointment tube came near, it became a race between my eye's reflexes and Roland. It was a right old performance – especially when he lost!

When I resumed looking for a flat, it became clear as 1997 went on that flats were now out of my price range. I started to consider buying my flat under the "Right to Buy" scheme and selling it after three years. The discount I would get in buying it would mean that when I sold it I could buy a two bedroom flat. Though I met my sister at my Aunt's funeral in 1997 and we chatted about our disagreement, our relationship was still tense and we have not spoken properly since.

I would definitely advise any disabled person whose parents have their own property to ask their parents what they are going to do when they pass away. If their parents put the money in trust for them, then nobody else can touch the money. This would avoid going through the difficulties I had to.

*Chapter Forty Four*
# On the Buses and in Public

In this chapter, I will tell you some of the funny things that used to happen when I used to go out and about walking and on the buses, when I was more mobile.

There was one occasion when my shoe came undone. I saw a policeman nearby and thought that he would be an ideal person to go and ask to help me. I went up to him and asked him if he could do my shoe up. He gave me such a look, and obviously did not know what to say to me.

I explained to him that I was disabled, and could not do shoelaces up, and would he be prepared to do it for me? He just stood there looking blankly at me for a good three minutes, until I said, "Well?"

In the end he said, "Yes, sure." I think, because I had a bag on my arm, he was frightened that I might hit him on the head with it!

Another time, I thought I was being followed. I went into the nearest house, pretending that I lived there. The person following me came in behind me, and said, "Can I help you?"

I felt all hot and bothered, until he said, "I live here."

I just turned round, walked out, and carried on walking home.

Sometimes I used to be at the bus stop when there were kids hanging around. They sometimes said, "If we give you the money, could you go and get us a packet of cigarettes?"

I used to refuse, but luckily they never gave me any trouble.

On another occasions, there was a lady who used to come round to everyone at the bus stop, asking for 10p. I gave it to her the first few times, and then realised that she was making a habit of it, and so stopped giving it to her. After a while, I found out that the police had their eye on her.

I used to be a regular customer on the 122 buses. I used to come out of Ruegg House, with a few minutes' walk to the bus stop. If there was a 122 bus coming towards me and I went to the edge of the pavement and put my hand out, if the driver knew me he would stop and pick me up there to save me walking all the way to the stop.

One of the 122 drivers used to bring a little girl with him, who used to sit in the space where the luggage goes. I used to talk to her, and sometimes she used to drop things on the floor, so I had to tell the driver. I got to know that driver well and eventually the driver was quite good to me and would stop and pick me up anywhere.

Another time it was raining. I was struggling to do my jacket up and a 122 driver got out of the bus, came over to me, and did my jacket up for me. Sometimes the 161 drivers were just as good, until they changed their route slightly.

I can remember one bad occasion on the 122 bus. We had turned the corner at Ladywell Road to go to Lewisham and I think it was a Friday. Some drunken boys got on the bus. One of them fell on me, and the woman behind me was very concerned about me. To be honest, I was all right, apart from my glasses. The driver saw what happened but didn't do much to help.

In the end, the other people on the bus got the boys off. The ironic thing was that the Police Station was just round the corner from where the boys got on.

On another occasion, I was on the bus and some young people got on and wouldn't pay their fare. The driver shut the door, pushed the alert button, and we had to sit there for about half and hour, while the police and inspector were sorting it all out.

Another time, on a hopper bus, the bus went around the corner and a lady fell off her seat. I had to laugh, but I couldn't show it. I don't think she was badly hurt.

On another occasion, I undid a sweet and went to throw the wrapper out of the window. As the bus was moving, the wind blew the wrapper back in and it landed on a lady's hat in front of me. I didn't know what to do – whether to tell her or whether to just leave it. I decided to leave it.

Another time on the bus, I felt some pain in my ankle. I kept rubbing it with my other foot. When I finished the journey and got back to Roland's place, I took off my shoes and socks to discover that I had been stung by a wasp. Rubbing it had made it even worse.

One time I will never forget. I was sitting by the door, and a man got on and sat opposite me behind the driver. When the bus started moving, the man put his arm round the corner and his hand under the plastic shield where the driver takes the fares, and grabbed some of the cash. I couldn't believe that he would do this in front of me, and in broad daylight. The driver did not notice anything and we were the only two passengers on the bus, so he got away with it.

One day, I was getting off the bus and a schoolboy took my bus pass out of my pocket. I told him to give it back as he would not be able to use it for himself, and he did.

Another day, I was standing at the bus stop and a lady took my purse out of my pocket. I felt her do it and asked her to put it back. She just ignored me and kept the purse. I had about £5 in it.

On another occasion, I lost my wallet with my bus pass in. It had a bit of money in it – about 3p. I decided to go to the police station. It must have been handed in because the police had it and gave it back to me. My 3p was still in there.

Once, I was on a 284 hopper bus, on my way to Lewisham. We were going around a one way system, instead of going straight ahead to the main shopping area. I was sitting behind the driver. The female driver hadn't noticed the bus stop was so near, so she had to stop quickly. I went forward and hit my head on the glass behind the driver, which shook me up quite a bit.

I got off the bus and a man who saw what happened asked me if I was all right. My glasses were bent, but apart from that I wasn't too badly hurt.

I decided to report this incident to the police. The police managed to find out the name of the driver, but I don't know whether she got into trouble about it. I think that if I had gone straight to the hospital, she would have been in real trouble.

I believe I was on my way to Roland's place. At that time, all the buses went on a bus route up Lewisham High Street and down Lewis Grove. The bus in front of us broke down, and there were other buses behind us. We could not move and a bus coming the opposite way was also stuck. We all just had to wait about half an hour for the police and London Transport to come out to deal with it. They eventually got it under control – they had about eight or nine buses to sort out.

In Lewisham High Street, there used to be a van that used to sell candy floss, and I used to love it. Slowly, I got to know the lady who sold it. I used to get my money out beforehand and then go up to her and buy the candy floss in a bag. This meant I could either eat it when I got home or on the way home. This lady was so nice to me. Sometimes, she wouldn't take my money.

Also in Lewisham High Street, there was the market. In the market was a fish stall and the lady who was selling fish called me over, her name was Peggy. She used to work in the fish shop near where my mum and dad used to live many years ago, and she recognised me. Slowly, I got to know other people in the market as I used to buy plums and pears and other fruit. They used to be very good to me and when my legs started to get a bit wobbly, they would come over to me and give me a helping hand to walk to the bus stop if I needed it.

When I used to leave the Centre to go home, before the 284 buses came out, I used to walk through the park. If you walked over the footbridge and turned left, you could come out at the back of Lewisham Hospital. If you turned right and walked straight through the park, you would pass a racing track and come out, more or less, at the back of Tesco's or Rushey Green.

On one particular day when I was walking through the park, I saw a man standing nearby with his trousers down. I felt a bit worried and wondered what to do. I decided to turn back and go back to the Centre and report it. I think they reported it to the police. This more or less put me off walking through the park. However, when my mum was in Lewisham hospital, I did walk through the park every day because it was a short cut and much quicker.

You could walk to the Centre from the Ladywell Road end on the 122 bus route; there were two roads – Malyons Road and Slagrove Road, and I used to walk down either of these roads. Later, when they brought out the 284 buses, I used to get off by Rushey Mead and walk between the houses. This would bring me out very close to the Day Centre.

I can remember once being in the Lewisham Shopping Centre, I was 47. I got stuck – my legs just wouldn't move. In the end, the security guard had to take me through the shopping centre and left me at the entrance. I had to ask someone else to take me to the bus stop. I believe it was a man who worked in the market who helped me to the bus stop.

Shortly after I moved into my bungalow, a man came to my door trying to get me to change over from LEB to another electricity supplier. I said that I wasn't really interested, but asked him to put some information through the door so that my friend could look at it later. The trouble was that he kept coming back and I could not get rid of him. Roland's sister, Marion, came over that day and he came back again. This time she answered the door and he still wouldn't go away. Marion rang up the company he came from to ask them to get rid of him otherwise we would ring the police. They promised that they would ring me back within half and hour. By this time, Marion had gone home as she used to live in Thamesmead. When they rang back, they apologised saying that they had managed to trace the person involved and had put a stop to him being such a nuisance.

One day I was trying to put some blue tack under my old phone to stop it from wobbling. The receiver came off and I accidentally pushed the button that dialled 999. Within 15 minutes the police were at my door. Hilda, my next door neighbour, came rushing out to see what was going on. When she eventually found out, she had a good laugh. I invited the police in because I thought this would be the best way to explain it to them. I showed them my telephone and explained what I was trying to do. I said to them that while they were here, they could put the telephone back for me. They gave me a funny look, but did put the phone back for me.

One day I was in Lewisham and it was pouring with rain. Roland and I went to stand in the doorway of a Wimpy bar. While we were standing there, one of the staff came out and gave me a portion of chips (he knew me because I used to go in there quite a lot to have meals).

On the day that Diana, Princess of Wales, died I was listening to the radio expecting to hear 'Good Morning Sunday' with Don MacClean, when the announcement was made that she had had a serious road accident in Paris. Later on it was confirmed that she had died as a result of the accident. This news had a tremendous effect on me – I don't know why. Over a period of time, I wanted to go up to Kensington Palace to pay my respects and to read what other people had written to her on the bouquets and flowers. At this point, I did not have my wheelchair and could see.

I made the journey by myself, travelling by bus up to Victoria and changing there to get to Kensington Palace. I was completely amazed and also amused by some of the poems that were written for Diana. As I was walking round, I could see a group of girl guides picking up all the cards and flowers. I stayed there for quite a long time before making my way back. To me, the trip was really worthwhile and I was very glad that I did make the trip. Roland thought that I must be mad!

In 2001 when I could walk a bit, one Saturday afternoon I booked a cab to visit my friend, Hilda. The cab came but he couldn't park near my bungalow. The driver told me he had parked around the corner and asked me if I could walk to it. Roland said, 'If it's just parked round the corner, Julia can walk there if she can hold on to your arm.'

As we began to walk, the driver said that he couldn't remember where he parked the cab. We kept walking and walking and I was getting tired and a bit worried. The driver said that he would leave me to sit on a nearby wall while he continued to look for his cab. By this time I wished Roland had come with me.

He came back about 10 minutes later saying he still couldn't remember where he had parked the cab. He had no mobile phone with him as he had left it in the cab. At this point, I told him to take me back home.

Roland took one look at me and said I looked like I'd seen a ghost, as I was quite shaken up. The driver apologised and Roland and I said that we would order another cab, after I had had time to relax and calm down a bit. Eventually I did get to my friend's house.

During the evening we rang up the cab company to see if the driver managed to find his cab and he had.

I must say that this was one of the worst cab drivers I ever had.

## Chapter Forty Five
# Moving to Woolwich

Roland and I were beginning to realise that I was spending more time at his place than I was at mine. I suppose in a way I didn't really like living on my own. In the year 2000, my legs started to play me up and I kept falling over. I was finding it difficult to walk without any support.

Roland was thinking about asking for a transfer to be nearer to me in Normanton Street in Forest Hill if I needed his help, as he lived quite a distance away. However, when he applied for a transfer the nearest he could get was Sydenham or Downham. To be honest, I knew deep in my heart that Roland really did like his flat and did not want to move.

I felt that I had nothing to stay for at the Ladywell Day Centre, apart from the WRVS and my friends. As my mum and dad had both passed away we thought that it might be a good idea to ask Lewisham Council to nominate me under the HOMES scheme for a transfer to Greenwich Council – this would mean that I would be nearer to Roland and he could come and give me help if I needed it. This was in 1998.

I applied, and Lewisham Council agreed to nominate me to Greenwich Council who accepted the nomination. Roland contacted Greenwich Council for me, explaining why I needed a move to the estate where he lived. He also wrote letters for me, explaining how my disability had started to cause me more problems and pointing out that it took him an hour or more by bus (as a non-driver) to see me, and that he was not in the best of health himself.

In October 1999, I was offered a bungalow in Kempt Street. Roland realised that it was next door to someone he had known for some years and whom I had met. Roland and I never thought that I would be offered a bungalow; we thought I would be offered a ground floor flat on the estate. A bungalow was much better.

The day before I went to look round, I was sitting on Roland's bed in his room and my mum appeared to me. She told me to take the property, even if I wasn't too sure of it at the time because it was boarded up, and also my eyesight was starting to fail me. She told me that I would be very happy there and wanted me to take it.

On the Monday when I was to look around the bungalow, Roland could not take me because he started his new job the same day. Instead, we asked Edina to come with me.

When we walked in I saw that mum was right. I could not see much as it was dark in the bungalow, as it was still boarded up. However, I was pleased with what I could see – There was a little lobby that led into the living room on the right; through an archway and on the right again was a fairly big kitchen; along a bit further was the entrance to my bedroom, which was very big, with an en-suite bathroom with walk-in shower – which was just what I wanted.

The electricity had been turned off and there was no light, and this was made worse because of problems with my eyesight. I just had to ask Edina lots of questions like – would my cooker fit? Can I have the gas hob taken out? Could I fit my washing machine in?

All the answers she gave were positive – "Yes, yes, yes!"

Hilda, my friend, and I had been praying for quite a while for me to find a place like this, and I knew I couldn't turn it down. Mum had been right!

That day I signed an agreement so that I could move in on the 18th October 1999. However I didn't move in on that day, deciding to keep my flat on in Forest Hill for a while, while my new bungalow was being decorated. I asked Denzil, a friend of Roland and Edina, if he would decorate it for me before I moved in, and he agreed. Edina helped me to choose the colours.

The living room was decorated in a peachy colour; the kitchen was painted in a fresh, light lemon; the bedroom was painted in a very light pink; and the bathroom did not need anything doing to it, except to paint the doors white.

I finally moved into my bungalow in March 2000. I stayed at Roland's place until it was finally ready.

By this time, my legs were getting more and more unbalanced. About a year before, I went to see my GP and she referred me to a Consultant in Cerebral Palsy. When I got the appointment, it was for a year later. Roland rang up the GP and managed to bring it forward a few months .

In January 2000 the Consultant sent me to Kings College Hospital for tests that included testing my nervous system and a body scan. They also wanted blood tests but by then it was too late in the day. They suggested I stayed overnight but I was not keen. Roland and I came back the next day. As it cost us £30 a round trip it was the most expensive blood test I have ever had!

When the results came through, we saw the Consultant back at Lewisham Hospital. He put my wobbly legs down to the effect of ageing on my Cerebral Palsy. In my own mind, I did not agree with him. I know the way my Cerebral Palsy affects me. I do not get the jerks unless I am trying to do something. I never jerk if I am just sitting down and resting (although it now affects me if I am sitting or lying down).

The Consultant put me on some tablets, which seemed to work. However, I still get the jerks now and again and sometimes they can get quite bad. Other times it is fairly mild. It always seems to get worse when it is the time of my period.

It was quite funny how I first met Edina. We both used to get on the same bus. She used to always go upstairs and I used to be downstairs by the door. We always used to say hello and goodbye to each other. She thought I used to live in Ruegg House in Woolwich, but I didn't. I was just visiting Roland.

At this time, Edina was working at Lee Green. Later, she got a job on the concierge in the reception area at Ruegg House. She was there to monitor who was coming and going in and out of the building, and to check the security cameras. Because Roland was already working in the concierge on the estate, she had got to know him.

It was a real coincidence when she found out that I was a friend of Roland.

As my legs were starting to get worse and I couldn't walk properly, I had to struggle to get to Ladywell (where the day centre was). The only way round it was to get someone who was on duty at the concierge at Ruegg House to walk me to the bus stop (by this time Roland had left and got a new job as a Housing Officer).

I would catch the 122 to take me to Lewisham. Then I used to get off and go to Handicars cab office, which was quite close to the bus stop. I would then book a cab to take me to the Ladywell Centre. Sometimes another member of the Centre would be at Handicars, and we used to share the cab. On the whole, though, I was on my own. I would then book the return journey to take me back to Ruegg House. The good thing about this was that I got to know the cab drivers on both journeys and they started to understand me.

This arrangement went well because in the end, I stopped going to the Centre every day and only went on Mondays, Thursdays and Fridays. Because I used to have a laugh with the staff in the Handicars office, I decided to write a poem about them, called 'Minicab'.

>Minicab
>Minicab, Minicab,
>So many about,
>Which one shall I pick,
>Past experiences come rushing back,
>The thought of minicabs,
>Will have to choose one very soon,
>As my legs won't walk me without an arm,
>My eye is seeing grey through cataract

> Oh dear, minicab which one do I go for,
> Handicars I see daily on my journey,
> Words flashing through my mind,
> Trusting, caring, understanding, friendly,
> Reliable, patient attitude,
> Thinking of disability and cost,
> Oh dear, don't want much do I?
> My body is trembling with fear,
> Can feel my heart beating fast,
> As I push open the big heavy glass door,
> Went to the counter and order a cab,
> Looking around while waiting,
> Clean, pleasant, with photos and rules,
> Feeling nervous wondering about the driver,
> Everything went smoothly as I had hoped,
> Slowly building a friendship with the staff,
> What fun and joy we have,
> My trust and confidence is growing,
> Handicars is the one for me,
> Handicars is the BEST!

On one particular Friday, I asked Helen, my communicator guide, to book the cab for the following day. They were quite rude and told her the price had gone right up – almost double what they had charged me in the past. They said the normal driver who took me had charged me less money than he should have done. I was surprised because actually I usually had different drivers every week and they all charged me the same rate. I could not understand their attitude as I had been a regular customer often using them two or more times a week. I stopped using them and Helen suggested that I use one that she knew, called Carlton Cabs, and I have been with them ever since.

Whatever cab company I have used, there were always one or two drivers who were a bit awkward, but the majority of them were really helpful. Now and again, when I used to get a moody driver, in my mind I used to say to myself – whatever would they do if they ended up like me: in a wheelchair, without full vision and hearing? They didn't know how lucky they were.

At Handicars, there were one or two drivers who I really got on well with, like Roger. I met his wife, who worked in Marks and Spencer in Woolwich. There was another driver called Dave, who left for a little while and then came back.

Another driver had a half-sister who was disabled. He often used to talk about her and I often wonder how they are getting on.

Going back to 1999, when I first took the bungalow on, we had to get the gas people in to change the meter from a card meter to an account meter. A card meter would mean I would have to rely on someone charging the card for me. The first time they came, they said they couldn't find the bungalow! The second time they claimed they found the place but no one was there although Denzil and his friend had been decorating my bungalow. When Roland contacted them it appeared they went to the wrong address. The third time they said they were coming, John's sister was here and it was cold. They still couldn't find the bungalow and Roland rang up the gas people. He told them that he was sure that they must have an atlas in their van, but they still couldn't find my road. In the end, Roland's sister waited in all day and then went home. What a boring day this must have been for her.

The fourth time, I was in the bungalow and I was looking out of the window and saw a man standing there. At that time I could walk a bit by holding on to things. I went to the front door and asked him if he was the gas man. He said that he was. I thought if I hadn't been looking out of him, he would have missed the bungalow again. In all it took 3-4 months to get the gas turned on, and without heating or hot water I could not move in. Roland made dozens of calls trying to sort it out. Thank God I did not have the same problem with B.T. or the electric people.

We decided to go to the Co-op to buy some furniture. We ordered two bedroom wardrobes and a display cabinet for the living room. What a palaver the delivery was. Despite promises it took ages to get it delivered. Roland had to complain to the Store Manager. When we did get them, Roland's brother-in-law came over to help him put it together. We found that one of the panels in the largest wardrobe flatpack was damaged. The salesman claimed it must have been damaged in transit and was not their responsibility.

Roland wrote to the store manager pointing out it was their responsibility as they had sold me the flat pack, and that as the panel had been in the middle of the flat pack surrounded by undamaged panels it had clearly been packed already damaged. He said that unless it was replaced, I would take advice from my solicitor. A departmental manager delivered a replacement shortly afterwards. That was the last time Roland or I bought anything from the Co-op.

This reminded me of what happened years ago, when I lived in Catford, when we went to MFI and bought an office desk flat pack for my computer. The top had been manufactured incorrectly and meant it could not be put together. Roland and his brother in law took it back and asked for a refund which they got after a lot of argument. On the way home from MFI, we saw a similar desk in a second hand shop in Brownhill Road and bought it. The shop delivered it for me within hours and it worked out a lot cheaper. I have still got it today!

When I moved in to the bungalow, I had a lot of books to take with me. In previous moves, Roland put a lot in a suitcase but it was hard to lift because it was so heavy. This time, we decided to tie them into bundles of 10 or 15 after he was advised to do this.

I agreed that I would need help from Social Services to assist me with living in the bungalow, as my disability had got worse. Roland took me to Greenwich Social Services at Nelson House in Woolwich, where a receptionist completed an initial assessment form and was told I would be given a full interview. Roland phoned them up every so often.

Almost a year later I received a phone call asking me to go to Nelson House for an interview. I asked if they could do a home visit, as by then I could not walk even short distances without support. She replied that they did not do home visits and if I could not get out to them, I would be placed at the bottom of the list again. When I told Roland about this, he was angry and phoned them up and when the social worker would not budge he phoned the Social Services Complaints Officer, who promised to investigate. She rang back and said she had spoken to the social worker who had promised to contact me and that Roland should contact her if I had not heard back from her within ten working days.

On the last day I received several leaflets (which I had already) including one giving advice on how to apply for assessment. Roland went up the wall and phoned the Complaints Officer, told her what happened, said he wanted to make an official complaint and that he intended to take it to the Chair of Social Services if immediate action was not taken. The Team Leader phoned Roland and apologised and said they had asked the Sensory Team to take my assessment over and that an appointment had been made for a Sensory Team worker to visit me.

At about this time, someone from the Occupational Therapy team came to the bungalow to have a look round and to see what I needed. I told them that I wanted a handrail on the wall opposite the kitchen and three more in the bathroom: one by the shower, inside the curtain; one on the other side of the curtain; and one by the sink. They also put a chair by the sink for me.

After a little while, I asked them to take the gas hob out, and they agreed to put in a new electric one, which was specially designed to help blind people. Because of this, they were also able to put a new worktop around it because they had to make a bigger hole. All the kitchen wires were also tidied away and out of sight.

In my front room there was a set of drawers, which were put flush against the wall between the front room and the kitchen. The drawers extended underneath the kitchen worktop. When they were putting in the new worktop for me, they wanted to take out a piece of wood around the worktop but found out that it would have left a big gap where the drawers were, so they had to put it back.

I later asked them to put in a new worktop over the washing machine to extend the workspace.

During the first three months living in my bungalow, I used to get myself ready before John came over and by the time me came, I was eating my breakfast. In my kitchen as you walk in, on the left-hand side I have got three drawers. There is a pull-out tray in between two of the drawers. I used to get a bowl and a spoon out and put these on the worktop. I then used to pull out the tray, get hold of a damp tea towel and lay this on top of the tray, and put my bowl on the tea towel to stop it from moving. I then used to pour out Sugar Puffs or Cocoa Pops or whatever I fancied that day into the bowl.

My kitchen chair was in between this pull-out tray and the fridge, so all I had to do was just turn around, open the fridge door and get out the milk. At this time, the milk top on a plastic carton was slightly different. There was a little seal around the lid, with a flap that you had to push up and pull. Sometimes I could do this quite well with my teeth. Some days I could not manage this and then I would get a fork and place it in the little hole near to the flap. I would then pull it towards me and it would start to come away from the top. I would then open the top by turning it.

Today there is just one ring that you turn, which is easier. However, now I can ask my PA to do this for me as I cannot do this anymore.

I have got a skylight in my kitchen, and the light bulb was very close to it and didn't really make any difference when it was switched on. Once again, I asked the Occupational Therapist if they could put a strip light into my kitchen instead, which they agreed to do. This was a great help.

The bungalow came with three alarm pull-chords – one in the living room, one in the bedroom and one in the bathroom. These are red. If I pull one of these chords, an alarm and a light flashes outside my front door to indicate that I need help.

We have had a few laughs with these chords. On one occasion, Helen wanted to switch on the light and pulled the chord and the alarm went off. I had to try to explain to her how to turn it off using the switch under the cupboard. We didn't get very far with this! My neighbour across the road heard the alarm and knocked at the door. Luckily, he knew how to switch it off and showed Helen how to do it. It didn't half frighten her.

On another occasion, I was having a house group meeting and one of the women went to the bathroom. Instead of switching the light on, she pulled the chord and set the alarm off. Everybody jumped! Before I had time to explain how to turn it off, my next door neighbour came rushing in to see what the emergency was.

Even Roland has set it off once!

Tricia, my Care Manager from Sensory Services Team, later got involved with providing me with help and things started to get better. Tricia organised for the Greenwich Association for People with Disabilities ("GAD") to provide me with a Personal Assistant. I really wanted somebody who was not too bossy, and would do what I wanted to do and would not 'take over'. Dot, the manager of GAD came over to see me with Jo. When I first saw Jo, I thought she was going to be a proper little madam by the way she came in and sat down! I could only see a little bit at that time. Jo asked Dot if she could have a look around, and then that was it. We just greeted each other and Dot explained to Jo what I wanted done: the housework, shopping and cleaning.

I agreed to take Jo on and she worked 2 hours per day – Monday to Friday. At first Jo worked from 3–5pm, then we changed it from 1–3pm and then it changed again from 1.30–3.30pm, which suited me better.

Jo turned out to be a very nice person – very good at her job, and would only do what I wanted or asked for. Now and again, she could persuade me that extra things may need doing and 9 out of 10 times I would agree with her. 4 years later, she was still with me, but on a 'direct payment' set up, which worked better for us both.

Tricia also suggested that I might benefit from having a Communicator Guide. This was a service they offered through SENSE, but has now been taken over by Social Services directly. A Communicator Guide is a person who communicates with me and for me by writing letters, making phone calls, reading the post and other items, using the computer and taking me out now and again. The first Communicator Guide I had was Anita. She was a very nice girl, but unreliable and often did not turn up or stay the full time. She left SENSE, and it appears she often claimed for hours she had not worked.

After Anita, Helen took over. She works approximately $2\frac{1}{2}$ hours per week. She is very conscientious and reliable and we have lots of laughs and fun. We really have become good friends and she has been with me for about 7 years as well.

In 2002, SENSE invited its service users to go on a trip to Kew Gardens. Helen could not come with me, so they arranged for a volunteer, called Julie, to accompany me. Helen picked me up and took me to Sidcup, and then Julie and I went up to Kew Gardens by taxi, which had been arranged by SENSE. We had a really good day and I bought some seeds for my flower beds. We walked round and touched and smelled all the flowers, and they also laid on a lunch for us, which was very nice. We then had a bit more leisure time to go around the garden before going home. We arrived home at about 6.30pm. I kept in touch with Julie for quite a while afterwards, but then we lost contact.

Tricia also agreed that I needed to get somebody in to cook the evening meal on Mondays, Tuesdays and Thursdays. On Wednesdays and Fridays, I could get a take away meal from 'Your Place', a church-run lunch club at our local Community Centre. Roland cooked for me on Saturday and Sunday and the school holidays when "Your Place" was closed.

Tricia agreed to give me a personal assistant for $1\frac{1}{2}$ hours, on each of the days I wanted. Their main task would be to cook me a meal. This was OK, but did not give much time to cook a big meal, like a roast dinner. On some occasions, I used to ask Jo to cook a meal for me in the afternoon, when she was here for 2 hours. I would then turn the oven off when it was done.

The first cook Tricia and Dot arranged for me to have was called Penny. She was really good because if she had any time left over she would help to feed me, which was very helpful. We got on really well together. Unfortunately, she had to leave as her husband became ill. We did have some good laughs together. Penny knew the receptionist at my G.P.'s. Penny and I had discussed a bad experience I had had 9 years ago having my smear test done. Penny spoke to the receptionist and I agreed to go with her to have a smear test done, and this time it was fine. I can thank Penny for this.

When Penny left, I got a replacement. Her name was Annette. I was quite amazed by her CV. She could offer every service that I could think of – bathing, housework, etc. apart from what I really wanted – cooking! When I asked her if she could cook, she said she was not very good at it but that she would give it a go. She did well, and cooked some good meals. Unfortunately, I felt that we did have a communication problem in that I found her accent difficult to understand with my hearing impairment.

Annette used to come for 1 hour on Saturday to help me get into a cab to go and see my friend.

I had another personal assistant who would come in on a Sunday, called Elizabeth. Her job was to put my shoes on, put my hearing aid in, cook my breakfast and take me round to the Church for the 10.30am service. This worked really well until one day, when she failed to turn up. Neither Elizabeth nor GAD contacted me. When she did not return the next week I phoned GAD, who told me that her grandson was ill and she was taking time off. GAD had not bothered to tell me or find a replacement. Elizabeth was away for weeks and I assumed her grandson was still very ill. GAD did not find me a replacement and I gave up phoning and waited for Elizabeth to come back.

Eventually I lost patience and rang GAD, only to find out that they had moved her to another client not long after she stopped coming to me. I never did get a replacement. I was also disappointed because I thought that Elizabeth and I got on very well together. I could understand her agreeing to it because it gave her more hours, but thought that she would have rung me up to tell me herself. This really made me consider using other services apart from GAD. I was worried that they might send me someone, without telling me first, and that, as I was partially sighted, I would not want to let them in. Thankfully that did not happen.

When Jo went on holiday, I often was not given a replacement. Her times were changed by GAD without my agreement or knowledge. Looking back I think that I was a bit too easy going and should have stood up for my own needs more.

There were a couple of times when Jo went on holiday that I did get two good replacements, who were organised by GAD. GAD communicated well with me on these occasions, and the replacement P.A.s were fine, generally. One, however, was a pain in the neck as she had a bad attitude and obviously did not want to do any work for me.

I came to feel that the more reasonable and accommodating I was the more GAD took advantage of me. On a few occasions they sent Jo elsewhere and left me with no one and did not even tell me what they had done. I decided to go on to Direct Payment. This meant that I would have more control over the people who worked for me and over the time they gave me.

I took Jo on direct payments but decided to let Annette go. In Annette's place, I employed my friend, Edina. She cooked my meals three times per week. She also covered if Jo was away or when Jo could not take me to appointments etc. She enjoyed cooking and her meals were excellent.

I am really glad that I made the move to Direct Payment as I have more control and flexibility over my care.

When I first decided to take on help, I was just like my mum. Because I am independently minded, I did not like the idea of having anybody in to do things for me. I did not like to have to rely on other people. However, as I got to know Jo and Helen, I suddenly realised how lucky I was to have these two people around me.

The other thing I was aware of was that as I was getting more and more help, Roland was slowly putting me more into the hands of my carers. At the time, I didn't know whether this would alter my relationship with him.

I suppose in a way it has altered our relationship. I have discovered that I have to change my attitude and my behaviour towards Roland, Jo, Helen and Edina as they all play different roles in my life and my relationship is different with each of them. This can be quite hard at times on my part.

I must tell you some of the things I got up to with Jo. One Monday, Roland had to come to hospital with me for an eye appointment. Jo was coming at her normal time of about 1.30pm. I decided to play a joke on her. When she arrived, she thought I would be gone. I told Roland to be quiet and hid behind the lobby door. When she came in I made a loud noise and she jumped out of her skin.

Another time I played a joke on her was when she was doing her NVQ. She had arranged to come in with her assessor at 9.00am and demonstrate how she would get me out of bed, give me a shower and help me get dressed. She rang me up to say that she was going to be late. As time went by I got bored and decided to get out of bed. I waited in my corridor and turned the lights out. When they walked in I made a loud noise and they both jumped out of their skin. When they came in, I pretended to be posh and acted like the queen. The assessor laughed her head off and could see the funny side of it.

One year, Roland and I decided to take Jo on holiday to Ireland with us, as our driver. Jo and I were to share the same room. Sometimes I used to get up early in the morning and crawl over to her bed and tickle her feet. I used to quickly try to get back to my bed. One day I banged my head getting in bed so quickly, and Roland came running in saying, "What are you two up to?"

One night, I was going to have a bath. I made Jo all wet on purpose. When it was time for Roland to give Jo a hand to get me out of the bath, the water had already drained away so he turned the cold water tap on and put the plug in. I got a cold bum! Jo just stood there and didn't know what to say. She was flabbergasted! In the end, Roland did get me out.

When Jo used to put my shoes and socks on, I used to give her one leg and then quickly give her my other leg to confuse her. I used to do this as well when she used to help me on with my jumpers. In the end though, Jo got quicker than me so I couldn't do it any more!

As Roland was getting older, and his job more stressful, he started to change. Because of this, our communication is not the same as it was 10 years ago. Sometimes I fall in to the role of a child, in order to keep things running smoothly.

I have found that the services offered by Social Services can be quite frustrating. When I first got involved with Social Services, I was offered lots of different care services. I turned these down at the time because of my ability to cope at the time and my independence. The real difficulties come in as your disabilities get worse. Because I turned down care in the past, it is more difficult to receive it later. The real problem is getting the right person to do the hours and the care you actually need.

It is down to me, under Direct Payment, to hire the staff I need.

Eventually, I needed to use a wheelchair to get around the bungalow and for going out. I am now in it all the time, but I can still transfer into a chair or into the bath, or into a car. I can also walk with the aid of another person holding my arm or hand for very short distances

Roland wanted me to have a Community Alarm wrist strap. At first, just like my mum would have done, I did not want to have one. Something happened to change my mind.

One morning, I got up and went to the bathroom to get washed. I had a shower and on my way out of the bathroom, I fell over and cut my head on the bookcase. I quickly got up and grabbed a pair of knickers and put them on the cut to try to stop the bleeding. I phoned Roland, who was luckily on his way round anyway. He ended up taking me to the hospital, where they glued the cut together to stop the bleeding. After this happened, I was pleased to have the Community Alarm.

The Community Alarm works by the user pressing a red button on a wrist strap or on a pendant (I chose a wrist strap). You can also press a red button on a box they install in your house. This contacts a control centre, who have a list of all emergency contacts. I then tell them who I need them to contact. They will then ring me back to confirm that they have contacted the right person and say what will happen next. If they cannot contact anybody, they will send someone round to help me – which I can accept if I want to.

One day there was a very embarrassing occasion which I will never forget, which did make me think twice about the Community Alarm. I was in the shower and picked up the shampoo bottle and dropped it. The bottle broke and shampoo shot all over the floor. I knew that if I tried to move from the shower to the chair, I would slip over. I therefore pressed the alarm button. I did not have my hearing aid in and could not hear properly. I asked them to contact Roland for me. Because I couldn't hear properly, and they obviously found me difficult to understand, not only did they ask Roland to come round, but they also came round, although I wanted to wait for Roland.

One of the girls who worked for the Community Alarm Service, Alison, goes to my church and knows me quite well. If I had been 100% sure it was her, I probably have allowed her in to help me, but because I could not hear her name properly through the entry phone system, I told her to go away.

Even though they didn't like the idea of leaving me in the shower, they still had to respect my wishes and do what I said, knowing that Roland would be on his way.

When Roland arrived, he was really cross when I said I didn't want to use it any more. Alison convinced me, when I met her at church the next time, to put it back on. She said that they often had had to deal with similar situations, and that I should not be embarrassed about it.

There have been some occasions when I have pressed the button by mistake, and have had to tell them that it was a false alarm. They do not mind this as it often happens with other people too.

After moving to Woolwich, I had to find another Church to go to. The Community Centre is just round the corner behind my bungalow. On a Sunday they hold a church service under Ichthus. The first time I went there, I really didn't like it. After a little while, I went back and the leader was quite friendly towards me and so were one or two other people. I started to go there more regularly. Roland used to take me to church, drop me off, and then come back for me, and I quite enjoyed this arrangement. However, as time went by we started to run into difficulties. At the time, Roland was not sure about his Christianity, but later on he became more involved.

Every year we went to a Revival Camp, held at Ashburnham Abbey near Battle.

This is held every year for Christians to get together with each other, from all over Great Britain.

The first year Roland and I went, I shared a room with Helda and Roland slept in a dormitory. This had rows of bunk beds in and Roland was sure that he did not want to get a top bunk, and managed to get a bottom one. To save a lot of time and hassle, he would get up early before the others, have a shower and go for a walk. Then he would come to the house where we were, and take over. We would go down to breakfast and he would stay with me all day.

This particular year, Roland committed his life to Jesus on the last night of Revival Camp. I had been praying for Roland for 16 years hoping that this would happen. I am glad he finally made it.

The second year we went, I shared a room with Deborah. She was lots of fun, and I could play up with her like I did with Jo on holiday. We had a great time together. Again, Roland and Deborah took it in turns to feed me. We used to let Deborah have a couple of nights off instead of looking after me. Roland had a room in the main house, instead of sleeping in the dormitory.

This particular year, I asked Deborah to get Roland a birthday cake. We put it in the kitchen and then took it in for supper and everyone sang happy birthday to him. When he got me on my own, he really told me off because he doesn't like things like that.

At these camps, we would choose a bible topic in the morning that we wanted to study all week. We would meet up at worship time, if we wanted to go. Then we would go to bible study, then have lunch and have the whole afternoon off. However, there were activities provided if you wanted to do them. We had supper at about 6–7pm and then a big worship evening every night.

I had an ear infection this particular year. Early Saturday morning, Roland had to take me to Queen Elizabeth Hospital. We had to get home for 12 noon to pick up the bus to get to the revival camp. We were a bit worried in case they said I couldn't go, but were glad when they said I could go so long as I remembered to put in my ear drops.

I think it was that year that I met Margaret West. She wanted my opinion and ideas on how I would improve the building and grounds to make them more accessible for people with disabilities.

The worst room in the building was the shower room. There were two shower rooms. It was ridiculous. As you walked in, there was a changing area and the shower. There was a shower chair in the corner, but if you sat on it, the shower did not reach over enough to wash you and the water went everywhere!

Because the water came out into the dressing area, I had to be very careful in case I slipped. To turn the shower on and off was even more difficult for someone like me who can't move their hands properly. You had to push, pull and turn – all at the same time. I don't know where they got this stupid idea from. If you are left handed like me, you had to lean over as it was partly out of your reach. In the end, I just didn't like the room as it made me nervous. As they had two shower rooms, I think they could have made one for right handed people and one for left handed. The building was supposed to be accessible to disabled people. To get into this building, you had quite a steep ramp to get up. When you got up the ramp, instead of pushing the door inwards, you had to pull it outwards, which is really difficult when you are in a wheelchair and up a ramp! You need very strong arms.

I passed all this on to Margaret but, unfortunately, I don't know how far this went. I passed on lots of other ideas as well.

I found out that Margaret lived in Sydenham and ran the Disabled Christian Fellowship in Lewisham. I also found out that she knew some of my old school friends. We did plan to get together, but never did.

The third time we went, we just went for the day with Neville. I saw all my friends like Pat C., Chris and Esther.

The last time we went was with Linda, again just for the day.

In 2003, Roland and I decided not to go as it was becoming more and more difficult with regard to accommodation and help that I needed. Nine out of ten times, we used to get the application forms too late. If this happens you have to go on a waiting list and get a place if someone drops out. We did not like this system because one of us might get a place and one might not.

In 2004, I was hoping to go down there for the day, but in the end could not find anyone to take me. My friend, Jill, was hoping to come with me on the last day, but unfortunately, this did not work out as we could not find anyone with a car to take us down there.

Every year we went to Highleigh Christian Conference Centre. The third time I went, Roland came with me, but could not be my carer all the time because he was male. I really felt as if a knife had gone through me because they did not tell me beforehand what they planned for me. Their idea was to get Roland away from me for the whole weekend, so that he could have a weekend to himself and to have time with God.

When we first went, we were picked up by Brian, a leader of the church, and his wife, Verena. They agreed to let Roland stay in the room next door to make it easier for me, as I was used to him helping me to get ready.

Because my legs were getting bad, we had to hire a wheelchair from GAD. At first, I was only supposed to keep it for one month, but in the end I kept it for about six months.

We had quite a good weekend as Mike (another leader at the church) took me out around the grounds and down the lane. This was lovely as the weather was really warm that year.

I will never forget that Sunday afternoon on the way home. Brian's car kept breaking down. In the end, they had to call out the rescue services, but everyone who went by who knew us hooted at us and asked us if we were ok. We had to take the car off the motorway and take it to a side turning. Then Brian dealt with the arrangement to get the car sorted. In the end we had to be towed home.

While Brian was sorting out the rescue services, Roland, Verena and I all had a good chat about all sorts of things. That year, I was studying world religion.

That night we didn't get home until after nine at night, even though we left quite early in the afternoon. Because we were getting hungry, Verena decided to go and get a pizza, which we eat in the car while we were waiting.

The second year we went, Graham and Liz took us. Graham was our housegroup leader and a member of the church and Liz was his wife.

Graham was Roland's housegroup leader. My housegroup leader was supposed to arrange for people to take it in turns to look after me. However this was not arranged. Therefore, the administrator had to organise this all at the last minute – people to look after me at mealtimes, etc. I started to get really angry because I was only allocated someone to be with me at mealtimes, and I needed someone there most of the time, as with my failing eyesight, I needed assistance to get from A to B. They had to go back to the drawing board to find more people. In the end, it worked out really well as I did get more assistance. I also ended up getting to know more people because of this, and they got to know me.

Roland and I payed for the carer who shared my room in the night time. Her job was to help me to get to bed and get me up in the morning. Actually, however, she only got me up in the morning and I was put to bed by whoever was with me that evening. I felt that this was a bit unfair as we had personally paid for this service. On the other side, we knew that she was reliable and trustworthy so in a way it was worth it.

In 2002, Roland had decided to be baptised, and we hired a Baptist church in Woolwich. Although a lot of people did not agree with this, I decided to be baptised again too. Evangelicals, Baptists and other born again Christian churchgoers are normally baptised when they are older and know what they are committing to. After you have asked Jesus into your life, you are turning away from your old path. You go into the water and the leader will ask you a couple of questions and you answer them. He then says, "I baptise you in the name of The Father, The Son and The Holy Spirit." He then pushes you under the water and you come up and get out of the water. You pick a song you would like them to sing for you. Then they will pray over you for a little while. After that, you get dry and dressed and that is it. You are then a born again Christian. You do feel very different after this has been done.

I wanted to be baptised for the second time because I knew that I had been rude to God, and had turned away from him. I knew that the only way I could convince myself that I wanted to go back to God was to be baptised again. A lot of people did not agree with this because normally you are only baptised once. I felt that just saying words would not be enough, and I needed to be baptised again.

During 2004, a lot of things happened. Roland decided to give up the church for the time being, which put me in an awkward position in a way. I asked the church to arrange for someone to pick me up to take me to church. At first, I used to have a PA who used to take me to church and someone would bring me home, but this later stopped.

I felt awkward because I had to keep asking for someone to come and pick me up. The ideal situation would have been that someone would always come to pick me up and I could just say when I did not want to go. By September 2004, I think they were slowly getting the message, which was good.

In March 2004, on Don Maclean's radio programme, Good Morning Sunday, he asked the question, "Why don't people go to church?" I got Roland to e-mail him to tell him that I don't go to church because I cannot get there as I am a wheelchair user. This was my main reason for not going even though the church was just round the corner. Also, obviously, my other disabilities of impaired vision and hearing, also got in the way. The week after I sent the letter, he read it out on the radio on Sunday and asked me to get in touch with him and give him the name and address of my church. At the time, I did not want to do that because I felt like I was going behind my church's back and did not know what sort of letter he was going to write. So I did not take up this offer.

When I went to Cyprus in April 2004 with Georgie and John we met up with Jenny Edwards, a member of staff at Through The Roof organisation. She said to me at breakfast time, "Was that you that sent the e-mail to Don Maclean?" I said that it was.

These are the main people who helped me, either to get to church, or when we went away to Highleigh or the revival camp:

Gail; Linda; George and Meryl (Meryl was a lovely person, but sadly died in 2004 of cancer); Angela and Graham; Mike and Anne; Lesley and Jonathan; Pauline from church; Tania; Brian and Verena; and Paul the caretaker of the Community Centre.

Gill was a special needs assistant and used to be a member of my church, which is where we met. She was learning British Sign Language at the time. I got on really well with her. We came up with an idea of organising a wheelchair dance in the church hall. I believe we had been trying to organise it for at least two years, and it still did not get off the ground! Gill now goes to another church, but still comes to visit me now and again.

Nearly all the people who helped me when I needed to get to church or to go away, all had experience of working or helping people with special needs or some sort of disability. It would be nice if people, unrelated to working with special needs, could have a bit more understanding, and not be afraid of disability. Maybe if the church encouraged able bodied people to get more involved with people with disabilities, barriers might be broken down.

I believe the church is slowly coming round to my way of thinking, but there is still a long way to go to reach the standards of the Churches for All Discrimination Act.

In October 2004, Lesley – the administrator for Icthius Church, slowly drew up a rota for people to take it in turns to come and pick me up, take me to church, sit with me through the service, and bring me home. We started a new house group in November, and sometimes at these meetings we would have a meal together. Because I need help with feeding, Lesley also organised a rota for people to take it in turns to feed me. The idea of this was to give Roland the freedom to attend these meetings, without having the responsibility of having to feed me every time.

I told Jonathon that if we were going to have a bible study class, maybe he could give me the bible passage beforehand, so that I could get somebody to read it to me before I went, or perhaps listen to it on my tape. This is because I could not always hear the readings at the bible study classes.

Once a month on a Saturday, Roger Foster and Faith, his wife, held a bible school in a church in Forest Hill, which I went to. This bible school was later sometimes held in a prayer house in Forest Hill. They knew a fantastic amount about the bible and it was so fascinating. I got to know quite a few people there that did not go to my church. There could sometimes be about one hundred people there.

In September 2004, a group of French people came to visit the bible school, and they needed an interpreter. It was hard work for the interpreter to keep up with Roger!!

Gail would be the main person who took me to bible school and brought me back. Before she did this, I used to make my own way there by cab and ask somebody to bring me home.

One Sunday morning when Roger was preaching at my church, he showed me up a bit by saying that I always sit in the front in bible class and that I am always there. After the service, Graham, my leader, called me a teacher's pet for a little while. Ever since then, Roger and I got on really well together. He and his family would always come up and say hello to me.

I think one of the main reasons I liked to go to Church is because I got on well with the leaders and some of the other members, and it also got me out of the house.

However, there are some things that I have been through with members of the church that made me a bit wary. Every now and again, I still felt that I had one or two problems. For example, if we went on an outing, I would not know who would be taking care of me until the day we went, and I do not like it that way. This made me wonder if they had actually organised it before hand or just asked someone on the day, and put someone in the position where they could not say 'no'.

I am still not sure whether this is the right church for me. I feel they are lacking in Pastoral care. In the past when I expressed to the Pastor/leader that I had a problem, they did not really bother to make time for one-to-one contact. I feel that it is usually down to me to make contact with the members of this church. With a few exceptions, it was a rarity for anyone from the church to knock on my door to make contact or to keep in touch.

Two of the main friends I made at the church were Gail, Lesley and Linda. They would keep in touch and pop down when they could. Later, Lesley became my PA and has also become a really good friend. Gail is also a very good friend.

It was not until Christmas 2005 that I found out something about Lesley and me. I just could not understand that every time I went around to her place or we went out for a meal, Jonathan, Lesley's husband, was the one who always fed me. One particular Christmas day while I was having breakfast at the Church Community Centre, Lesley said that she was going to feed me. I was so shocked that I asked her why she was doing it that day, as she had never done it before. She said it was because she was scared of my disability. She was not scared of me as a person but did not have the confidence to feed me. When I told her that it made my day that she was feeding me, she was over the moon.

After I had been in my bungalow for about a year, I asked my brother-in-law, Paul, if it would be worthwhile for me to upgrade my computer or should I buy a new one. I really liked the one I had at the time. He said that it would be better for me to get a completely new one. In year 2001, my Auntie Trudy died and left me some money and so I decided to buy a new computer with the money.

Roland and I went around different computer shops. I believe that one shop was called Candy. They had a lovely computer there. We were all ready to pay for it, but I wanted a bigger monitor or screen. Because this was not part of the 'package' they refused to sell it to me. We then went to Dixons in Woolwich, and found the same computer there. I signed a cheque for Roland so that he could go to Woolwich and write-in the correct amount on the cheque and order it. However, because I was not present to sign the cheque there they would not accept it. Roland suggested that they did not deliver until the cheque was cleared but they still said no. This was on the Saturday. On Monday morning, I decided to ring up Dixons and have a word with the manager. I said something like this:

"If you think my friend, who is partially disabled himself, is going to push me all the way down to your shop just to sign a cheque, which takes me a long time to do, and then push me all the way back, you've got another think coming! So – what are you going to do about it?"

After this he said, "Tell your friend to come back and ask for me, and then I will accept your cheque." When Roland went down with the cheque the salesman found it was out of stock.

Roland and I went to PC World with his sister and brother in law. Roland ordered the computer package with his new credit card which he had got partly to avoid another "Dixons" and I paid him by cheque

I was sad for quite a long time afterwards when I had to give my old computer away as I had got attached to it!

I had my new computer for a while, and then Tricia, my Care Manager, told me about a computer class that I could do at home. She asked me if I would like to have a bash at it and I said that I would. Tricia filled in the appropriate forms and sent them off. After a few months, I was contacted by Tracey F., who belonged to an organisation called U Can Do IT. This organisation would teach people to use the computer at home and were able to give you up to two hours per week, up to a total of 20 hours over the whole course. For this course, I only had to pay five pounds.

As Tracey got to know me, she started to realise that I had already done a lot of work on the computer, and so we decided to concentrate on how to use the internet and e-mail.

Because of my eyesight, we had to change all the background and letter colours so that it became easier for me to see, write and read the text. She then introduced me to a package called Supernova. This can be downloaded from the computer for twenty minutes at a time, just to sample how it works. If you decide it may be helpful, you can then buy the package on line or over the phone. I tried it and decided to buy it.

I find Supernova very useful as it reads out instructions and text that I type in. I was quite lucky with Tracey, as she gave me an extra few hours because it took a long time to make adjustments to the colours on the screen to make it easier for me to use.

Supernova did have one or two faults however – one being that it repeatedly gives you information that you have not asked for and may not want.

Tracey and I still keep in touch by e-mail.

I do not know how I got involved, but Woolwich College started a Supernova course for people who wanted to learn more about how to use the package. Helen took me down there for an interview, and it was a lot of palarva parking the car as there were not many spaces, even for disabled parking. However, we managed it in the end. We went for the interview and Helen filled in some forms, which I signed, and I agreed to give it a go. The person at the interview, who dealt with special needs, arranged for transport for me for the following week.

The black cab took me there for my first lesson, but I did not get much done because the teacher spent most of the first lesson raising up my keyboard so that it was at the right height and putting yellow stickers on the keyboard, to make it easier for me to read. Jo came in with me during the afternoon and stayed with me and took me home. The third week I went, they had booked the cab to take me home as well.

I was not allowed to be left alone and the teacher had to stay with me until the cab arrived. The teacher was moaning his head off because he had to get back to his class to pack up and the cab was late. It turned out that the Special Needs Co-ordinated had arranged for the cab to come at 3.30pm instead of 3.00pm. Because the teacher was complaining to me, I said that I could ring my P.A., Jo, and ask her to come and pick me up.

I told them that if Jo came to pick me up, and then the cab arrived at the same time, I would have to go home with Jo and the cab would have to go back without me. The funny thing was that the cab got there just before Jo did. I knew that Jo was on her way, so I refused to get into the cab.

The first two or three sessions had not been a good experience. The real reason I decided not to continue with the course was because I could not learn to touch-type because of my disability. I had already done my word processing course at Lewisham College and did not want to have to go back to the beginning again. It would take me such a lot of time to type in the first paragraph, using only one finger. All I wanted to do was to learn about Supernova and how I could use it to make my life easier.

I got really cross with the teacher and told him about my idea. I told him that I did not agree with the way they were running the course. The teacher we had at Lewisham College would type out the text for us, put in on a disc, and then all we would have to do would be to call up the text we needed and do the alterations using the correct commands. This saved a lot of time for people with Cerebral Palsy who cannot use two hands on the computer keyboard. The teacher at Woolwich expected us to type all the text in ourselves first. This is fine if you can touch-type, but not if you have one or more disabilities, like I have.

When I told him about my thoughts on this, he just looked at me. I could tell he was not really interested. Because of this, I decided to leave the course. Nobody, even the Special Needs Co-ordinator, bothered to get back to me. Helen and I sent her an e-mail, which she did not respond do.

*Chapter Forty Six*
# Blindness

On Sunday 17th October 1999, I was sitting on the floor in Roland's flat reading my bible for a project I was doing (The History of Disability), when all of a sudden, I went blind in my right eye. Roland could not take me to the doctor's the following day, so he asked Edina to take me to my G.P. in Perry Dale. After the doctor saw me, we had to wait outside while she phoned Kings College Hospital to make me an urgent appointment for that day. They finally made the appointment for 3 o'clock.

Edina and I had already made arrangements to go and have a look at a carpet for my bungalow in Woolwich, which Edina did not want to put off. So what we ended up doing was going from my doctor's to Woolwich, choosing all our carpets, and then getting something to eat. Then we took a cab from Woolwich to King's College Hospital.

When I got to King's College, they did quite a few tests. They told me that I had glaucoma and that was what had caused the blindness in my right eye. They told me that they would do everything they could bring the pressure down in my eyes to save my left eye. Unfortunately, there was nothing that they could do about my right eye.

My Consultant thought that he may be able to save my left eye by doing some laser treatment. This did work for a little while.

In 2001, they decided to do the operation to help my glaucoma. I went into hospital for the day at 7.30am on Friday 17th August. I had my operation early that afternoon. When I started to come round from the operation, they had to put me on a drip because I had not eaten for about 18 hours. I was weak and could not come round properly from the anaesthetic. They had also put me on a drip before the operation for about half an hour.

I came home the same day with a patch over my eye, and had to go back to Kings College again the next day at 11am. I did this and was told that everything was ok. I was told to go back to Lewisham Hospital on the Monday at 1.30pm. The Consultant at Kings College told me I had to put some drops in my eye 6 times a day. Eventually, this went down to 2 times a day. It was a nightmare trying to get the drops into my eyes.

A week or two later, the doctors thought my eye was healing up too quickly. They had to take me in again, and put me out. They then had to give me an injection in the corner of my eye to stop it from healing up too quickly, as slow healing was more beneficial for my eye. Even though I had a general anaesthetic, I was home sooner than I was the last time. Roland left me there to go back to work, and I had the same nurse I had last time to look after me. I was very pleased as she really did cheer me up.

Different nurses had been assigned to come to my house at certain times to put drops into my eyes. This meant that I always had to be in at certain times – 11.00am, 1.30pm and 3.00pm.

It was Helen's, first day working for me when one of the nurses asked her if she could put in the drops to save her coming back later in the day. Helen had to ring up her boss, who said that she should not be administering the drops. You could tell by the look on the nurse's face that she wasn't too happy about this and that she had to come back later at 1.30pm. After this I warned Jo that the nurses might ask her to do this.

The second week Helen came, we decided to go and walk over Woolwich Common and on into Queen Elizabeth's Hospital café for a coffee and a drink. We had to be back in time for the nurse to put the drops in my eye (12.00 noon on that day). After we had finished our drinks, we started to walk back.

Helen took a wrong turn and was directed by an army cadet to go through a gate at the end of a field. When we got to the gate it was locked, so we had to go all the way back to the path to get back on the right track again. We finally made it back to the bungalow, but the nurses had already been and gone. Helen rang up the nurses and was told that we would have to wait until the next dose was due (which Jo, my Personal Assistant, would give me).

When Helen had her old car, the boot would not open. The only way she could get the wheelchair in when we went out was to put it on the back seat. I didn't mind, but I was a bit worried in case she pulled up too quickly and the wheelchair would come flying forward and bang her head and knock her out!

A couple of years later, she changed her car to one that was slightly smaller. This time, she had to put the wheelchair in right behind her seat, which was a bit safer. Once when we took Molly out for a meal, Molly sat in the front and I had to squeeze myself in on the back seat. That was quite funny.

Sometimes Helen used to bring me in a cream éclair. On one particular day, we were eating it and my one stayed on the plate and Helen's one slipped off and fell on the floor! She had to throw it in the bin – poor girl. I did offer her a bit of mine, though.

On November 29th, 2002, I had to go and have a cataract operation. I had to go to and have a pre-op examination where they had to check me over and do some tests on my eye. I asked about putting eye drops in my eye, and the nurse gave me a new idea. If you screw your eyes up and put the drops in the corner and then open your eyes, the drops just run in – and this is much easier. She asked Roland to have a practise with some drops of water, and it did work. Roland and I thought why on earth didn't they tell us about this method before?

I then had to go in and have the cataract removed from my left eye (they would not remove the cataract from the right eye as I was already blind in that eye).

The cataract operation and the glaucoma left me with some complications. There was a small split at the top of my eye which was too small to be stitched. They were hoping that it would heal up by itself. However, the problem was that every now and again, it started bleeding and then I would go blind for a couple of days. As days went on, it would start to clear and by the evening my sight was a bit clearer still. This condition usually lasted about two or three weeks before my sight improved enough for me to see again.

I had a follow-up course of eye drops, but decided not to involve the nurses this time, and for Roland and Jo to put the drops in for me.

Because of my blindness, I now had to find a new way of dressing. I used to feel the labels to see which way around my clothes were. To make sure I got my knickers on the right way round, I would make sure that the label was either on the right hand side or at the back in the middle. Then I would be sure that they were going on the right way round. Some brands would put labels on the left. M&S would be stitched on the right, Littlewoods and other brands would be at the back, and some others would be on the left. Nine out of ten times, I would like the knickers with patterns on as you could be sure you had them on the right way round because the colour inside the knickers was slightly paler than the colour outside.

With regard to getting my bra on, I used to get Roland to do it up before hand, and then I used to put my feet in first and pull it up over my bum and put it up over my body. I had to make sure that the label was always on the left.

If I had to put a jumper, sweatshirt or tee-shirt on, I had to find the label at the back, put my arms in and just pull it over my head. If my jumpers did not have a label, I would feel for the seam because it was always on the left hand side, so I could tell that I had it on the right way round.

To put my socks on, I would put them on my feet and then use the wheels of my wheelchair to pull them up into the right place so my heel fitted.

Because of my failing eyesight, a lot of people had suggested that I learn to read Braille. I said that it would be a good idea, but that I did not think I could do it as I had numbness in my hands. Also with my

Cerebral Palsy, it would be difficult to keep my hand going in a straight line.

Tricia suggested to get something called Articles for the Blind, which is a tape of current news, and Talking Books from the Royal National Institute for the Blind ("RNIB"). For the Talking Books, you fill in a form, listing what books you like, and they then send you a big machine and tapes, which are the size of a video cassette. The first one I listened to really put me off, as the reader put no feeling or emphasis into the story. The reason why I kept on receiving these tapes was because they were supposed to be changing soon to a C.D., which hopefully might be a lot better – in fact, on the day I wrote about this service changing to C.D.s, I received a letter informing me that it was my turn to receive a C.D. player and that all the books would be transferred to C.D. The result is fantastic!

At first, I enjoyed listening to Articles for the Blind, but I don't enjoy them as much now and do not listen to 9 out of 10 that are sent to me. This is because the people's voices were too varied in pitch. Some were loud, some were quiet and some read so quickly that you could not get the gist of the article.

One day in 2003, Jo and I were messing about on the internet, looking up information about books for the blind. We came across a charity called Calibre, who produced books for the blind. We made some notes about it and passed these on to Roland, who e-mailed Calibre to get me registered. I could go through a list on the internet and pick out as many books as I liked. My choice would then get registered on their records. They will then send you one book of your choice, and when you finish it, you send it back and they send you another one four days later. If you have requested a specific book and it is already out, Calibre will go through a topic list that you have marked, and will select one under a heading that I have chosen, and send one through, hoping that I will like it.

In October 2004, my left eye was still playing me up – bleeding and getting worse all the time. Lewisham Hospital and Kings College Hospital began talking to me about having another operation. They gave me about a month to think about it. The thought of having another operation did not really please me as you can never guarantee what the outcome is going to be.

The day after the hospital told me this, Roland told me that he wanted to have a whole weekend off. When we came back from our holiday in Ireland last year, my lighting outside the bungalow was not working and it was quite dark in the evenings. Roland offered to stay with me at my bungalow until the lighting was fixed. He started staying with me in September 2003, and I slept on my put-up bed. However, this situation carried on for over a year, and I got very used to it.

Over the time that I have known Roland, I realise that he does love me, but as a very good friend. He is a very caring person. During the last part of 2004, we began to get on each other's nerves. Because Roland was now doing so much more for me, I felt that I had to let Roland take the lead in most situations around the bungalow and with my care. This began to make me feel that I was no longer an equal in our relationship, and was beginning to slip into a role that I was not comfortable with. It also changed the atmosphere between us.

Roland made a suggestion about me getting more hours of care, so that he could have the whole weekend off – he did not say how long he wanted this to go on for. Of course, this started to make me feel upset. He could not talk to me comfortably about this and would get quite short with me when I wanted to discuss it. This felt like a knife was going through me and that my life had been turned upside down again.

As a result of all this, I began to think again about making myself more independent by doing everything I could by myself. This included putting myself to bed, getting up in the morning, having a shower and washing my hair – I had to make quite a few changes.

When I go to bed, I go to the bathroom, and get undressed while sitting on the loo. This gives me more freedom of movement for my arms. Some jumpers I can pull over my head by pulling on the collar and others I lift up from the bottom. I pull my bra down to just below my hip without undoing it. Then I push my shoes off with my feet, and move them out of the way. I then take my trousers off, and socks off. I leave my wheelchair at the door of the bathroom, and put all my clothes onto it. I would then get up, get hold of the door handle, reach out with my other hand for the handrail, and then sit down on a seat by the sink and clean my teeth.

I have to use a certain type of toothpaste and at first, I could take the top off the toothpaste but could not put it back on again. I finally found a way of doing it. When I undid the toothpaste, I would keep the top in my hand and squeeze the toothpaste into my mouth with the other hand. Then I would put the top back on to my toothpaste, put the toothbrush into my mouth and clean my teeth. This worked perfectly. Since that time, the pump dispenser has been invented, which is easier for me. I still use the same method of putting the toothpaste in my mouth first.

I would then go back to my wheelchair in the same way. I would then go to my bedside and put my wheelchair at a certain angle. I would then pull my bra down and take it off over my feet. I pick it up by the left strap and hang it on the left-hand handle of my wheelchair. Next, I get my nightie on. Sometimes it can be a pain sorting out the back from the front, but I get there in the end. And finally I get into bed! Sometimes, Roland comes over and gives me a hand to tuck me up.

Getting up in the morning is like this: I take the clothes off the wheelchair and put them on the bed. I then go to the loo, by putting the wheelchair against the door again. I then repeat the same thing for getting to the sink and have a wash. I use apricot face cleaning pads, and sometimes it can be a bit of nuisance getting them out of the box. I just keep fiddling about with them until I get one out. If I drop the box on the floor, I have to be very careful how I bend forward to pick it up or find it. I have to find it with my feet first and then bend down to pick it up. If I am not very careful the chair could tip up. I then have a wash, and clean my teeth in the same way as before. I then go back to my wheelchair and come over to the side of the bed where my bedside cabinet is. I pick up my deodorant and undo it with my right hand and put it on with my left hand. To put the top back on again, I put the deodorant in my right hand and put the top on with my left. Sometimes to make it easier I used to roll the lid up the top half of my legs to do it up. Now I roll the lid against my jaw to undo it. To do it up, I put the deodorant in my right hand and put the lid in my left hand. I then turn it with my thumb to do it up. This works well.

 I then pick up my bra which is on the left handle of my wheelchair. I can tell the front of the bra by putting the middle of it to my lip, where I can feel a bow at the front. I then have to fiddle about with it to find the correct armholes. To make sure I haven't got the bra twisted, I follow around the top part of the bra with my lip until I come to the ring where the strap is. I can then pick it up with my right hand and I know I have got it right. I then bend down and put my feet in first and pull it up over my body and put my arms in. Eventually, I managed to find a quicker way than this. To save all this work, when I took my bra off, I would put the left arm hole on the wheelchair arm, and the right armhole I would lay on top of my trousers so that I could see it quite clearly.

 When putting on my jumper, I would find the label in the normal way. If I had got it on back to front (which would happen quite often), my quick way around this problem would be to take the jumper off, pull out my right arm and push it through my left armhole while my left arm is still in it. I then would take out my left arm when my right arm is about a quarter of the way in and put it in the right armhole. I then put the jumper back over my head.

 After this I put my socks on. I used to use the wheels of my wheelchair to straighten my socks out, but now I use the footplate, which is also very good for helping to push my socks on. I then take hold of my trousers and put one leg at a time through the holes. Because I have to lean against the seat of my wheelchair to balance myself when I stand up, there is no way I can pull my trousers up because the seat is in my way. The only way round it is to make sure that I pull most of the trousers up above my knee, where the seat level is. I then pull up one side at a time over my hips. This makes it very difficult to tuck my jumper in. Some days I can manage to do it myself, but most days I have to wait for

Roland to come over. Roland always has to put my shoes on, unless they have a Velcro strap.

At first I used to be able to walk from the bathroom door to the shower, but I can no longer do this. When I could no longer walk to the shower, I would crawl to the shower handle and pull myself up. I now find this a bit more difficult to do without Roland being there. I found that I could crawl to the shower and get in ok, but getting from the shower chair to the other chair where the towel was was a bit nerve racking as I could not get hold of the handrail properly and could not see it properly. I was always concerned that I was going to slip over.

Once again, I had to put my thinking cap back on and I eventually found another way around it which works perfectly.

I take all my clothes off my wheelchair and put them on my bed. I also put the cushion on my bed. I put my bra on top of my trousers so that I can see it when I get dressed again. Then I go to the bathroom door, go to the loo, get back into my wheelchair, unbolt the door and take the wheelchair in with me. I then turn left to get out my apricot face cleanser. I move the chair by the sink out of the way and grab hold of my hand towel and put it on my lap with my cleanser. I take all the towels off the chairs in the bathroom and put them on the floor. I leave one maroon towel on a bathroom chair. Then, I turn to the left to get level with my shower seat, sideways on.

Next, I pick up the shampoo bottle, which Roland has left on the shower chair for me. I finally realised why I could not pick it up off the floor. This was because instead of lifting the top up, you have to push one side of it down and the shampoo will come out of a little hole at the side. This would make it very slippery and when I tried to pick it up with my finger and thumb it would slide up again. Now, I always ask Roland to leave it on the side of the chair.

We moved the other mat in the bathroom because my wheelchair would not go over it. I have to pick up the shampoo bottle with my right hand, while holding my cleanser (making sure I have got the brakes on!). I have my left hand fee to get hold o f the left handle of the shower chair. I can then stand up or pull myself up, turn round and sit down. I then put the shampoo and cleanser on my lap. I fold the handtowel in half, and put it in my wheelchair so it doesn't get wet and rusty. I then take the brakes off and push the wheelchair as far out of the way as I can.

Next, I switch on the shower by pressing a button, and make sure I am sitting on the edge of the chair to make a quick get away as it comes out cold at first. Once it warms up I get back under it again and have a lovely warm shower, and wash my face and hair.

When I have finished, I press the button to turn the water off, pull my wheelchair in towards me, put the brakes on, get hold of the left side of the handrail for the shower seat, pull myself up, turn around and sit myself down in the wheelchair. I then go over to where the towels are on the floor. I put one on my legs and one for my top. I dry my legs by rubbing them together with the towel and use my hands to dry behind my legs.

For most people, putting on knickers in the morning is something that you don't even think about. However, finding my knickers can be a pain in the neck. They can get all twisted and so I had to come up with a way of dealing with them to help me become more independent again. What I did was to get Jo to sort them all out and put them back in the drawer in a certain order. When I opened the drawer, the waistband would always be in the same place. When I got a pair out, I would pick up the right-hand top corner and put this corner in between my teeth. I would then climb over the other side of the bed to get out of bed. I would then take my nightie off with my knickers still in my mouth. I then get in my wheelchair, go to the bathroom, take my knickers off and put my clean ones on. This makes sure that I do not get my old ones mixed up with my new ones. If I do drop them, I would know which way up they should be because I had been holding them in my mouth and one corner would be a bit damp.

After about a month of trying to get undressed in the bathroom, I realised that there was some water leaking from the toilet onto the bathroom floor. This made the floor slippery and one day I slipped and hit my elbow on the handle of the toilet. This really hurt. Roland was in the bedroom on the computer and did not really come to my aid. Within a couple of minutes, I had slipped and knocked my elbow again. This time, Roland came in to help me.

In the end, I decided that it was not a very good idea to get undressed in the bathroom. I had to go back to the drawing board. I decided to get undressed in the bedroom, while sitting in my wheelchair. This went really well until I came to taking off my trousers.

I realised that I did not have enough room to get my trousers off over my feet because the footplate of my wheelchair got in my way, even when the plates were folded back. I could have folded the footplates around the side of the wheelchair, but this would make quite a lot of work for me because I would then have to turn the footplates back again. This meant I had to put on my thinking cap again.

Again I found another way round it. After I had used the bathroom, I would sit on the loo, kick my shoes off, pull my trousers down and then I would have all the space around me to pull the elastic waist down over my feet. I would then transfer to the wheelchair and come into the bedroom again to finish getting undressed. This was the end of that problem, and so far I have not had any more problems.

As I have told you in a previous chapter, my dad always tried to get me to write with my right hand, but instead I learnt to write with my left hand as this came more naturally to me. Because of the blindness in my right eye, it is almost impossible to read my writing as I go along, when I write with my left hand. This problem is made worse by the way I write and hold my pen because of my Cerebral Palsy. Because of this problem, I eventually had to learn to write using my right hand. All I do now, is to just sign my name at the bottom of letters or cards. I no longer write like I used to. When I sign my name, it is not often that it comes out perfectly, but most of the time it is recognisable as my signature.

The letter that I dislike writing the most is the letter 'a'. This is very difficult because of the curves in the letter. I used to use a writing guide, which is a piece of plastic about the size of a cheque book. It had a space cut out of the middle which was where I put my signature. I had to ask someone to put the signature guide in the correct place and hold it down for me, and place my pen and hand at the correct position. I then would sign along the edge of the guide. I am just grateful that my signature does not contain a 'p' or a 'y' because this would be very difficult to write. In the end, I found it easier to write without the writing guide.

My friendship with Roland changed a lot during 2004. In some ways he really started to annoy me. I put this down to stress at work and also looking after me. There were times when he got shirty with me without realising he was doing it. An example of this would be where he would come in the morning and tell me something, which I would not hear because I did not have my hearing aid in. He would say that he would tell me later. When I would ask later, he would sometimes say that he couldn't remember and this would really annoy me.

Another example is, when I am ready for bed, Roland would be on a computer game in my bedroom and would not come and take my plug-holes (hearing aid) out, but would stay and finish his game off first. This would make Roland late for bed.

If we watched something on T.V., and Roland did not like it, he would tell me he was going on the computer in my room. This would leave me on my own and sometimes I would ask myself why he is here. It is Roland's company that I value most. I am hoping that in future, when Roland settles into his job, he will find it less stressful and our friendship will start to improve again. Roland does pay for the internet connection and half the cost of our weekly shopping.

Because I know that Roland is not going to church at the moment, I feel that this is having an effect on him, which he doesn't realise.

An example is, one day Roland came over to my bungalow really early. I was not completely ready, and I was expecting him to ask if I wanted him to give me a hand. However, he didn't. He went straight into the kitchen and made his breakfast. I told him that it would have been nice if he had offered to give me a hand, and things would have been done a lot quicker. Instead, I was left to struggle. Although I have told

Roland that I want to be more independent, I often wish that he would give me a bit of extra help.

At first, I was trying to please Roland by being more independent, so that life would be easier for him. I now feel that I want increased independence for myself, and not to please Roland.

Sometimes, our situation makes me feel really angry. Roland sometimes doesn't appreciate that I also do things for him in our relationship and it is not just one-sided. He uses my washing machine, uses the shower here (so that he is not late for work) and watches his choice of T.V. programmes sometimes (not that I mind, because I can close my eyes and switch off).

I really do believe that this started happening after I had spoken to one of my friends, and Roland either overheard some of the conversation, or the person I was speaking to could have related to Roland what I said. The conversation was about Roland caring for me, and how our friendship had changed because of this. I told my friend about how I felt that I was more relaxed with Jo and Helen than I was with Roland and I said that Roland was "outside" these relationships. Roland told me that he knew about this conversation and that it really hurt his feelings. I told him that I didn't mean it in a hurtful way and I did apologise, but I also remembered that he had also said some hurtful things to me in the past.

While Jo was working for me, I did not really know what to buy Roland for Christmas one year. I hit on a fantastic idea of booking up two driving lessons for him. I asked Jo if she could help me to organise it. Jo went through the Yellow Pages and found a driving school and explained the situation to them. They were happy to oblige. I asked Jo if she could pay for these lessons on her debit card, as I did not have one at that time. She was very happy to do this, even though she shouldn't have, as she knew she would get her money back. The driving school said that they would send her a voucher for the driving lessons.

We then decided to make it even easier for Roland, and got a driving licence form to put in with the voucher. Everything went well. The only thing we had to do was to keep out eyes out for the post, to make sure we saw the voucher before Roland did. Again, that worked out really well as it came one day during the week while Roland was out. Jo and I hid them and on Christmas day, when I gave Roland his present, he was so stunned and surprised he did not know what to say. He was over the moon with his present and surprised that I would think of doing such a thing.

I also arranged for the driving school to pick up Roland after work on a Friday, for his first lesson. All Roland had to do was to ring the driving school to confirm the arrangement. Unfortunately in the end, to the disappointment of all who knew about this surprise present, Roland did not take it up and never took the lessons.

In my eyes, I think that Roland could have been too nervous as he had tried driving lessons years ago when he was a lot younger. Alternatively, he could have been worried that if he did pass his test, he would have to take me here, there and everywhere – but this was not my intention.

Because Roland and I have been friends for over eighteen years, I do believe that he cares for me very much and will always be there for me. Although we have our ups and downs, I do really appreciate him.

My latest experience with the community alarm service was that on 7th February 2005, I got out of bed to get washed and dressed, began to get dressed, went to get a clean pair of knickers out of my drawer and the cabinet toppled over on top of me. The telephone receiver fell off, but thankfully the phone stayed put, and so did the community alarm box. I tried to put the cabinet back, but I could not because it was too heavy. I didn't really know whether to press the alarm or wait for Roland. I decided to press the alarm. The community alarm people said they would come out to help me. While I was waiting for them, I made sure that I put my underwear on! They arrived within about ten minutes and soon sorted me out.

When they left, at around 6.30am they locked the top lock on my front door. When Roland arrived minutes later, he realised that something had gone on because he had to unlock the front door, which is never normally locked. When I told him what had happened, he didn't laugh, as I expected, but asked why I hadn't waited for him to come.

My cat, Rosie, was really good and came on my bed to keep me company, and disappeared when she heard the community alarm people come in.

I now feel unafraid to call the community alarm service as they were very good with me.

During the period of time when I could not see I did not feel confident when I used my telephone. I tried to tried to dial 198 which connects you to a special service for people who cannot dial the numbers themselves. This is a really efficient service, but you do need to know the number you want them to connect you with. I pressed 4 instead of 1 and had to go back to the beginning again. It used to take me a long time to find the 9 and if my hand jerked I would have to start all over again. However I did get there in the end. I do wish they would make the number 189 as it would be a lot easier to find!

In the past when speaking to an operator on 198, I had problems saying the number 6. My way around this was that I would explain to them that there was a number that I could not say properly, and that when I come to it, I would spell it out for them. Some operators were really understanding and you could tell that they had the patience to listen. However, on two occasions I got a man who did not have much patience. The minute I started to explain how I would do this, he disconnected us. This really made me swear. Luckily I could press the redial button, and then I got a girl who was very helpful.

The best way I found of getting around the problem of saying number 6 was to link it with the next number – so I would say "sixty-one" or "sixty-two". But between you and me, I haven't tried it with sixty-six yet!

I was very grateful for this service which helped me communicate with people before I had my last eye operation, which enabled me to see a lot more.

## Chapter Forty Seven

# Rosie

During the period 2003 – 2004, I had been thinking about getting a pet. Knowing that I was like my dad, who would like something for a little while and then get fed up with it, I wasn't really sure about the whole idea. I thought about getting a dog from Dogs for the Blind, Dogs for the Deaf, or Dogs for the Disabled. I decided against it because I thought it would be too much work for Roland and my other carers.

Quite a few of my friends kept saying to me that a cat would be the right pet for me. At first, I thought about getting a kitten because you could raise it the way you wanted it to be. But then I decided against it because kittens can be a bit wild and I would be afraid that I would run it over with my wheelchair (even though people said that the kitten would soon get out of the way)!

Edina, Hilda and Georgie were all for me getting a cat. In the end, we went behind Roland's back. Jo rang up a lady who had cats for sale. She was so rude to Jo – not only about me being disabled but also about the area I live in. In the end, Jo got so mad that she put the phone down on her.

Jo rung me up that evening to tell me, and asked me if Roland was in. I said that he was, and she said that she would tell me more tomorrow. Roland started saying that it was not like Jo to say something like that, and began to suspect that there was something going on. In the end, Jo said she knew a friend, also a PA and also called Jo, who was a member of the Cats Protection League. This friend had a cat called Rosie and one other cat.

Rosie was a feral cat, which meant that she was wild. Jo, at the Cat Protection League, had looked after her for nearly a year since she was a very small cat. She had decided that she wanted to find a new home for Rosie, as she needed a lot of attention. My PA, Jo, told her that I was interested in getting a cat, and they both thought that Rosie might be the one for me.

I knew that if I could not cope with a cat, Jo would take the cat back and there would not be a problem.

I decided that I would like to have a cat, and Jo and her husband brought it round to my bungalow.

The week before, Jo and I had gone out shopping to get a litter tray with a lid on it, some cat litter and a food tray. We also got some dried food, which was a lot easier, and some cat toys.

When I met Rosie, I could not see the colours she had, but she is between a tortoise shell and a tabby, with a ginger line around the middle of her waist. She also has a bit of red in her colouring. She is quite small and very cute. I made up my mind as soon as I met her that I wanted her. Jo did give me some warning that she might go into hiding for a while and may take some time to settle down. For the first week or so, she did go into hiding.

Roland and I got a bit worried when she went behind the TV, and so Roland got her out the first time. He then decided to block her route behind the TV. Then she found another way to get behind the TV from the windowsill. This time, Roland said that she could get herself out. I got worried about this because there were lots of wires behind the TV and thought that she might get tangled up or get an electric shock. I did not say any more to Roland and waited for Edina to come round. Edina said that if a cat can get itself in, it can get itself out again. However, in the end, she did get Rosie out for me.

Rosie then found another hiding place in the bedroom, which I did not mind. After about three weeks, she became more confident and started to move around the bungalow more and sit on my lap. In the end, Roland said that it was a crafty move between me, Jo and Edina to get the cat moved in!

Rosie does have one or two habits. She loves to have her tummy rubbed every time you stroke her, which is quite unusual as she likes you to do it every time. If she sits on the floor or on my lap and puts her paws up, it means that she wants attention from Roland or Jo, my PA.

If I am sitting on the settee with Roland, eating my dinner, and Rosie wants some of my dinner, she will put her paws up. We started giving her a little bit of meat, but found out that it did not really agree with her, so we stopped doing it.

She now goes to sleep on my bed and always sleeps close to my feet or close to my legs.

When Roland was staying here and got up to go the loo in the night, Rosie would go up to him and touch him with her paw for some attention. Once she got some attention, she would soon go back to sleep.

Rosie would always sit on my lap in the armchair or the settee, but never when I was in the wheelchair. However, as time went on, she got more confident and will now happily jump onto my lap and sit there while I am in my wheelchair. If she is on my lap when I am having my breakfast, if she tells me she wants a bit then I give her a tiny bit. After that, she gets down. She gets on well with all the people who come to visit me, and she will let them stroke her. She is a great companion and I get a lot of fun out of her.

Rosie likes to get underneath my settee, where a hot water pipe runs under the floor. Because she likes it there so much, we decided to keep some of her food in the kitchen, but put we an extra portion of food and drink under the settee. Because she eats dried food, this can be left under there without it going off. We later put her food on the other side of the room and just left the water under the settee.

Before Roland goes to work in the mornings, he helps me to get into the armchair. The minute Rosie hears the radio go on, she jumps onto my lap and stays there all morning, or until I push her off to get the telephone, or go to the loo. When Jo used to come in, she used to have to play a game with her to get her off my lap. She played games with her on my lap or on the floor.

When I go out of a room and Roland comes in, Rosie will look at Roland as if to say "Oh, it's you." When I come back in, Rosie will wait for me to get settled and jump up on my lap. Rosie and I sometimes have a race to see who can get on to the settee or armchair first.

During the daytime, she is just like a little child. If I am taking a long time in the bathroom, she will come in, miaowing, as if to say "Hurry up!" When I get to the armchair, she always tries to get there first and to get in my way.

Sometimes in the night time, when I am awake, she comes up close to me and I have to make a fuss of her. Then she will go back down and go to sleep at the end of my bed. She also does this first thing in the morning.

I have never known a cat who likes her tummy rubbed as much as Rosie does!

One day, Roland went to get a glass of milk. He put it on the floor by the settee and Rosie came along and started drinking from it. In the end Roland had to throw the glass of milk away.

When Tim, my PA, arrives in the morning, Rosie will run into the bedroom, jump up onto the bed and Tim will rub her belly before doing anything else. Rosie does get a little tiny bit of meat every time we have our food. It is like being a food tester! She will then go away and have a sleep. This is the best way to keep her quiet!

One of the reasons that Rosie is so special to me is that she was one of the last and nicest things that Jo did for me, and she reminds me of her.

## Chapter Forty Eight
# A Very Nerve Racking Day

As you already know, I had been waiting to go into hospital for an operation to drain the blood away from the back of my left eye, at King's College Hospital. I had been turned down twice because there were not any beds. I got so worked up wondering when I would be admitted that it made me feel ill.

On Wednesday 23 February 2005, I was still waiting to see if there was a bed for me. Jo kept ringing up every half-hour after 3pm, as the hospital had instructed us to do. Finally, at 4.30pm we were told that they had a bed for me.

In the meantime, Roland was calling me every now and again to see if we had heard anything.

Jo agreed to pick Roland up on the way to save him time coming back to the bungalow and then going up to hospital with me. The hospital had told us to get there by 6pm. Jo said that we may not be able to make it by then, as we were coming from Woolwich. However, I believe that we did make it on time.

We were taken to the ward, which was quite nice – a women's ward with only about 12 beds. As I could not see, Jo described the ward to me. There was a Chinese nurse there, who was a bit rude. Another nurse came to take over, who was much better. Roland thought that the first nurse's attitude had to do with the fact that she may not understand too much about people with disabilities.

The doctor came around to give me all the details about the operation and I had to sign the consent papers there and then. The doctor told me about haemorrhaging, going blind and having a gas ball put in my eye. A gas ball in my eye would mean that I would not be able to fly and would also have to lay on my front for 15 minutes every hour. This would have been quite an ordeal for me.

The doctor could not say what the outcome of the operation would be until after he had finished the operation itself. I looked at Roland and then Jo. They both said that they could not decide for me and that I had to make up my own mind. They questioned whether I was satisfied with just seeing a little bit of light – enough to see my whereabouts – or was I prepared to take the risk and have the operation, even if there was a chance that I could go blind.

In my mind, if I did go blind, I could possibly have got more care. I wondered whether I could still carry on living at home on my own. I was not too worried about going on holiday. I cried for a few minutes and Jo comforted me. I calmed down and started thinking logically. I looked at the options – it will either get better, or I will go blind. If I were to go home and not have the operation done, I would keep wondering if I should have done it. I decided to go for it and if it worked, it worked. I signed the papers.

The next thing I knew was that they wanted to put a needle in my hand so that I would be all prepared for the anaesthetic the following morning. I did not want to go to sleep with a needle in my right hand, as I sleep on that side. Roland and Jo helped me to get undressed while the doctor went to get a needle. He put the needle in my vein and put a bandage around to protect it.

Needless to say, I didn't get much sleep that night. I managed to get Roland to take out my hearing aid and give me my medication before he left.

I said goodbye to Jo and Roland and then it was up to me to try to get comfortable. I could not do this, so I just lay there. A nurse came over to me and told me not to have anything to eat anything from breakfast time until midnight. I was so glad that Jo had cooked my dinner and I had eaten before I arrived at hospital. I did have some bananas and custard in hospital which Jo had given me beforehand.

The nurse would not let me go the toilet and said that I had to use a commode. I knew that I would not be able to do this. I managed to hold on.

I went down for the operation at about 12.30pm on Thursday 24th February, and got back to the ward at about 2.45pm. When they tried to put me on the operating table, which was quite narrow, I told them that I could not lay flat on my back with nothing underneath me, because I would be too tense. I also asked them to keep my left hand flat, as this is the most comfortable position for me.

When I woke up in the ward, I realised that I had a needle in my other hand as well. This made me feel very tense as I now had a needle in each hand. I was desperate for the toilet and was also trying to cope with my cerebral palsy. There was no way that I could go to the loo on the commode, no matter how hard I tried. I eventually gave up this idea.

That night, Roland and Jo came in to see me and were surprised to see how lively I was. I had a sore throat and this made me more talkative because I liked the sound of my own voice with a sore throat! When they went to kiss me goodbye, Roland put his hand on my left had, where the needle was, and pushed down into my vein. This made me wet the bed a bit. I was glad in a way and I told him to do it again! Of course, he would not, so it was back to square one again. The nurse had to change me and clean me up. I still could not get comfortable because I was so cold. An extra blanket was put over me.

In the end, I kept wetting myself all through the night. If they had put me in a wheelchair and had taken me to the bathroom they would have saved themselves a lot of work changing the bed!

At about 3am I was getting so fed up that I made the nurse take the needle out of my hand. I wet the bed again, and I told them to wrap me up warm again because I was freezing. They got me a duvet and I felt relieved that at last I could turn over and get some sleep.

The next morning, which was a Friday, the operation went ahead as planned. After my operation, one of the nurses, Lydia, gave me my breakfast. I decided to have a little bit of porridge but did not expect to have it together with toast and marmalade. It was quite a mixture! The night nurse, Helen, was really good and did her best to comfort me. However, this still did not help my problem with going to the toilet.

Lydia washed me and got me up and dressed and put me in my wheelchair. While waiting for Roland and Jo, I kept calling the nurses to take me to the loo. Then Chris, the male nurse, came over and took me to the bathroom. He was behind me and I told him to come around to the front of me, take me by the hand, and guide me to the toilet. He did this and then left me to it.

It was such a relief to go to the loo. I then pulled the bell and Chris came back for me. On the way back to my bed I asked Chris what the time was. It was around 11.00am. When I arrived back at my bed, Roland and Jo were already there, wondering where I was.

I told Roland that we had to see a doctor in the Normandy building, but in the end we did not have to do this. We just had to go to another ward, but we did have to wait a bit. I had some dinner there, and had to pick what I wanted. After I had ticked my choice on the menu, the nurse took me to see a doctor in another ward. This was a nerve-racking moment because he was going to take the eye patch off. Would I be able to see, or would I be blind? The minute he took it off, I could see – and what a relief it was. I had made the right decision. The next thing we knew was that we had to go back to the main ward and wait for the eye drops to arrive. While we were sitting there waiting, I had my dinner. I had chosen fish and chips and cheese and biscuits. For supper, I chose fried chicken with vegetables followed by a pudding. We were hoping that we would not be there for dinner, but unfortunately we were.

Jo decided to feed me, but the peas went almost everywhere. I told her not to worry about feeding me the peas. While Jo was feeding me, a nurse arrived and told me that we might have to wait over four hours before we could get the eye drops. We did not want to sit there for four hours, so Jo suggested that she would take Roland and me home and then come back in four hours' time to pick up the eye drops and my tablets. After the four hours were up, Jo went back to hospital with her dad, who could meet someone nearby while Jo went into the hospital.

At around 6.00pm we got a phone call from the hospital saying that Jo had been given the wrong eye drops. Jo and her dad had to go all the way back again! By the time she got back to me, it was quite late. After she went home, Roland and I started thinking about getting her some flowers and a bottle of something, instead of chocolates. Luckily, we were able to do this over the internet and were told that they would be delivered the next morning. Jo came in the next day, which was Saturday, to work her normal 2-hour shift. That was when she told me that she had decided to go to Spain that afternoon.

I looked at Roland and he looked back at me, as much as to say, "Oh, well". We just had to keep our fingers crossed that the flowers would come before she left.

At around midday, I was listening to Money Box on Radio 4. I said to the Lord, "You've got roughly an hour to get those flowers to Jo, so get a move on!"

At about 1.15pm my phone rang and I could not get there on time. Jo left a message on my phone, sounding quite emotional and saying that the flowers were beautiful. I managed to dial the 1471 number and then press 3 to redail. I then managed to talk to her. This was good and it worked out well in the end. I told Roland and he was over the moon too.

After two weeks of Jo being in Spain, Edina and others were surprised that she had not been in touch with me. During the second week I felt that I had been abandoned and used to look out for the post to see if she had sent me a card. In my eyes, and in other people's, Jo used to think a lot of me. I felt sure that she would send a card just to say that she had arrived and was getting on well or just to give me an update on the phone. After two weeks, I rang her mobile number, without telling Roland. Something inside me just told me to do it. My batteries were low and I could not hear very well. The mobile I dialled had been left behind by Jo. Someone answered and recognised my voice – it could have been Jo's mum or sister. They were going out to Spain the next day and I asked them to pass on my regards to Jo. They said that they would tell Jo to get in touch.

Jo did tell me before she left that she might not come back until her boyfriend was ready.

If Jo comes back, my feelings towards her will not change. However, if she does not come back and I get a new P.A., I will endeavour not to become such good friends with them just in case they move on.

At the end of March 2005, I realised that it had been nearly five weeks since Jo had left for Spain and I still had not heard anything from her.

At this point, Roland also began to have second thoughts about whether Jo would get in touch with me.

I had to advertise for a new P.A. and had eight applications by the end of March. Neither Roland nor I thought that any of them were suitable – seven of them could not drive and the eighth person could, but had no insurance. We resolved to keep trying. Because Jo was such a professional in her job, it would be very difficult to replace her.

In April 2005, I did manage to get in touch with Jo. She said that she was coming home for a couple of days in May. I don't think that Jo realised that I was being put under pressure by my care managers to find a suitable replacement for her. She said that after she came home for a couple of days, she would probably return to Spain as her boyfriend may have good job prospects.

What I decided to do was to try to get my care managers to try to employ someone temporarily from Monday to Friday, for six months, and to employ someone permanent to come each weekend. The care managers did say to me that I was making it a bit too easy for Jo. I felt that I wanted to give Jo a really good chance to make up her mind.

When Jo first told me that she was thinking of going to Spain, Helen, my communicator guide, also said that she had a new job and that she might be leaving too. I thought – oh no, I can't stand this! However, Helen and I came to an agreement that she would continue to come for an hour in the afternoon. I am so glad I did agree to this because after six months she left the LSA job she had in the mornings to look after her niece. She could then give me back the two-and-a-half hours I usually had, which meant that I did not have to go through finding another new person!

I wanted to be as fair to Jo as I had been to Helen, and this is why I held Jo's job open for such a long time.

When I went on holiday to Portugal in May 2005, Jo came home for a long weekend. She was very upset as a lot of people she wrote to, including me, did not receive the letters she sent to them. She had to return to Spain before I got back from Portugal because of an interview for a job there.

Roland had a good chat to her mum over the phone, so that he could tell me the latest when I returned from holiday. Her mum said that Jo really wanted to tell me herself that she might not be coming back. She also explained that as Jo lived in a newly constructed area in Spain, a lot of letters had not been getting through.

Jo and her boyfriend, Tom, have now moved out of that area to a more well established area.

I tried to call her on her mobile, but could not get through. I just got a Spanish message. Jo texted Roland to tell him that I could ring her up the next day – which was a Sunday. Roland forgot to give me the message, so I asked him to text her back to ask what the best time was to ring her. She replied straight away that I could ring her that minute. We had a good chat, and she got the job she wanted – as a waitress in a local restaurant. She said that it was very hard work after having so many weeks of relaxing! She had to spend seven hours on her feet, non-stop.

I am looking forward to next time she comes home for the weekend, and hopefully I will be there!

I did eventually employ a new PA, called Caroline. She seemed a very nice person, but unfortunately it did not work out and she left after five days. During the same week, Roland was taken to hospital on the Friday because he had some fluid on his leg. We came to a compromise with the Doctor that he could come home for the weekend, as I really wanted him to meet Caroline. He then went back on Sunday evening.

It took me quite a while to find somebody else to take over as my PA. After interviewing four people on one Wednesday, I found that none were suitable. Then Michelle, who is in charge at Choices, knew another PA called Eileen, and I managed to interview her the next day. Jill, my care manager, and I knew that she was the right one for me as we got on straight away. However, we had to wait for a police check to go through before she could start. In the meantime, her mother, who had a disability, became ill. Eileen decided to resign to look after her mother full time. I was sad to loose Eileen, because I just knew she was the right one. In October 2005, I was back to square one.

As far as my care was concerned when Roland was in hospital, everything went really well. Edina was on night shift, so this made it easier. She would come in in the morning after her night shift, and would help me to get dressed and put on my shoes, etc. She would then give me my medication and put in my plugholes (hearing aid). She then gave me my breakfast. She came back again in the afternoon to cook my dinner. During the evening when she was working, she would have a break, come over to me during her break and give me my tablets and eye drops, and take out my plugholes.

On Monday night, I forgot about taking out my hearing aides. It was really late and I realised that if I tried to turn them off, it would take too long. I decided to push my community alarm. Edina had just got back to the office to do her night shift. When I spoke to Alison, at the Community Alarm Centre, I asked her if she could get hold of Edina on her mobile phone.

When Alison spoke to Edina there was some confusion as Edina did not know who she was, and had only just come from my house. Edina's imagination ran away from her and thought that I had fallen over. Alison explained that I was fine, but I needed my plugholes taken out. We all had a good laugh and Edina came back to me and then went back to work again.

Roland came out of hospital the following Tuesday, but was told that he might have to go back in again for more tests.

One day I was talking with my care manager, Jill, when she visited me at home and my friend Lesley popped in to see me. She was coming to tell me off for not having let her know that Roland had been in hospital. She would have been happy to come in to do some extra jobs for me. Lesley did not realise all the problems we had had about getting a PA to do my cooking, etc. She said that she would be quite happy to come in to do my cooking. Jill spoke to Lesley about this and we then all agreed that Lesley would be the right person for the job.

I can really have a good laugh with Lesley and I get on really well with her and her husband, Jonathan. We are sometimes like sisters and her husband feels like a brother to me. Lesley often asks me over to her home to have dinner and invites Roland too. Jonathan picks us up and drops us back off again. Despite not always being in the best of health herself, Lesley always does her best to meet my needs and generally puts other people in her life before herself. Lesley and Jonathan are both wonderful.

Tim started visiting me, as a friend, on a weekly basis in 2006. This was just a friendly visit for a chat. At the time I did not realise that he was interested in the job as my PA. When he told me, I agreed to take him on. As he had a car this was an advantage as well. Some of the members of my church did not agree with Tim being my PA because he was a man. However, Tim knew what he was letting himself in for and I knew he could do the job. He is a good worker, but unfortunately we do have differences which we have both learned to cope with. Most of our disagreements are due to our different opinions about the bible and our beliefs, but sometimes we clash about other things as well. At other times, Tim can be a great help when I'm feeling really down.

## Chapter Forty Nine
# Hopes for the Future

With regard to my future, I have been thinking ahead. I still believe that I could get healed – don't ask me how or why, but it is just something I believe could happen.

I am very happy in this bungalow. There is an old people's home which is not used any more on this estate, and which cannot be knocked down. This was going to be shared between Greenwich Sensory Services, Age Concern and another group to provide help as a day centre for people with hearing impairment, and for the partially sighted and blind. This was to take place sometime in 2006, which would have been lovely as it was just across the road from me. However, by the end of 2006 this had still not happened and we wondered whether the plans had been changed. We later found out that this was not going ahead.

I have already mentioned Georgie and John, whom I met on holiday. We telephone each other every week. They would love me to move to Bournemouth to live nearer to them. When I went to visit them for a week in 2004, they took me around a respite centre where I could stay to see if I liked the area, and to see what respite care was like in case I needed it when I was older.

The inside of the residential home was very clean and tidy, but felt much too big for my liking. I did enjoy my stay, but to spend a week there would be difficult because of my blindness. It would be completely unfamiliar and I would have to rely completely on guidance from other people all the time. I was worried that I may feel isolated because of this. Georgie and John realised this and I decided at the time to wash that idea out.

A few months later, I was going through a bad patch with Roland (over care). Georgie and John had found another place down in Bournemouth, which was like Bargery Road, where people would share a house but you would each have your own room. This would have been better for me. The house was split into two groups: one group would be independent, like I am, and in the other group there would be more severely disabled people, needing more care. The only problem with this accommodation was that you would have to stay there for a minimum of six weeks. This was so they could get to know you and you could get to know them. After this time, you could decide if you wanted to stay there or go back home.

I liked this idea very much, as there is a lot going on in Bournemouth for people with disabilities. Maybe in the future I will consider this again. The other good thing about this particular place was that I could take my cat, Rosie, with me. However, I would feel like I was sharing her with the other residents, and I would be upset that she wouldn't feel like 'mine' anymore.

In 2005, I went to Bournemouth again with Georgie and John and we looked around James Burns House, which is a home for disabled residents. I was introduced to some of the residents and staff, and I quite enjoyed myself there, and had a bit of dinner. One of the residents said that someone was moving out soon, and that he wouldn't mind having me opposite him. This made me feel welcome and I also liked the way the home was organised and run.

The next stage was to get Roland to come down and have a look round. He agreed to do this, and we went down to visit again in October 2005. Roland mentioned that I needed to be aware that I would be moving from a bungalow to one room again. He also picked up on the attitude of one of the residents, who thought he was a bit of a 'know it all'.

When we came home, we got a piece of paper and wrote down all the strengths and weaknesses of the home. We were concerned whether my care manager at Greenwich Sensory Services would support this move or not.

The strengths about the move would be that I would have a key worker working with me, I would have staff on duty 24 hours a day and I would be able to tell staff what I wanted with regard to activities and they would be able to organise it for me. I would also be able to take part in disability awareness training, which is one of my strengths and favourite areas.

Edina was surprised when I told her in January 2005, that Roland and I had not been out together for about a year and a half. It would have been nice, but it doesn't really bother me. Really and truly, Roland is with me a bit like my dad was with my mum. At the moment, we do not go out on our own, but this might change. A lot of this has got to do with Roland not having much free time.

Another thing that concerns me is that when Roland talks about caring for me, he refers to it as 'work.' I cannot relate to this because when you are looking after someone, you do it because you care about them. I think this is what makes me think that in the future, we will always be friends, but I will have to get more and more care in from outside, and eventually Roland will be more in the background.

In 2004, I did a presentation on disability awareness from my own experiences. I was asked to do this by Liz, a member of my church, who also used to work at my G.P.'s surgery as a nurse. The presentation was at Charlton Athletic Football Ground in the conference suite, to about two hundred people.

The way we planned it was to tape the presentation on video and then show it so everyone could see. We made a date to meet up in one of the health centres. I was asked lots of questions and the interviewer was amazed at how quickly the tape was made (she thought that it would have taken much longer with lots of re-takes).

On the day, there were about two hundred people there. We showed them the video and everyone was very impressed, including my G.P. who had come to see it.

A lovely surprise was that they gave me a copy of the video presentation and also a gift voucher.

I did a crafty thing with the voucher – I exchanged it for money with Roland. I then went out and bought a special teddy bear for my collection with the money. This bear will always remind me of the presentation.

Roland mislaid the gift voucher and it took me about a year to find it – in fact Jo, my P.A., found it! I told Roland the vouchers had been found and he spent the money on some Christmas shopping. However, I could have been crafty and spent the voucher at Homebase!

I went to the Christmas carols at church in 2004 and Liz came over to me to ask me if they could have a photograph of me to put on a poster to advertise their NHS disability services. I gave her my permission if she promised that she would take a good picture of me! She agreed, and it went ahead.

Who knows, it could open the door to other things.

During the year 2003, Jo was doing her NVQ Level 2, and asked me to help her out a lot with it, in order to enable her to complete the sections on personal care, hygiene and leisure. During this time, I played lots of jokes on her. I was amazed to see how close the assessor watched her do the hovering. She was literally right behind her. If Jo had taken one step back, she would have trodden on the assessor's foot.

Another part of the assessment was for Jo to prepare and give me my lunch. This went really well. I had two favourite sections of the course. One of these was when Jo had to help me to have a shower. She did not usually do this. She had to guide me into the shower and make sure that I had all the towels and clothes I needed.

I said to her assessor, "I am going to behave like a queen, and Jo is going to be my servant." This made the assessor laugh.

As part of this section, Jo was also supposed to get me out of bed. Because both Jo and the assessor were a bit late arriving that morning, I decided to get up. I left all the lights off and went near the door. When I heard them coming in, I screamed and they both jumped out of their skins.

My second favourite section of the course, was when Jo took me to the gym. While I was on the bicycle, the assessor had a quiet word with Jo.

Jo told her that I would be all right on my own and that they could leave me for a while, while they had a chat. The assessor was very surprised by this. I am pleased to say that Jo passed this NVQ Level 2 exam.

There is one thing that I do wish for, and that is for my sister, Pauline, and I to become more like sisters in our relationship, instead of having a big 'gap' between us. It would be nice to meet my brother-in-law and my niece again as well. When I think about my sister, I get the impression that she still sees me as she did before she left home. I don't think she realises how much I have changed and what I have achieved in my life. I do try to keep in touch with Pauline by e-mail.

There are a couple of things that I would like to do in the future. I would love to do a parachute jump and have a go at abseiling. I would love to be on 'This is Your Life'. I would also like to go around the world and visit Canada, America, Australia, New Zealand, Hong Kong, Sweden and Norway. I would also like to meet some of my favourite people – Cliff Richard, David Jacob, Michael Crawford, Don MacClean, Gervaise Phinn, Daniel O'Donnel, Cilla Black and Dana.

In 2007 Linda Smith and I were listening to Premier Christian Radio in our own homes separately.

We were listening to a lady called Suzanne, who believed in the power of spiritual healing. Linda rang me up to tell me to contact Suzanne and that she would pray for me. I could not dial the number because they said it too quickly so Linda made the call for me. Suzanne rang me back to pray with me. The following Sunday, Linda and I decided to go to Suzanne's church service. I went forward for healing prayers and Suzanne asked if she could have a word with me afterwards.

After the service, we went to find Suzanne. She told me that she had dealt with a lot of people with Cerebral Palsy and other disabilities and I was amazed at what she told me, as it seemed to make sense to me.

We both know that God is going to hear me but we don't know how, where or when. So it doesn't matter how many healing ministries I go to, because God has already set the time for me to be healed. Suzanne said that all I had to do was to spend more time in prayer with Jesus and reading the bible and the day will come when I am complctely healed – God has got it all in his hands.

I believe in this prediction of healing more than any of the others I have heard.

In the future, I would like to spend more time working on disability awareness, try to get back to having a good relationship with God and wish that, hopefully, one day I will be completely healed.

I believe that one day I will be worshipping and the Lord will touch me and say, "Now is the time." This was told to me by my Pastor in Church.

At the moment, I have just got to wait for the right time.

# Conclusion

From birth to the age of forty-seven, I was coping quite well with my Cerebral Palsy. Then, however, my life was turned completely upside down when I became partially sighted. It completely changed again when I became a wheelchair user.

Because I had experienced these things in my life, I learnt a lot about disability. The courses that I had taken also improved my knowledge of disability.

I have learned a lot about mum and dad's relationship through my own experiences.

Since I moved to Woolwich, I definitely realise who my real friends are. There are certain people who have kept in touch, but there are some people who I only keep in touch with when I make the effort to contact them. I saw the same pattern when my mother became ill with M.S..

I don't know whether moving to Woolwich was the best decision for me overall. Sometimes I think that I should have stayed in Lewisham, as I had all my friends around me. However, on the positive side, I now have my bungalow, which I do not think that I would have been given in Lewisham. I also got to know people like Jo, Helen and Edina, who have helped me and are my friends.

If my mum and dad were alive today, I wonder how they would feel about the way I am now – partially sighted and a wheelchair user. I know one thing my mum would say – "Why didn't you go to the optician's earlier?"

If I had my life over again, I don't think I would have stayed at the Ladywell Day Centre quite so long. I think I would have moved on earlier, as I feel that I wasted a lot of time there.

Looking back at all the places I have lived in, I think the place where I had most fun and laughs was at Bargery Road. Because I shared this house with other people, there were always other people to talk to, and there were always home-helps coming in and out every day.

Where I am now, I don't have as much contact with the people around me. Although I have a nice, big bungalow to myself, I lose out on contact with people in the community. The main people I have contact with are the people who work with me and care for me.

The purpose of writing this book was to show people how I cope with my own difficulties, disabilities and ups and downs.

The past 24 years of my life has been spent with Roland. He has sorted out all my personal details, such as banking, living arrangements and has always been there to give me support in all sorts of ways.

Despite our ups and downs, I hope that Roland and I will always be best friends. I really appreciate the way he has looked after me, helped me and supported me over the last twenty four years. I will always think the world of him.

Over the years I have put together a list of the important factors to remember when dealing with people with physical disabilities. I thought that it would be a good idea to include this in my autobiography.

GENERAL HINTS ON DISABILITY AWARENESS

1. Do not make assumptions about the existence or absence of disability. Some people have hidden disabilities, such as epilepsy.
2. The effects of a specific disability often vary from individual to individual.
3. Remember, some disabilities are unpredictable, being very disabling at times and only mildly disabling at other times.
4. Do not assume lack of intelligence or learning difficulties because of a physical appearance, mannerisms or behaviour.
5. You can never fully understand what a disabled person goes through. You can only empathise to a degree.
6. Treat adults as adults. Do not patronise or treat them as children just because they need help.
7. Talk directly to a disabled person rather than through a companion.
8. When offering assistance to a disabled person, wait until your offer has been accepted before helping. Listen to what they say – do NOT assume you know best.
9. Try not to discourage disabled students from doing things for themselves, just because YOU are inpatient.
10. When talking to a wheelchair user, sit down if possible to get down to their eye level.
11. Do not lean on a person's wheelchair; it's part of their body space. Think how annoying it would be if someone leant on you.
12. Do not start pushing someone's wheelchair without their permission.
13. Wheelchair users who usually propel themselves may need help negotiating obstacles or when they are tiring.
14. Do not smoke when helping. Smoke in a disabled person's home only if they give you permission.
15. Disabled people have the same sexual desires and needs as everybody else. Do not assume because they are disabled they are asexual.
16. Alert the deaf person before you talk to them so that they can pay attention.
17. When talking to a deaf person, look straight at them. If you don't, they cannot lip read or use what limited hearing they have. Avoid standing in front of windows – the light can obscure their view of your face.

18. Hearing aids do not restore normal hearing; they only help by increasing the volume of sound (this can include background noise).
19. When assisting a blind person, ask before you give them help and let them take your arm – not the other way round.
20. To help a blind person sit down, place their hand on the back of the chair.
21. Respect their privacy, as you would expect yours to be respected.
22. Remember people with disabilities deserve respect from you, as you do from them, but remember people with disabilities are people, not saints. They have their 'off' days, just as you do.

www.ingramcontent.com/pod-product-compliance
Lightning Source LLC
LaVergne TN
LVHW021559070426
835507LV00014B/1859